£2.50

VIEW OF WALTON HALL IN THE DISTANCE; OF THE ANCIENT RUIN; AND OF THE CAST-IRON BRIDGE.

CHARLES WATERTON:

HIS

HOME, HABITS, AND HANDIWORK.

REMINISCENCES OF AN INTIMATE AND MOST CONFIDING PERSONAL
ASSOCIATION FOR NEARLY THIRTY YEARS.

BY

RICHARD HOBSON, M.D., Cantab.,

LEEDS.

SECOND EDITION
CONTAINING A CONSIDERABLE AMOUNT OF ADDITIONAL MATTER.

WITH SIXTEEN ILLUSTRATIONS
ENGRAVED FROM PHOTOGRAPHS OBTAINED WITHIN THE GROUNDS AT WALTON HALL.
BY SAMUEL SMITH AND THE LATE W. LYNDON SMITH, ESQRS.

"MULTIS ILLE BONIS FLEBILIS OCCIDIT,
NULLI FLEBILIOR QUAM" MIHI.

"He died lamented by many good men,
By none more lamented than" by me.

LONDON :

WHITTAKER & Co. ; SIMPKIN, MARSHALL, & Co.
LEEDS: H. W. WALKER, AND JOHN SMITH.
MDCCCLXVII.

Dedication.

―――――

TO SIR WILLIAM JARDINE, BART.,

L.L.D., F.R.S.L. & E., F.L.S.

OF APPLEGIRTH, DUMFRIESSHIRE;

MEMBER OF THE PHYSICAL SOCIETY OF EDINBURGH

BOTANICAL SOCIETY OF EDINBURGH;

METEOROLOGICAL SOCIETY OF SCOTLAND;

SOCIETY OF ANTIQUARIES OF SCOTLAND; MICROSCOPICAL SOCIETY

OF EDINBURGH;

ANTHROPOLOGICAL SOCIETY OF LONDON;

BERWICKSHIRE NATURALISTS' CLUB;—

HONORARY MEMBER OF THE NATURAL HISTORY SOCIETY OF

NORTHUMBERLAND, DURHAM, AND NEWCASTLE-UPON-TYNE;

TYNESIDE NATURALISTS' CLUB;

COTSWOLD CLUB;

SOUTH AFRICAN INSTITUTION, CAPE OF GOOD HOPE;—

MEMBER OF THE AMERICAN PHILOSOPHICAL SOCIETY OF PHILA-

DELPHIA;

ORNITHOLOGICAL SOCIETY OF GERMANY;

PRESIDENT OF THE DUMFRIESSHIRE NATURAL HISTORY AND

ANTIQUARIAN SOCIETY, ETC., ETC.

MY DEAR SIR WILLIAM,

IN HAVING PERMISSION TO DEDICATE THE FOLLOWING PAGES TO ONE SO HIGHLY ESTEEMED BY OUR LATE MUTUAL FRIEND, IS MOST GRATIFYING TO ME, AND, I AM THOROUGHLY CONVINCED, WOULD HAVE BEEN EQUALLY SO, DURING LIFE, TO HIM WHOSE DEATH WE DEEPLY MOURN, AND WHOSE LEISURE HOURS WERE ARDENTLY AND UNCEASINGLY DEVOTED TO THAT PARTICULAR BRANCH OF SCIENCE WHICH YOUR LABOURS HAVE SO COPIOUSLY ENRICHED.

I AM, MY DEAR SIR WILLIAM,

YOURS FAITHFULLY,

RICHARD HOBSON.

. . . "*OMNE VOVEMUS*
HOC TIBI; NE TANTO CAREAT MIHI NOMINE CHARTA."

"All this I dedicate to thee; that this my book may not be deprived of a name so great as thine."

PREFACE TO THE FIRST EDITION.

THE readers of the following pages may, in all probability, enquire why I have taken upon myself to issue to the public this little Volume.

In anticipation of such very natural and reasonable interrogatories, in the present instance, I am determined to clear the decks and take time by the forelock, by stating that my replies, which are simple, shall be now expressed, and, I trust, that they will be generally satisfactory.

The late Mr. Waterton's tastes in the science of natural history, and the more especially, in consequence of his ardent and enthusiastic partiality for ornithological pursuits, were so similar and naturally so closely interwoven with my own,—they so agreeably harmonised, particularly in the ornithological department of this system, and were always worked out in such mutually familiar confidence for upwards of a quarter of a century,—that no surviving friend ever possessed similarly favourable opportunities which I so long and so absolutely monopolised, for acquiring an intimate and a positively detailed knowledge of the Squire's every-day habits, of witnessing his marvellous manipulating faculty, and of ascertaining his general and unreserved sentiments, particularly on all subjects associated with any branch of practical natural history.

Another reason, and one which I am delighted and proud to entertain and express, is my absolute love for the Memory of the man who was so warmly, so faithfully attached, and so abiding a friend.

It also gives me infinite pleasure to enumerate a third and very important reason, viz., that the chief part of what I have written had the careful and generous sanction of Mr. Waterton himself, as to its accuracy in dates and in facts.

I can easily conceive, that the purely English reader may complain, and probably not without some apparent reason, that the following pages are loaded with too great a profusion of Latin quotations, but this was one of the Squire's habitual peculiarities, and therefore, not to have introduced them, would have been incompatible with the profession on my part, that I would endeavour to faithfully delineate the true character of the man.

Mr. Waterton's Latin quotations were so frequently

mingled—so naturally and happily interspersed in his ordinary conversations with me, and apparently, with such an ease and freedom of expression, that I had, very repeatedly, extreme difficulty in remembering even a moiety of them.

I respectfully crave the kind indulgence of those who may peruse the following pages, and who may have calculated upon a more elaborate production, that they would deal gently with their Author, whose limbs were stretched on a bed of severe sickness, and whose life was in imminent danger at the very moment when the melancholy and ever-to-be-lamented accident occurred to his old friend, which so speedily cut short his earthly career,—terminating a life full of years, and distinguished as justly, as it had been profusely adorned to its close, by the highest esteem and veneration of all who had the good fortune to enjoy his friendship.

Independently of sickness, as an irresistible preventive to the final accomplishment of my anxious wishes, I deeply regret that unavoidable delay in the completion of the Illustrations, and other unforeseen circumstances, have unfortunately occurred to interfere with and materially delay the publication of this sketch of "the Home, Habits, and Handiwork" of the far-famed subject of this Memoir. I can now, however, with some degree of certainty, and with a vast amount of pleasure truly quote the poet :—

" Inveni portum, Spes et Fortuna valete ;
Sat me lusistis, ludite nunc alios."

" I 've reached the harbour, hope, and chance, adieu !
You 've played with me, now play with others too."

RICHARD HOBSON.

LEEDS, *August,* 1866.

PREFACE TO THE SECOND EDITION.

THE Author having been called upon, for so early a re-publication of this work, its original purchasers are entitled to explanation why this second issue should contain so much additional matter and yet be issued at less cost than the first.

On a careful re-perusal, however, he was mortified to discover the omission of many temporarily forgotten incidents familiarly exhibiting the genuine characteristics of "the old Squire" which were apparently worthy of record.

When apprised of the demand for another Edition, retrospective occurrences were reconnoitred, which showed that in justice to the living as well as in admiration of the memory of the dead, many endearing amenities and essentially characteristic eventualities claimed a merited insertion in its pages, the admission of which he trusts, will exculpate him from the charge of any less worthy motive, the sundry preparations for a first edition being always much more costly than any re-production, even with additional matter.

The Author tenders his cordial thanks for the frankly expressed approbation of the volume already before the public, not only by those with whom he is personally acquainted, but by many distinguished individuals, on whose friendship, or even acquaintance, he has no claim.

LEEDS, *January*, 1867.

LIST OF ILLUSTRATIONS.

CONTENTS.

CHAPTER I.—PAGE 1.

CHAPTER II.—Page 30.

CHAPTER III.—Page 80.

CHAPTER IV.—PAGE 106.

CHAPTER V.—PAGE 146.

CHAPTER VI.—Page 176.

CHAPTER VII.—Page 209.

CHAPTER VIII.—PAGE 241.

CHAPTER IX.—Page 271.

CHAPTER X.—PAGE 300.

CHAPTER XI.—Page 325.

NATURAL HISTORY IN THE MUSEUM.

EVERY Quadruped, Insect, Bird, and Reptile has been prepared and mounted by my own hand. I have collected them at intervals, in Guiana, in Brazil, in the West Indies, in the United States of North America, in Italy, and in England, from the year 1812, to the present time, 1855.

The specimens have all been done upon an entirely novel principle, discovered by myself, so that their original features have been perfectly restored,—the full brilliancy of their plumage retained, — and every part of them secured from the effect of damp, and from the depredation of the moth.

Reader, you are referred to the "Essays" and the "Wanderings," placed here to assist those who visit this Museum. They contain nothing but the absolute truth, although, on their first appearance before the Public, much disbelief and sarcasm caused me to regret that I had ever sent them to the Press.

Poor Captain Stedman, who in days long gone by, headed the Maroon war in the wilds of Surinam, met with no better a reception when he gave his Adventures to the world. But later times have done justice to his memory. I take my leave of you, in the lines which that brave and enterprising Scotchman penned for his own grave-stone :—

> " This, Stedman leaves to you,
> As you would be done by—do.
> The rest—*memento mori*,
> So ends poor Stedman's story."

CHARLES WATERTON.

WALTON HALL, *April 5th*, 1855.

CHARLES WATERTON:

ETC., ETC.

CHAPTER I.

THE materials collected in this little Volume, which are designed to afford a brief Memoir of a highly esteemed and recently departed friend, have been chiefly furnished by a very frequent, an intimate, and a most confiding personal association with the deceased for nearly thirty years.

Recollections, of a man whom we have venerated for his excellence—of kindnesses lavishly bestowed upon us—of frequent and agreeable intercommunion with a spirit having kindred tendencies to our own, are intellectual enjoyments occasionally anticipated but rarely realised. Reality, however, now and then supersedes the shadow. Under such circumstances, that man, who has been so fortunate as to mingle with and to enjoy the friendship of the late MR. WATERTON, would be callous indeed if he could not dwell on the remembrance of this privilege with unalloyed satisfaction. A feeling of such a character has

B

long existed within me, which prompted me to put my thoughts, in an occasional leisure hour, on paper, in order that they who have known Mr. Waterton merely by name, or only as a naturalist of wide-spread fame, may not, in future, be altogether unacquainted with, at least, a few of the many excellencies of this truly remarkable man, nor entirely ignorant of the peculiarities and very interesting scenery which surrounded WALTON HALL during the period of his life and residence there. "*Ea sub oculis posita negligimus; proximorum incuriosi longinqua sectamur.*" "Those things which are placed under our eyes we overlook; indifferent as to what is near us, we long for that which is distant."

"'Tis distance lends enchantment to the view."

It is an acknowledged fact, that the man who travels abroad overlooks the beauties of his own country, and this is a remarkable proof of what I have stated as regards Walton Hall. I have frequently heard men of travel say, when in the grounds, on their return from the staircase and the grotto, and a *tête à tête* with the hospitable master of the mansion, that they had no conception of the existence of so much that was really fascinating in their own neighbourhood. "We have," they would say, "often travelled hundreds of miles, and have been weeks from home, not having experienced half the gratification during the whole of that period, which we have here realised in a single day, and then, there is the Squire himself, the sight of whom we would not have missed on any consideration. What a kind creature he is, how quaintly, and yet how well he expresses himself, and how anxious he has been that we should thoroughly enjoy ourselves, and what is still more important, how capable he is of carrying those wishes into execution."

Experience convinces us that much mental gratification may be derived from an endless variety of rational and entertaining sources, which are abundantly and legitimately within our reach, and may be indulged in according to individual taste.

> "Tell me, Trebatius, are not all mankind
> To different pleasures, different whims, inclined?
> Milonius dances whilst his head grows light,
> And the dim lamp shines double to his sight;
> The twin-born brothers in their sports divide, —
> Pollux loves boxing, Castor joys to ride."

My good friend, Mr. Waterton, judiciously selected his amusements from, and limited his desires, chiefly, to the more immediately surrounding and interesting objects of natural history for the attainment of happiness,—and in this he was successful, whilst he was also contributing to the gratification of thousands of others.

A love of change seems to have been a primary element in the human heart; and if the variety be well chosen, it has, in all ages, been acknowledged to have afforded incalculable mental enjoyment as well as the most permanent satisfaction. Horace, who was no mean judge of human nature, very truly observes,—

> *"Denique non omnes eadem mirantur amantque."*

"All men do not admire and love the same things." The angler frames and encourages laws in order to multiply the finny tribe—the fox-hunter cares for the vulpine race—the knight of the trigger revels in the game battue—the manorial owner of his countless heathery acres, mountainous ranges, and wild ravines, delights to maintain and multiply the cervine herd, whilst the master of the leash preserves and fosters the timid hare.

" Mutual vouchers for their fame they stand,
And play the game into each other's hand."

In this land of acknowledged protection of interests—in this age of affirmed civilised humanity and ostentatiously boasted freedom from barbarism,—where are the benevolent, to attempt to shield the feathered tribe from ruthless destruction ? It cannot be denied that very many birds, which, in consonance with ordinarily established rules, we may fairly claim as indigenous to our soil or to our climate, have, within the last half century, almost entirely disappeared, whilst not a few species have literally become extinct. Wilful and wanton destruction prevails, not only among the lawless multitude, but also, to a disgraceful extent, among others, whose adult years, whose education, and whose position in life, leave them not the plea of youth nor of ignorance to justify, nor even to extenuate their inhumanity. In fact, we are continually meeting with this species of wholesale and indiscriminate cruelty, publicly chronicled as if praiseworthy acts. For instance, it was recently stated in a provincial newspaper, that Mr. —— was so fortunate as to shoot the male of some very rare bird, but was exceedingly annoyed that he had been so peculiarly unfortunate as to be unable to kill the female, and, that "this grievous disappointment was the more especially mortifying," he observed, " as they were, very probably, the only pair of this species within the United Kingdom." Now we have here an assumed gentleman, committing one very flagrant and unpardonable act, and, even after time for reflection, very much regretting that he had not the power, nor the opportunity, to perpetrate a second act, even more inhuman and more reproachful than the first. Fortunately, however, in the West Riding of Yorkshire, there has been, at least, one solitary and noble exception to this unrestrained barbarity;—and witness the result, nay, I may add, the happy and positively beneficial result, which I shall now endeavour to briefly recount.

" *Mors ultima linea rerum.*" " Death, the closing limit of human affairs," has very recently numbered (May 27th, 1865,) with the dust of his ancestors, the Squire of Walton Hall. " *Pallida mors æquo pulsat pede pauperum tabernas, regumque turres.*" " Pale death, with impartial foot, knocks at the cottages of the poor and at. the palaces of kings."

This esteemed, talented, and humane, but avowedly eccentric man, was passionately devoted to natural history pursuits. He, " none but himself could be his parallel," was not a closet but a field and telescopic ornithologist, and invariably distinguished as such, in every sense of the word. He would never, excepting in specially necessary instances, permit a gun to be fired within the precincts of his park, which is extensive, its circumferential walls measuring three miles. The ground, within these walls, has an agreeably undulating surface, is well wooded, and is enlivened by a splendid sheet of water. No boat, under any circumstances, was, during the life of the subject of this Memoir, ever allowed on the lake from September to May, nor were any fishermen permitted to prosecute even their passive vocations for this lengthened period; consequently, all land and water-fowl had a perfectly unmolested and secluded retreat for upwards of six successive months. It was a singular coincidence that the boat, containing the dead body of the naturalist, should be the first that could legitimately claim permission to be navigated across the lake, agreeably to the rules enacted by the Squire himself, during life. Thus, the dead appeared to be obedient to the laws previously laid down by the same body when living.

This benevolent privilege — that is, a combination of privacy, protection and freedom from annoyance — was extended also, to every animal within the park, with the exception of what Mr. Waterton designated the "Hanoverian" rat. Even the fox, although at enmity with many of the Squire's prime favourites, was always secure, as regards life, within this domain. This, however, is not surprising, as Mr. Waterton was himself a keen sportsman in the heyday of youth, having, for a considerable period, been a daring rider with the late Lord Darlington's fox-hounds. This early association with his equals in the hunting-field, innoculated the Squire with those elements constituting an open, a manly, and a gentlemanly bearing, as well as a generous warmth of heart, and I may truly add, that this benignity of character was so firmly and perennially established, that it increased with his years. Mr. Waterton was always a staunch preserver of foxes, notwithstanding what an arch enemy may have stated to the contrary; and he rigorously maintained the same conservative feeling to the close of a long life.

There were many seductive inducements within the park, which, doubtless, the keen scenting properties of the fox enabled him to discover. Notwithstanding that the surrounding wall of this domain is ordinarily an insurmountable obstacle to the wily fox, yet, on one occasion, a gate having been carelessly left leaning against the outside of the park wall, sly reynard was able, in using this gate as a ladder, to gratify his curiosity by venturing an intrusion to the interior of the park. The cunning culprit, however, was speedily detected by the Squire himself, who was delighted to have an opportunity to set his uninvited visitor at liberty, so that when released, and left to his own crafty resources, he might, at some future period, not only gratify his neighbours in scarlet, but be himself equally pleased that reynard should have a fair chance to save his brush "in the open," either by his game defiance of danger, or by some *ruse* or *finesse*, with which he is so plentifully supplied by instinct.

To the uninitiated, as to the topography of this district, I may state, as regards the locality of Walton Hall, that the residence of the late Mr. Waterton is about three miles south of Wakefield, and a mile and a half distant from the

Oakenshaw Station on the Midland Line of Railway, and the same distance from the ruins of Sandal Castle, memorable for the great battle on Wakefield Green, fought on the 31st December, 1460, between the Queen's army and the forces of the Duke of York, who, in consequence of the taunts and menaces of the Queen, was tempted to imprudently come out of his castle, in which he was perfectly secure, to meet the Queen's army, four times superior in number to his own.

It was here where Lord Clifford cut off the head from the dead body of the Duke of York, on the battle-field, and having, in contempt, put a paper crown upon it, presented it, on the point of his lance, to the Queen, who directed him to place it on the walls surrounding York.

It was at this eventful time that this noble lord so disgraced himself by plunging his dagger into the breast of the youthful Earl of Rutland, second son of the *then* Duke of York, in his anxious flight from the field of battle, to endeavour to save his life, being but a stripling of twelve years of age.

Sandal Castle was built in the reign of Edward II., and was afterward the property of the Duke of York.

> " Where York himself, before his castle gate,
>   Mangled with wounds, on his own earth, lay dead ;
>   Upon whose body Clifford down him sate,
>   Stabbing the corpse, and cutting off the head,
>   Crowned it with paper, and to wreake his teene,*
>   Presents it so to his victorious Queene."

The mansion is situated on an island, surrounded by a

* Anger.

BOULBY'S SUN-DIAL IN THE GROUNDS AT WALTON HALL.

beautiful and extensive sheet of water. The lake is somewhat on the western side of the park, having a circumscribed stone and mortar wall, with an elevation varying
from nine to sixteen feet. This property is in the town-
ship of Walton, and in the parish of Sandal Magna. The
late Mr. Waterton was lord of the manor. Within the hall
there is a neat but plain chapel, which was, up to the death
of the old Squire, served by the Roman Catholic priests
from St. Anne's in Leeds. The chief part of the estate
abounds in iron-stone, coal, terra cotta clay, and an
abundance of excellent stone for building purposes. The
land is generally good, with a fair proportion of various
kinds of timber upon it, of luxuriant growth.

On the southern side of the mansion, on a slightly
elevated mound, stands a most complete and very beautiful
sun-dial, deserving of careful observation, inasmuch as it
reflects great credit on the sculptor, the late George Boulby,
who was a common mason at the contiguous and rural
village of Crofton, in 1813. As a work of art, and,
especially when it was well known to have been executed
by a totally uneducated man—by a common mason, not
only devoid of inculcated literary attainments, but by one
having had no guiding artistic instruction — by a man
having to earn, "by the sweat of his brow," the few shillings sufficient to enable him to secure some of the works
of the philosopher of Athens—by one having to entirely
depend on self counsel so as to elevate him in his financial
and social position. I venture to say, considering all these
formidable disadvantages and impediments, that this specimen of sculpture is a wonderful development of innate

talent, and must be admired and applauded, for generations in futurity, as a relic of the excellence of the scientific execution of the common stone mason.

This dial is composed of twenty equilateral triangles, which are so disposed as to form a similar number of individual dials, ten of which, *whenever* the sun shines out, and *whatever* may be its altitude in the heavens, are always in use, and ever faithful time-keepers. On these separate dials are engraven, severally, the names of cities in all parts of the globe, which are placed in accordance with their different degrees of longitude, by which arrangement, the solar time, at each of the cities recorded on the different dials, can be simultaneously ascertained. Boulby was truly a self-taught sculptor. "*Abnormis sapiens,*" "wise without instruction." In early life he saved a little money, with which he purchased some of Plato's works, and was so struck with Plato's observation, that every solid contained twenty equilateral triangles, that he hewed out a globular stone, and reduced that very stone to the dial here described. On one occasion Mr. Waterton, having to pass Boulby's house, on returning home from the hunting-field, accidentally saw this dial in the stonemason's yard, for which Boulby asked a mere trifle. The Squire, delighted with the execution and the ingenuity of this simple-minded man, generously presented Boulby with twenty guineas by way of purchase, when the ingenuous and unaffected mason was infinitely more delighted to have the honour of his own artistic skill exhibited at Walton Hall, under the patronage of the Squire, than with the douceur which the sculptor erroneously considered far beyond its value.

Very near the sun-dial, is a subterraneous passage leading to two boat-houses, which are entirely concealed under part of the island on which the house stands. They are capacious, with well-arched roofs lined with zinc plate, thus affording complete protection to the boats in every variety of weather. Within these houses most convenient arrangements are made for slinging the boats to the roof, when required to be kept dry, or to be painted. They are easy of access by a commodious flight of steps leading down to the edge of the lake, where there is a jetty causeway, by the aid of which ladies can enter the boats without difficulty.

Four large sycamores, on the island, effectually screen the mansion from the bitter north-west blast, and have, from time immemorial, afforded most admirable roosting branches, especially for pea-fowl, (delicacies which I have occasionally enjoyed on the dinner table at Walton Hall,) whilst the decayed trunk of a fifth sycamore, for many previous years tenanted by a pair of saucy jackdaws, always maturing their offspring in perfect safety, has recently paid the last debt of nature.

On the northern side of the island, close to the cast iron bridge entrance and at its southern extremity, is a ruin, covered to a considerable extent with ivy, the northern gable end of which has its foundation on rock in the lake. This ruin was, in times far distant, the principal, and, indeed, the only pass to the island, by a swivel bridge. In its gable still hang the veritable ancient doors, ornamented by their original, antique and huge hinges, bolts, knocker, and other appendages of a former age. These doors, upwards of two hundred years ago, stood the test of Cromwell's fire-arms, and were found sufficiently strong to resist the besieging influence of that daring Puritan.

There is a traditional legend at Walton Hall, stating, that Oliver Cromwell was signally repulsed in attempting to cross a portion of the lake in order to sack the mansion, the present ruin, which is close to the bridge then forming a part of the entrance approach to the old family residence—that he and his party were in possession of fire-arms which they freely used, but apparently of so small a calibre, and at so great a distance from the house, in consequence of the intervening water, that neither the mansion nor the surrounding premises suffered any serious damage—that Cromwell was vigorously and efficiently opposed by Mrs. Waterton, in the absence of her husband—that the Lady and her whole household acted with great heroism, inasmuch as they gallantly mounted, and as valiantly fired a swivel cannon ball across the water upon Cromwell's party, and thus by this shot, broke the leg of one of his confederates, who was said to have been standing by a tree at the side of the carriage road, and that in consequence of this occurrence, together with the fear that the investing party might gain a landing on the island and discover the cannon, Mrs. Waterton directed it to be plunged into the lake for concealment. This oral communication, handed down from one

generation to another, seems, recently, to have been
singularly and forcibly confirmed by circumstantial
evidence of a strongly corroborative character. The nature
of the evidence is this, that a swivel cannon was actually
found in the lake when dredged in 1857, and that it
was discovered precisely where it is reasonable to
suppose the besieged party would place it for concealment; and also, that a ball, since that date, has been
dug up, embedded in the earth, at the very spot where
the man's leg was said to have been broken. What
renders this supposition still more conclusive is, that the
ball which was found in the earth at the exact place where
the man was said to have been shot, accurately corres-
ponds with the calibre of the reclaimed swivel cannon.

In the outer surface of the ancient doors, which are
fixed in the gable end of the ruin, on the northern side
of the island, bullets, which were shot by Cromwell's
party across the narrow portion of the lake, still remain,
around one of which a brass plate is fixed, with an inscription engraven upon it, recording this signal event.
Cromwell then destroyed the wooden draw-bridge and
took away the carriage and draught horses, and in consequence of being deprived of her horses, Mrs. Waterton,
at a fête subsequently given to her for her intrepid
conduct, had a yoke of six oxen harnessed to the family
carriage.

On the top of the ancient gable the foundation of
which juts into the lake, is erected a stone cross, at the
base of which, and at an elevation of twenty-four feet

above the level of the lake, a wild duck, on two occasions, nested and hatched her young. These periods of incubation frequently spoken of to me by Mr. Waterton, had, evidently been, from his mode of reference and relation, watched by him with much interest, added to which was his great amazement by the safe descent into the lake of such young and tiny creatures from an elevation of twenty-four feet.

This ruin is enclosed on the south by a freely-grown yew fence, so that the birds, within this barrier, may consider themselves thoroughly concealed, and, always free from disturbance, which peaceful and retired condition is doubly necessary during the period of building, incubation, and nurturing their offspring. For the encouragement and protection of the starling and the jackdaw specially, there is erected, within the yew fence, a thirteen feet high stone and mortar-built tower, pierced with about sixty nesting berths. To each berth there is an aperture of about five inches square. A few, near the top of the nesting portion of this tower, are somewhat larger and are intentionally set apart for the jackdaw and the white owl. The remaining number, in the lower portion, are each supplied, at the entrance, with a square loose stone, having one of its inferior angles cut away, so that the starling can enter the berths, whilst the jackdaw and the owl, being larger birds, can not gain admission, so as to annoy their less powerful neighbours, which molestation jack's natural tendency to mischievous propensities, would lead him to adopt. But when Mr. Waterton desired to examine the eggs or the young, or to have the interior of the berths cleansed, this could always be done by the removal of the loose stone. At the base of the nesting portion of the tower, a projecting stone flange encircles the lower tier, so that cats and all vermin by their being unable to surmount the flange, may be prevented reaching the birds or their offspring.

This decayed edifice has also afforded, for many years, a safe and unmolested retreat, and comfortable roosting-berths, for a beautiful rumpless fowl and his jet-black mate, as rumpless as himself, which were stationed on the island for the purpose of proving and victoriously confirming the accuracy of the Squire's opinion, written and publicly expressed on a disputed question, relative to the utility, inutility or application, if any, of the oil-gland in birds.

To those readers who may not be versed in ornithological anatomy or physiology, I should explain, that the oil-gland in birds is situated at the extreme end of the back, above and anterior to the tail; and has acquired that name because it secretes a semi-unctuous fluid. It had been hitherto universally maintained, with great pertinacity by ornithologists, that this secretion was an essential requisite as an application to be used by the bird itself to its own feathers, in order to beautify it by giving a shining lustre to its plumage, as well as an oily surface to the feathers, for the purpose of resisting the penetrating properties of water during wet weather, to which birds are so frequently exposed. Mr. Waterton always contended, and established the accuracy of his war of words by the birds themselves, viz., that the "rumpless fowl," which had neither tail nor oil-gland, had, notwithstanding, plumage as beautiful and as capable of resisting water as those birds which are furnished with both tail and oil-gland; but the Squire never professed to have discovered, in a physiological signification, the definite use of this organ. All that he asserted was, that this gland was not originally designed for the purpose hitherto erroneously supposed. Inasmuch, however, as the oil-gland only exists in conjunction with the tail, assuredly it may be reasonably inferred, that it is in some way connected with the maintenance, the support, or the growth of the tail.

The old ruin is fertile in objects of curiosity. Within the fence, and on the ground, there is a poison trap for rats, singularly simple and effective, and one of its cardinal virtues is that it destroys only what you desire should be destroyed. This trap is constructed from a circular and somewhat obtusely formed conical flag-stone; and its under surface, or base, is hollowed out from the centre of the internal roof of the stone, to within two or three inches of its circumference. At, and from its external conical apex, a hole is drilled in a perpendicular direction, downward, through the stone, large enough for the admission of a poisonous powder, which act is all that the "setting" of this trap requires. From the outer margin and at the base of the extreme circumferential line, a hole is drilled horizontally through its parietes, large enough for the admission of a rat to pass to the hollowed-out central portion of the stone, by which the "Hanoverian" has free ingress and egress to and from the poison, which, being in *dry powder*, cannot be dragged away and exposed to the risk of its being taken by any domestic animals, poultry, or game. This stone should be about two feet diameter at the base, and so heavy, as to prevent its being accidentally moved, and thus unintentionally expose the poison beyond the range of the "Hanoverian." The enticing and fatal powder used by the Squire, was a mixture of brown sugar, oatmeal, and arsenic. It is of essential importance that this combination should be well triturated in a mortar, so that not an atom of the arsenic be left uncombined with the other two tempting ingredients, otherwise there will be very little chance of capturing the crafty "Hanoverian."

Within the boundary of this yew fence enclosure, is located the swivel-cannon to which I have already alluded, as well as the identical ball which, it is presumed, disabled one of Cromwell's party.

Here, also, attached to the wall, and adjoining the ancient doors in the ruin, in a retired corner, the Squire always had a snug little box, comfortably prepared within for his favourite cat, wherein to find shelter during winter, or in which to snooze when in idle mood or when desirous of retiring from the scorching heat of summer, or, when threatened with an apoplectic seizure from plethora, the consequence of profuse feeding and superfluous attentions bestowed by Mr. Waterton.

Inasmuch as the island, on which the house stands, is closely surrounded by a sheet of water, it seems reasonable to suppose that this residence would be damp, but, this very natural supposition is not verified, indeed, the island itself is remarkably dry, and a spacious stone path-way affords an ample and excellent foot-path from the front door to the cast-iron bridge. Of course, the lake itself affords an inexhaustible supply of soft water for all culinary and cleansing purposes within a few feet of the kitchens and the laundry, which is an incalculable convenience and benefit in a variety of ways, as well as an immense advantage in an economical point of view.

The surface of the island is rich in verdure, and the mansion is supplied with an abundance of fine water, from a crystal spring at a little distance in the park, by ingenious artificial means, the water being conveyed under the lake to the house.

During the life of the late Mr. Waterton's father, he, for many years, kept a few deer on the island, providing them with such additional food as they needed beyond the scanty supply of grass which they were able to pick up within their limited boundary. One of these, however, became savage, and of course, terrified the whole household;—consequently, they were one, and all, discarded.

The front entrance to the hall is a somewhat eccentric one, consisting of folding doors within a plain but well-designed portico, supported by four stone pillars, specimens of the stone obtained from a quarry on the

FRONT VIEW OF WALTON HALL; SURROUNDED BY THE LAKE.

estate. Each door, in its upper panel, has a circularly raised wreath in its centre, originally designed to contain Mr. Waterton's crest, but which is yet blank. The family crest is an otter, with a fish in its mouth, the motto being—

"Better kinde fremd than fremd kinde."

On each of the lower panels is the Maltese cross, and a little above the centre of each folding door is a knocker. These two rappers are ludicrously strange-looking appendages. They are cast, in the similitude of human faces of a very extraordinary character, from bell metal, so as to yield an agreeably harmonious and powerful tone when used; one face representing mirth, and the other misery. The former is immoveably fixed to the door, so that when you have wound up your feelings to give a smart rap-tap-tap, according to the fashion of the day, and are suddenly and unexpectedly disappointed by not being able to raise the knocker you have laid hold of, this face seems to grin with intense delight at your failure; and when you then, somewhat confused, resort to the other face, to rap on its forehead, this rapper appears to scowl upon you as if suffering intense agony from the blows you have just given it. This humorous conception, so admirably executed, was modelled by the united ingenuity of Mr. Waterton and the late Captain Jones. "*Trahit sua quemque voluptas.*" "Each man is led by his own tastes." Within, and above this door, that is, in the vestibule, is a singularly-conceived, and inimitably-modelled, representation of

the nightmare, which is also the production of the same
amateur artists. This horrid incubus has a human face,
grinning and displaying an exact appearance of the
frightfully formidable tusks of the wild boar—the hands
of a man—satanic horns—elephant's ears—bat's wings
—one cloven foot, the other that of an eagle widely
expanding its terrific-looking tallons, and the tail of a
serpent, with the following very appropriate, and
significantly communicative, motto,—

> . . . . *"Assidens procœcordiis*
> *Pavore somnos auferam."*

"Sitting on the region of the heart I take away sleep
by fear."

I have just previously alluded to Mr. Waterton's
crest and motto, in a casual way, the meaning of which
appears to be somewhat dubious, never, so far as I know,
having been literally deciphered. If I am correct in
this supposition, it would, perhaps, not be deemed pre-
sumption to endeavour to suggest a probable, or, at all
events, a possible signification of this motto, in the
hope of stimulating some one, better able, to more correctly unravel the mystery.

> "Better kinde fremd than fremd kinde."
> "Better friendly strangers than deceitful friends."
> or,—
> "Better among strangers than estranged kin."

That is, it is better to deal, or associate, with persons,
between whom and you, there is no natural relationship, but who may, notwithstanding, be friendly disposed,

than to depend upon kindred who have already shown apathy, hostility, or neglect. The Saxon words *cynne* and *fremd* are susceptible of the applications I have here given them. Probably these, and similar words, may have been more familiarly used in Shakespeare's time, and have suggested the smoother, but scarcely more intelligible phrase, put into the mouth of Hamlet,—

"A little more than kin, but less than kind."

Inasmuch as the otter and the fish inhabit the same element, nay, the same stream, there seems to be a sort of natural expectation of friendship between the two, and on this ground, the fish having discovered the destructive and devouring tendencies of his supposed *fidus achates*, may well say—

"Better friendly strangers than deceitful friends."

Cicero did not hesitate to affirm, "*Præstat amicitia propinquitati.*" "Friendship is better than relationship."

The island is circumscribed with a supporting and protecting division between the water and the soil, by means of a very strong stone and mortar wall, the passive power of which is still further increased by numerous and substantial abutments,—all this magnificent masonry having been designed and completed by the Squire. This wall is not in the slightest degree offensive to the eye, from the mansion, nor from any part of the island, as a dead or gloomy object, because the grassy surface of the island has an elevation of upwards of six feet above the level of the lake, so that, from the windows, even on the ground-floor, you look down on the lake.

At the northern entrance of the mansion, there is a spacious hall, on the left of which vestibule, is a large oblong dining-room, having three windows to the north and two to the east, and, communicating with which is a door into the hall, another into the drawing-room, and a third into the passage leading to the kitchens. The drawing-room is large and well proportioned, with three windows to the east and a triple bay plate-glass window to the south, all commanding a fine view of the lake as well as of its surrounding and undulating park. The breakfast-room is small, and has a northern aspect. The remaining part of the ground-floor is occupied by the grand staircase, with its small ante-room at its base, the housekeeper's room, store-rooms, servants' hall, and lofty and well ventilated kitchens. The walls of the staircase are largely supplied with paintings, whilst the centre-part of the staircase itself, from the highest to the lowest portions, is filled with a vast variety of subjects in natural history. It is very spacious and well lighted, and also beautifully arranged for the display of its contents. It ascends to the third story, terminating in a room of considerable extent, with a northern aspect. The first and second tiers are lighted by an immensely long window, on the southern side of the house. In this unique, measureless, and charmingly lofty space, objects of deep

THE CAST-IRON BRIDGE APPROACH TO WALTON HALL.

interest crowd on the eye at every step, and can be well seen in every part of it.

The original approach, by the old swivel-bridge, to the island, from the park, has been superseded by Mr. Waterton having thrown a fixed and substantial, yet light-looking cast-iron bridge over a narrow portion of the lake, which is probably about thirty yards in length, and affords a most convenient communication from the park to the mansion, whilst it forms an ornamental object in the scenery.

About a hundred yards from the bridge, and on the banks of the lake, stands a Lombardy poplar of considerable notoriety, inasmuch as it has been twice struck by lightning, and in connection with which, a singularly providential circumstance occurred. On the evening of the 10th of August, in the year 1842, on the Squire's return home from my house, during an awful thunderstorm, he observed, on his arrival, seven fishermen taking shelter under this poplar. His presence of mind, which rarely forsook him, "*omnium horarum homo*," "a man ready at all hours," prompted him, at once, to direct these poor fellows to instantly leave so dangerous a position.

"*Intonuere poli et crebris micat ignibus æther.*"

"The heavens thunder, and the sky flashes with vivid lightnings." No sooner had the fishermen obeyed Mr. Waterton's call, than the tree itself was nearly rent in twain by a flash of lightning. Its lacerated condition, however, under the constant and skilful care of the naturalist, has been wonderfully restored, although still exhibiting the extreme severity of the electric visitation it had sustained.

This tree was planted in 1756, by the late Mr. Waterton's father, being a gift to him by a friend at Burgh-Wallis, and, when a mere twig, was brought thence, by him, in his pocket; which circumstance, in addition to its being associated with the providential occurrence to which I have already alluded, always furnished a powerful and attractive interest for special protection to this eventful poplar, which was nursed by the Squire with the tenderest care for many years; indeed, it may be said to have been long held in a sort of reverential esteem. In addition, as this individual tree has twice suffered in a similar way, from the same cause, the idea very naturally suggests itself, that its peculiar position, as regards locality, or its pointed and spire-like apex, may have attracted the electric fluid, and thus have acted favourably, as a conductor, and, consequently, proved a fortunate means of hitherto rendering the house scathless.

There appears to be a singularly comparative immunity worthy of record in the female sex from this character of death, which is stated by M. Boudin, to the Academy of Sciences in France. For instance, from 1854 to 1863, out of 800 individuals killed in this manner, 243 only belonged to the female sex, *i.e.* 26·7 per cent.

In several instances lightning struck groups, consisting of males and females, when, the latter were always more or less spared.

In 1853, 15 out of 34 persons, killed in the fields, were, at the time, under the shelter of trees, and from 1841 to 1853, out of 107 individuals struck by lightning, 21 were in the same position.

If we estimate at 25 per cent. the proportion of victims injured beneath trees, we find that out of 6,714 persons killed or wounded in this manner from 1835 to 1863, 1,678 might have have escaped, had they avoided the neighbourhood of trees during storms, and yet how invariably do people, either from ignorance, thoughtlessness, or from being regardless of known danger, rush into the very position affording them the least possible immunity, or the least chance of escape from peril.

Within a few yards of this poplar, the lake has its artificial under-ground waste-sluice, by which, simple but efficient means are arranged to adjust the precise quantity of water required to flow from the lake, so as to preserve its surface always at a certain previously determined height. This concealed sluice, at a little distance from the lake, issues out a visible stream, affording all that could be desired for Mr. Waterton's observations in natural history, and especially so in one particular department, as it furnished an admirable opportunity, to cultivate a more minute and really practical knowledge of the mysterious habits of our little beaver, the water-rat. The water-rat, unlike the "Hanoverians," was a special favourite with Mr. Waterton, and years gone by, he generally secured them in this stream for natural history purposes by his bow and arrow, but, great dexterity, precision of eye, and eagle-winged rapidity were necessary to achieve the fatal issue, as, the velocity of this rat, by its nimble-footed bound from land to water, reduces this act of destruction of life to a flying shot. The stream then passes forward to some more distant pleasure-grounds, through one of the loveliest grottoes, probably, in England, and, at length, after being crossed by two or three naturally formed stone bridges, and having its banks gracefully fringed by groups as well as by isolated rare and beautiful ferns, it flows through a large and well-secured trap reservoir, formed, in order to intercept, and safely retain, any fish that might escape from the lake during a flood, beyond which reservoir, the stream makes the best of its way into the Calder.

Here, close to the fish-trap reservoir, is built a substantial hovel, in which the keeper may shelter, during the night, whilst attending to the protection of his pheasants and other game, or whilst watching the fish reservoir during a flood, when the water occasionally rushes from the lake in a torrent, bringing numbers of fish in the stream to be caught in this trap.

As a lasting proof of the considerate kindness and care manifest for the poor, who were permitted to fish

in the lake for their own pannier, and often, poor
creatures, for their own immediate dinners, the Squire
erected a circular and substantial hovel, in which they
could eat their "bit of bread," or obtain shelter from
the occasional pitiless storm. This fisherman's hut is
encircled, excepting a small space by which to enter
on the south, by a finely-grown yew fence; and its
roof is formed of an immense flag-stone, supported by
three stone pillars, whilst, upon the roof, stands the
ancient "frumenty stone," the letters and figures, "T.
K. W., 1679," being engraven on its anterior surface,
these initials indicating Thomas and Katherine Waterton. Within the cavity of this stone, at the date
described, many a load of wheat has, doubtless, been
triturated by hand, in order to furnish "frumenty,"
which at that period, as now, was so much prized, and
so generally used, at the season of Christmas.

Mr. Waterton had very great pleasure in putting in
requisition the stone with its original inscription for
two reasons, the former, because he had so great a
reverence for his ancestors that he was always
delighted to pay a tribute of respect to their memory—
the latter, because he entertained a decided preference
for antique reminiscences, and for ancient over modern
usages. In addition, it was an object of considerable
interest by affording a practical opportunity of comparing
the former laborious, slow, and imperfect method of pul-
verising wheat with the present easy, speedy and perfect
one.

Ever mindful of the comfort of others, the Squire, many years before his death, permanently fixed an easy and refreshing arm chair in this hut, in which the exhausted and half-starved fisherman might rest his wearied limbs ; or, in which the naturalist visitor to the mansion might, whilst surveying the lake and the land scenery at his leisure, unobservedly watch, the wild and unrestrained habits of the various land and water-fowl, and thus, without any trouble and without the least physical exertion, pick up a variety of that character of information which would be both pleasing and instructive to him, and which it was so difficult to obtain elsewhere, and especially in so luxurious a position.

At a trifling distance from the fisherman's hut, in a south-easterly direction, there is a small pheasantry, its central portion being a clump of yew trees, on thoroughly dry ground, which have had their lateral and inferior branches lopped off, whilst the whole mass is surrounded by an impenetrable holly fence.

About a hundred yards from this little snuggery, there is another and much larger pheasantry, but of a similar description, its central portion also consisting of fir and yew trees, which form a complete and very extensive awning, and, consequently, an admirable retreat for the pheasants, as well as a secure hiding-protection and a perfectly shaded and concealed place for their food, from the pigeons and rooks, which sustenence had to be supplied to them, during

THE STABLE DEPARTMENT, AT WALTON HALL, COVERED WITH

the severe winter months, not only for supporting life, but as an inducement to permanently remain within the park and not expose themselves to be appropriated by poachers.

On returning from the larger pheasantry, towards the well-built and well-arranged stable department, the front of which is ornamented by two splendid vines, yielding excellent fruit during a fine season,—also, close to a small oblong sheet of water, filled with all sorts of fish, and gracefully decorated on its surface by the widely-expanded leaves of the water-lily, through which pond a nice under-ground current flows into the woods and pleasure-grounds below, you pass "John Bull and the National Debt," a singularly unique combination, and well worthy of a very minute examination.

> "*Dicam insigne recens adhuc*
> *Indictum ore alio.*"

"I shall record a remarkable event, which is new, as yet, and untold by the lips of another."

This "*lusus naturæ,*" or, what I may describe as a very extraordinary phenomenon, is interesting, not merely because there is not, in all human probability, a known similar instance, but because it is itself a marvellous example of nature's power in accommodating herself to circumstances, notwithstanding their extreme deviation from her ordinary course.

CHAPTER II.

MANY years ago, this property, like many other private rseidences, had, at that time, its own corn-mill; but, when this inconvenient necessity no longer existed, the then unserviceable building, with all its useless appliances, doubtless shared the common fate of such cumbersome structures.

It would appear, that in disposing of these materials, worthless at that period, a mill-stone had been removed, with a view of putting it out of the way, into what had evidently been an old orchard. The diameter of this circular mill-stone measures five and a half feet, whilst its depth averages seven inches throughout, and its central hole has a diameter of eleven inches. Apparently, by mere accident, some bird, or probably a squirrel, had dropped the fruit of the filbert tree through this hole on to the earth, as, in the year 1812, the seedling of a future filbert tree was seen rising up through the hole. In subsequent years, as its trunk gradually ascended through this central opening, annually increasing in diameter, its power to raise, at some future period, this ponderous mass of stone from the earth, was speculated upon by many parties, totally disinterested, excepting by a laudable curiosity. The contemplated future power of this sapling was frequently expatiated upon by *the* naturalist himself, whilst examining it with his friends, when three knotty questions, involving the future, were usually dis-

"JOHN BULL AND THE NATIONAL DEBT," A LUSUS NATURÆ IN THE
GROUNDS AT WALTON HALL.

cussed with great earnestness; and not unfrequently, nay, generally, the friendly disputants ultimately arrived at as many varying conclusions.

The *first* question was, Would this filbert tree continue at all to eke out its existence, when so tightly encircled by the unyielding stone? The *second* was, Would the tree, if it did survive, ever be able, during its upward growth, to raise so enormous a weight, in any appreciable degree, from the earth? The *third*, and probably the most doubtful one, was, Would the mill-stone be able to resist the continual expansion of the trunk of the tree, without itself being rent asunder?

Two of these questions, so natural to ask yet then so difficult of solution, have been now unequivocally set at rest. The tree not only continued to live for many years, but it soon became evident that its upward growth gradually and perpendicularly elevated the monstrous mill-stone along with it. This had been an anxious and an eventful period for the Squire, but the result was exceedingly gratifying, by his previously expressed anticipations being progressively realised during his life.

In 1863, the aerial position of the mill-stone, assuming a somewhat crinoline form, was found, by careful measurement, to be nearly a foot from the ground, and appeared, evidently, a very unwieldly incumbrance to hang round the trunk of the filbert tree. This fortuitous occurrence, and destructive position, as well as the singularly unique altitude for a mill-stone to occupy, coupled with what *must* eventually be the result of the fatal grasp of this ponderous, hard, and inelastic mass of dead matter, induced, Mr. Waterton to name this extraordinary combination, "John Bull and the National Debt." We can not, for a moment, doubt, that this accidental and unnatural union was, for a long period, a great discouragement to the healthy growth of vegetation, simply from its grasping embrace. Nor can we doubt that the weight of the stone has been a most disastrous drag round the neck of the filbert-tree, whatever eight hundred millions sterling may have been around the neck of our nation.

In November, 1864, Mr. Waterton writes,—"The millstone tree has undergone an odd transmutation. The parent stem has died; but, perceiving a radical shoot trying hard to work its way outside of the stone, I cut away the parent stem, and bended the shoot back again to the centre. It grows well, and will inherit its father's situation shortly, and become John Bull the 2nd."

On our way to the grotto, you pass another union at variance with the harmonious laws of nature, viz., two trees, the spruce fir and the elm, which were, originally, planted side by side, but which, by the Squire's own hand, had been annually twisted round each other, and have, consequently, in some parts, grown one into the other. Horace had warned future ages in reference to an atempt to reconcile things which are adverse to the established course of events.

> .   .   .   .   *" Pergis pugnantia secum*
> *Frontibus adversis componere."*

"You are trying to reconcile things which are opposite in their nature."

The process of training, in this instance, in order to endeavour to force by artificial means, an unnatural union, has resulted, as must have been anticipated, in a miserably stunted growth of both trees, and therefore, this manifest failure of any beneficial conjunction of interests, was by Mr. Waterton, always facetiously pointed out as an apt illustration of what he deemed the absurdity of the union of "church and state;" hence, this sobriquet was given to the union of these trees.

> . . " *Non ut placidis coëant immitia, non ut*
> *Serpentes airbus geminentur, tigribus agni.*"

> . . . " Nature, and the common laws of sense,
> Forbid to reconcile antipathies ;
> Or make a snake engender with a dove,
> And hungry tigers court the tender lamb."

I have a suspicion that the Squire well knew what would be the suicidal termination of this union, and that it was originally designed and carried out in order to support his favourite crotchet of a thorough disapprobation of the union of Church and State, as we seldom passed it, on our way to the grotto, without his slily making some jocosely caustic observation in derision, or indicating his ostracism by a jeering expression of countenance, as if to draw my attention to the absurdity of the junction, or, of the "two rolled into one."

Passing along an avenue in the wood, where, in trunks of trees, artificial nesting boxes were prepared in hidden recesses, for the brown and the barn-owl; and where the relics of wooden imitation-pheasants are

D

perched here and there on the surrounding trees, so as to delude and mislead the poachers in days gone by, you come rather suddenly to a termination of this avenue, where the road bifucrates. "*Hic locus est, partes ubi se via findit in ambas.*" "This is the spot where the road divides into two parts;" one path slighty diverging to the left, towards the fish-trap reservoir, whilst the other, turning at right angles, leads to the lovely and charming grotto.

Here, at this junction of the roads, you come to an ancient stone cross, meriting observation. This curious remnant of Saxon art was, some time ago, accidentally discovered in the neighbouring town of Wakefield, where it had, from time immemorial, been in constant use, having formed an humble door step, in one of the ancient houses in that town once called "merry Wakefield." No one appeared to be able to afford any information how this cross came to be put to such ignoble use. After many applications, possession was at length obtained of this beautiful specimen of the old Saxon crosses, now so extremely rare in England.

Directly in front of the junction just named, you have an immediate view of a most magnificent clump of the spruce-fir, a specially favourite nesting retreat for the ring-dove, the brown owl, the kestrel, the jackdaw, the magpie, and the jay, as well as for a host of the ordinary British birds, which flock to this sequestered place for shelter and to secure a safe retreat from man. These firs, which are of remarkably fine growth, are pruned to the height of seven or eight feet from the ground, consequently, they form an unbroken canopy above, affording

"THE GROTTO," IN THE GROUNDS AT WALTON HALL.

a most fascinating and delightfully refreshing promenade in summer, and, in winter, a complete protection, by warding off the chilling blast from every point of the compass.

In description, we have now arrived in the immediate neighbourhood of "the grotto," a little earthly paradise, where the Squire and I, sitting in front of the larger temple, have beguiled many an hour in natural history pursuits, for upwards of five and twenty years, ever charmed by the varied music of the feathered tribe, in addition to our being deeply interested in silently watching the diversified habits and distinguishing peculiarities of the numerous birds in view, when nesting or maturing their offspring, or when temporarily sojourning here.

The grotto is embosomed in wood, to the extent, and at the precise distance from its centre, to enhance, in the greatest possible degree, its many charms. It is a flower-garden excavation hewn out of solid rock. In its base, it is graced by a small temple, having an obtusely formed conical roof, supported on stone pillars, and covered with ivy. In its centre, is a table, which is surrounded by benches for the accommodation of visitors to these grounds. On the rocky summit of the grotto, and on its brink, stands a large and circular temple, its roof being lofty and spherical, and supported by eight stone pillars. When pic-nic parties assembled here, which they did from a distance of many many miles, they usually availed themselves, if the weather should be unfavourable, of the larger temple for dinner, and for dancing.

In these pleasure-grounds, such gatherings of friends, forming large parties, were numerous and frequent in the spring, summer, and autumnal months, as every arrangement had been considerately made to meet the wants, and to afford the necessary comforts for pic-nic parties.

During the life of the late Mr. Waterton, any party, having a card of admission for a special day, always had the park reserved for themselves during that day, which afforded an agreeable privacy and a greater scope for positive enjoyment. Occasionally, these pic-nic parties numbered several hundreds, and were accompanied by very excellent bands of music, when frequently, dancing was the order of the day, either on the turf,—under the canopy of the spruce-fir grove,—in the base of the grotto,—or in the larger temple, which is about one-third of a mile from the hall. On such occasions, if the late Mr. Waterton appeared, even at a distance, during these happy, rural, and festive gaieties, the Squire was always greeted by the bands playing, and the whole multitude joining in chorus, "The fine Old English Gentleman;" having selected the portions peculiarly applicable to the high-spirited and generous-hearted "old Squire:"—

> "I'll sing you a good old song that was made by a good old pate,
> Of a fine old English Gentleman, who had an old estate ;
> And who kept up his old mansion at a bountiful old rate,
> With a good old porter to relieve the old poor at his gate,
> Like a fine old English Gentloman, one of the olden time.
> His custom was when Christmas came, to bid his friends repair
> To his old Hall, where feast and ball for them he did prepare ;
> And though the rich he entertained, he ne'er forgot the poor.
> Nor was the houseless wanderer e'er driven from the door
> Of this good old English Gentleman, one of the olden time."

There was ever a manifest warmth of feeling, and a genuine energy of voice displayed, which afforded an abundant proof of gratitude for the generous reception they had met with. Although these gatherings were sometimes apparently unwieldy in number, yet seldom or never was the slightest damage sustained in any part of the park, or any impropriety of conduct indulged in. On taking their final departure, they usually congregated at the cast-iron bridge, in front of the Hall, and played and sang "God save the Queen," as their last grateful offering, with a heartiness and enthusiasm, that would have animated the heart of a stoic.

More private, and more aristocratic *symposia* were, now and then, concentrated in the park at Walton Hall, to have a day of thorough and unrestrained enjoyment, 'who rarely bade adieu without showering down numberless blessings on the venerable octogenarian, for his own sake, associated with ardently expressed wishes, that the good old man might live many years, enjoy life, and generously afford them future pleasures. Ovid has truly beautifully, and most appropriately, embodied all their wishes, in two lines :—

> " *Di tibi dent annos! a te nam cætera sumes,*
> *Sint modo virtuti tempora longa tuæ.*"

"May the Gods grant thee length 'of years! 'all other blessings from thyself thou wilt derive, let only time be granted for thy virtues."

On the brink of the precipice, hewn out of rock,

and forming the posterior portion of the grotto, in front of the larger temple, and in a southern aspect, sat the Squire on sunny days, ever minutely perfecting his knowledge in natural history. *The naturalist* would be here seated for a lengthened period, even without his hat, under a scorching sun, looking down upon the smaller temple—on a shaded site—upon the stream, which glides silently along from the lake, to the fish-trap reservoir—upon an artificial nesting tower, for the starling and jackdaw specially,—and upon the splendid grove of the spruce-fir, tenanted by a vast variety of the feathered songsters, all pursuing their own instinctively individual vocations and habits, peculiarly allotted to them by nature's unerring laws. This scenery has really a soothing influence, which must be experienced in order to be thoroughly appreciated.

Hundreds of times in this enchanting alcove, fascinating the naturalist by a happy combination of nature and of art, have I shared my old friend's enjoyment. With extreme pleasure have I heard him, in an unaffected enthusiasm, recount and dilate upon his daring ornithological adventures in the vast and interminable forests of that unparalleled country South America. Riveted to the rock on which we have rested, have I intently listened to the autobiographical description of his solitary exploring career, primarily conceived and contemplated in admiration of the feathered tribes, originally cultivated in his father's grounds, subsequently nursed into a fundamentally growing and increasing attachment, and, at length, ripening into an unflinching determination, on the part of the naturalist, to be able to say, in these dark, dreary, and boundless forests " *Veni vidi vici.*"

The Squire, seeing that his numerous incidents of travel were deeply interesting to me, would fondly dwell upon many and various expedients and manœuvres resorted to in order to gain possession of those birds which were rare and difficult to approach. He would recount the peculiar and apt character of arrangements in detail necessary to be devised by himself and adjusted with the natives in order to secure what was required by his ingenious and decoying contrivances, so that he might be able to obtain the shy, the cunning, and the seldom seen birds. All these designs evidently emanated from a master-mind, and from a proficiency in that special craft or vocation, into which the naturalist had launched his bark, and to which, he was so ardently attached. He would describe the characteristic flight of the minutest humming birds, mere atoms of creation—the dust-shot destruction of one of these beautiful particles of vitality by a single pellet, which was the very perfection of shooting for future preservation of the bird.

Mr. Waterton's innate, or, as it were, indigenous knowledge of, and influence over uncivilized man, enabled him to gain the confidence of the natives to a surprising extent, so that they served him with greater courage, with more zeal, ingenuity and fidelity, than English servants would have done.

I could gather from the Squire, that if a frown was

needed to intimidate, it was evident that he was in immediate possession of one. On the other hand, if a smile was an essential requisite at the moment, his countenance was instantly clothed with a gracious and an alluring one. His great object, therefore, was never to allow a native to see that *he doubted*. If the Squire doubted, *they hesitated*, and he was no longer supreme. Mr. Waterton speedily discovered this trait in their character, which put him in possession of an influence rendering him capable of surely accomplishing all he required, without which power, his exploring excursion would have been a fruitless one.

Even the hundred lunatics, from the Wakefield Asylum, who were wont to be kindly permitted by Mr. Waterton to have their harmless and frolicsome merriment — their dancing, and their dinner, within the grotto — were always greatly delighted, and even tranquillised, so as to temporarily forget their pitiable and frequently unhappy condition, and one and all to declare the grotto to be an elysium.

Above, and behind the larger temple, in the wood, is an artificially prepared trunk of an ash-tree, set apart for the owl, a very favourite bird with the Squire; and, in a portion of this trunk, which was decayed, there was a cavity, in which an ox-eye titmouse yearly nested, hatched, and matured her young, for a long period. Mr. Waterton attached a door hung on hinges, to exactly fit the opening in the trunk, having a hole in its inferior portion, for the admission and escape of the titmouse, when the door itself was closed. The Squire seldom omitted visiting his little favourite daily, and was in the habit of opening the door, and gently and delicately drawing his hand over the back of the bird, to give her a convincing proof that he was her friend, — a little confidential intercourse between the two, which I have, with great pleasure frequently witnessed. On one occasion, after the titmouse had raised her offspring to maturity, and for that season, had deserted her habitation, a squirrel, unfortunately, selected this tempting excavation for its nest; and although, early the following spring, every relic of the lining of the squirrel's nest was carefully removed, yet, from that period, no bird ever ventured within the cavity, in order to restore it to its original use.

The temples at the grotto—the excavated rock which forms it — the tea-room — the owl and the jackdaw-tower, and the keeper's hovel at the fish-trap reservoir were all fabricated by Jack Ogden the keeper, and his master. Jack was originally a mason and an excellent workman, as well as, naturally, a very clever fellow. Early in life he was strongly tainted with poaching propensities, which accomplishment being whispered into the ear of the Squire, Jack was speedily installed "keeper for Mr. Waterton," a post of honour and eminence, of which Ogden was always proud, which he never disgraced, and, the duties of which he discharged most faithfully. He was passionately attached

to his master, and the balance of approbation between
Jack and his master, was always so equally poised,
that the Squire was ever ready to cry quits. Ogden
was gifted with brains to invariably discriminate his
master's wants, whilst they were of a character that
enabled him to fulfil all reasonable ones, and the Squire
was never known to ask an unreasonable one. Mr.
Waterton was wont to say that Jack Ogden was the
very perfection of the man he needed in the South
American forests. Poor Jack died a little before his
master, deeply regretted by him as well as by many of
this faithful keeper's friends, during his reign at
Walton Hall. Jack was a crack shot, and clever in
breaking either pointer or retriever, and was well up
in all the little generally hidden mysteries of the
accomplished keeper. He could use the casting net
very adroitly on the lake, or from its margin, and could
handle the oar and steer his boat like an old sailor.

It is somewhat singular that Ogden had scraped together
a certain amount of knowledge relative to the Battle of
Wakefield Green, and the troops assembled at Sandal
Castle, coupled with the cruelty of Lord Clifford in mur-
dering the youthful Duke of Rutland. The name of Clifford, again incidentally introduced, suggests the propriety
of alluding to a very singular and interesting circumstance
recorded in the following letter to my friend, Mr. Salvin,
who stands so distinguished in the art of hawking, a
pastime in such high favour to the end of the Saxon era.

It happens that I had the pleasure of being intimately
acquainted with the late Mr. George Walker, and can,

therefore, thoroughly corroborate Mr. Salvin's impressions that our friend's unerring perceptivity might be emphatically depended upon.

REMARKABLE RECOGNITION.

"About the time Dr. Whitaker wrote the history of Craven (a district in Yorkshire), he and some of his antiquarian friends opened several ancient graves at Bolton Abbey and other places. At Skipton they peeped into the tomb of Admiral Lord Clifford, and as I have been told, a curious circumstance connected with it, from one present on the occasion, viz., the late Mr. George Walker, of Killingbeck Hall, near Leeds, I think it worthy of record. Mr. W. told me that they found the Earl, who had been embalmed, quite perfect and dressed in the costume of the day, in high crowned hat, plume and frill, &c., but no sooner was he exposed to the air than the remains began to shake like a jelly, and in a few seconds all gave way, and this extraordinary sight (bringing one back to the days of Elizabeth), collapsed into dust. Mr. W. who was a person of great observation, and who was a naturalist, a sportsman, and an amateur artist, was very fond, at this period, of making pedestrian tours through the country, and he informed me, that the day after his curious introduction to the Earl, he visited Chatsworth, and, whilst looking through the pictures, he had the pleasure of putting the housekeeper right, for she had got her story wrong about the portraits, and pointed out one which she said was this identical Admiral

Lord Clifford. Upon this, he said, 'I must correct you; (here pointing to another picture) this is the Admiral, for I saw him only yesterday, and if necessary, I could swear to him.' "—F. H. SALVIN.

Near the smaller and lower temple, and on the brink of a precipice above it, there stands, in a prominent position, a cross, said by the Squire to be the first that was erected and exposed to public view in England after the Reformation.

Ever anxious to gratify all, and more especially the juveniles, Mr. Waterton kindly erected, on the border of the spruce-fir grove, a chair-swing, of truly noble dimensions and of extensive sweep, in which many a buxom country girl has joyously received the swinging attentions of her devoted swain, in this secluded little valley.

The Squire frequently alluded to his old favourite the "Ox-eye," as if grieving for the loss of a valued friend, telling me how many visits he had known the parents pay to their young in one hour during the subsistency of their numerous brood within the tree. Mr. Wieber has stated, that "at half-past three o'clock in the morning in July," he "carefully watched the blue titmice feed their young, six in number. From 3.30 to 4.0, they fed them twelve times—from 4.0 to 5.0, twenty-five times—from 5.0 to 6.0, forty times—which was astonishing as, during the whole of *this* hour, they flew to a plantation at a distance of more than one hundred and fifty yards from their nest. From 6.0 to 7.0, they fed them twenty-nine times. During a part of this hour they fed every minute. From 7.0 to 8.0, they fed them twenty times. During this hour, it rained heavily. From 8.0 to 9.0, they fed them thirty-six times, and from 9.0 to 10.0, forty-six times. During a part of this hour, they fed them twelve times in five minutes. From 10.0 to 11.0, they fed them thirty-seven times, from 11.0 to 12.0, thirty-nine times, from 12.0 to 1.0, twenty-four times. From 1.0 to 2.0, they fed them twenty-three times, from 2.0 to 3.0, thirty-four times, from 3.0 to 4.0, eighteen times, from 4.0 to 5.0, twenty-nine times, from 5.0 to 6.0, twenty-five times, from 6.0 to 7.0, twenty times, and from 7.0 to 8.30, twenty-five times. They now stopped, after having been almost incessantly engaged for nearly seventeen hours in their labours of love, and after having fed their young four hundred and seventy-five times." The Squire was always delighted to carry out experiments of this nature himself, whilst time, opportunities, inclination, and suitable locations were at his command.

Passing from the grotto to the northern side of the lake, you find here and there, *en route*, in the wood, several trunks of trees, about fifteen feet high, fixed in an upright position. These trunks, being decayed, are hollow, and, for that very reason, were selected for the purpose for which Mr. Waterton intended them. The decay having rendered the cavities within the stems pervious to rain, they were protected on their summit by an artificial roof so that the hollow portions might be kept perfectly dry. Holes were purposely pierced in the stems, leading to the cavities, in order to afford a free entrance for birds to occupy them for the purpose of nesting and hatching, and to provide for them a secure retreat from vermin.

In the month of May, 1862, the Squire pointed out to me three birds' nests within one cavity, viz., the nest of a jackdaw, with five eggs—that of a barn-owl, with three young ones, very near to which, (the owl's resort,) were several dead mice and a half-grown rat,—and, eighteen inches above the nest of the owl, in a little recess, was a redstart's nest, containing six eggs. The barn-owl and the jackdaw must have passed in and out at the same hole, and therefore, in all probability, were on neighbourly terms. The redstart might have entered and returned by a small hole a little higher up, and then have descended to its nest; but at all events, it inhabited the same cavity, all three birds dwelling under the same roof, and, in fact, in one room; we must also remember that this was a voluntary act on the part of each of these birds.

> "I shall not ask Jean Jacques Rousseau
> If birds confabulate or no;
> 'T is clear that they were always able
> To hold discourse—at least in fable."

In an unreclaimed state, birds, although of different species, are not generally disposed to quarrel with each other; neither do the savage race of animals, of the same species, object to associate with one another. Juvenal tells us " the ferocious tiger agrees with his fellow, and the bear consorts with the bear."

> . . . . . " *Tigris agit rabida cum tigride pacem*
> *Perpetuam, sœvis inter se convenit ursis.*"

On the same day, in a tuft of rushes, just within the water and on the edge of the lake, we carefully examined a water-hen's nest, into which, when the old bird had left it, we could see very distinctly. It contained nine eggs and four very recently hatched young ones, a larger number of eggs, by four than Mr. Waterton had ever before known. Water-hens were great pets with the Squire, daily during winter coming upon the lawn in front of the mansion, to be fed by him from the windows. They are singular birds, as regards their apparent pertness, and the very extraordinary rapidity of their physical movements, especially as to the precipitant or jerking motion of the tail ; and are not less remarkable for their pertinacious and adherent constancy of attachment to their nest and its contents, when once they have fairly commenced incubation.

I will narrate one out of many instances, which have occurred at Walton Hall. In the year 1825, when a willow was being stubbed by the workmen, on the "little island" in the centre of the lake, they found during their labour, the nest of a water-hen containing seven eggs. They moved the naked nest, with its eggs, a distance of three yards, and there left it on the bare earth. Notwithstanding this rude interference, the old bird, so soon as the workmen had gone away, gathered together the dried and dead grass, which had been previously used as a foundation for her original nest, and at once instinctively commenced her new labours, by tidily arranging, and propping up with this *debris*, the shattered remains of her former domicile; she then again took possession of her nest, and hatched her seven chicks in due time.

We afterwards discovered, in an artificially prepared trunk of an old ash-tree, the nest of a brown owl, in which was one addled egg, the young owls having flown. Mr. Waterton remarked that it was singular, but in all the brown owls' nests that he had examined, he had never found more than three eggs, and, that in every instance, one out of this number was addled.

Whilst stating the Squire's observations about the *eggs* of the brown owl, I am reminded of his opinion as to the carrion-crow sucking the eggs of other birds. He did not deny that the carrion-crow would suck eggs, and also devour the young of birds recently hatched, but he much doubted their being so frequently destructive as they were represented to be, otherwise, he thought he should have seen signs of such instances, occasionally, in the park, considering the many opportunities afforded him, and he had not seen a single case sufficient to convict the carrion-crow, whilst he had repeatedly seen instances where the accused had not availed itself of opportunities which had occurred.

For instance, in 1852, a pair of water-hens built
their scanty nest at the head of the lake, by merely
placing, in various directions, one twig upon another
on the surface of the water, but only to such an
amount, and extent, that it would float sufficiently
to sustain the female and her eggs, without there
being any solid foundation whatever under the nest.
Its watery site was in a very secluded spot, being in a
sort of little bay, and scarcely under the influence of
even a more than ordinary breeze, whilst it was made
still less so, from its immediate proximity to an abundance of luxuriant rushes at the edge of the lake.
In this openly exposed nest, without the least attempt
at concealment by its builders, and directly under the
nest of a pair of carrion-crows, in an alder-tree, the
water-hens hatched their eggs, and reared their young,
without any apparent molestation from the carrion-
crows. Now, during the lenghtened period of incubation, when the water-hen would, of course, frequently leave her nest in quest of food, the carrion-
crows must have had many opportunities afforded
them to slily pilfer an egg from the water-hen's nest,
or, subsequently, to lay hold of so delicate a morsel
as a newly hatched chick, yet no such cruelty was
perpetrated, clearly proving that the destruction of
eggs or chicks is not an every-day criminal act with
this "bird of prey."

On the southern side of the lake, and in front of
the drawing-room windows of the Hall, is an extensive

E

and carefully protected heronry; a rare and valuable acquisition to the grounds of a naturalist in the present destructive age. This heronry afforded the Squire an ample opportunity of becoming familiar with the habits of a bird, about which, it is now next to an impossibility to gain reliable information. An open swamp is preserved, in its native boggy condition, between the heronry and the house, in order to tempt the herons to spend a portion of their time in it, so that they themselves, should constitute, not merely additional ornaments to the scenery, but highly interesting objects, in a scientific point of view. In this favourite swamp, the herons could be seen, in perfection, through the telescope, from the drawing-room windows, by which means the Squire became intimately acquainted with all their little peculiarities, an immensely instructive, and a most interesting advantage, and one which few, if, indeed, any other naturalist possesses. Their habits were not merely seen and narrowly watched collectively, but individually, and not only when engaged in the marshy ground, to which they appeared to give a preference, but also when they retired to the dry banks to rest and to plume themselves,—which cleansing and embellishing operation was minutely attended to every day.

Here was a pre-eminent opportunity to occasionally watch the herons, when in search of their finny as well as of their amphibious prey along the shallow and rushy margin of the lake, also to scrutinize the mode of carrying out nidification in all its rude simplicity of architecture;

to investigate the special character of materials forming their nest, and to ascertain the precise kind of food supplied to their young.

It is acknowledged that the young heron is a great delicacy on the table, if killed at a proper time, and cooked by a *connoisseur* in the Art. They should never be killed for the table until they have had, for the longest possible time, the benefit of the moonlight nights to gather flesh by fishing, and when killed, the bird should be enclosed in an earthenware jar, and buried underground for several days, by which means their brown colour becomes white, and the fishy flavour vanishes.

Herons are remarkably speedy in the act of nidification, generally constructing their nests in two days, and it was no uncommon thing to find in the same nest, eggs, the young just hatched, and some nearly full-fledged young ones. During these periods, there would always be one of the old herons prominently posted in the heronry on the watch, to ward off the carrion-crows and magpies from attacking the young herons; and, when in defence of the offspring, whether her own, or those of another, she would daringly and indeed irresistibly, give battle to the intruder in protection of the helpless progeny over which she had been appointed sentinel.

Her onslaught on the interloper was made more terrific by a fiendish screech added to a descent so fierce and furious, that her enemy generally retreated in rapid flight so as to seldom suffer even a scratch; but, on one occasion, the keeper was witness to a heron spiking a retreating magpie through its back, when her sharp pointed bill became temporarily so firmly transfixed in the back of the magpie, that in this entangled condition they descended several yards before they became separated, when the magpie fell headlong into the swamp near the heronry, and was drawing its last breath when the keeper reached it. Herons, in their early stage of life, are extremely clumsy and awkward, without, of course, any knowledge of balancing properties, when the branch containing their nests is under the influence of a high wind, and are, therefore, frequently tossed out of their shallow and unprotected tenements, and, consequently, now and then, die from sheer starvation, as well as from the violence of a fall from so elevated a position. In the Island of Islay, herons build on the ground, and, consequently, escape the dangers of the shallow nest.

When such disasters did occur at Walton Hall, it was Jack Ogden's duty to gather up the fragments, in the form of the benumbed and the maimed, in order to replace them in their own special berths, if sufficient vitality remained to give Jack a reasonable hope of resuscitation. After a stormy night, the Squire was on the look out for Jack with the halt and the maimed, or, at all events, to receive a report of their number and the intensity of any unfortunate catastrophies that might have occurred during the boisterous night, when grief or joy betrayed his mental impressions, in accordance with his faithful keeper's announcement.

It is worthy of remark that, some years ago, the heronry was in the wood, on the northern side of the lake. It,

however, became desirable to cut down a few trees, in
order to benefit the growth of the remaining ones in
this part of the wood, which was quietly and carefully
accomplished, and, of course, not in the nesting season;
yet, from this time, the herons commenced to change
their quarters, and all apparently agreed to occupy the
southern, the opposite side of the lake, where every
possible care was bestowed upon them, so long as they
remained within the walls of the park; but, unfortunately,
herons take long, I believe, extraordinarily long flights,
generally during the evening, in search of variety of food,
and in the morning on their return home, are, consequently, much exposed to the merciless public, who spare
no pains to destroy these interesting and harmless birds.
It is not, however, in their long flight, that they are shot,
as they fly too high to be killed *by shot*. They usually
suffer by being surprised in their fishing streams, where
they are suddenly pounced upon whilst fishing little
shaded rivulets. Their commencing ascent, from the
stream into the air, when disturbed, is so slow, that
they seldom escape, even, an indifferent shot. They are,
in general, shot, not because they are required for the
purpose of being "set up" as specimens in the science of
ornithology, nor because they are wanted for the table,
nor because the bird is suspected of doing injury in any
way, but simply, that he who kills may boast that he has
shot a heron.

This heronry at one time, in consequence of its
position, and also of its trifling distance from a most
destructive influence (soap and vitriol-works), barely

escaped annihilation. If it had been where it formerly was, viz., on the opposite side of the park, the trees forming the heronry must have succumbed to the abominable effluvia arising from these works, unless an injunction had been obtained : — the odour from which (the soap and vitriol-works), was disagreeably offensive, as well as very detrimental to both animal and vegetable life. Some of the Squire's finest trees were literally destroyed, and many hundreds very seriously injured. Mr. Waterton being anxious, if possible, to avoid law, took Terence for his guide, who contends that "it becomes a wise man to try every thing that can be done by words, before he has recourse to arms." "*Omnia priùs verbis experiri, quam armis, sapientem decet.*" Reasoning and persuasive measures were therefore, adopted on the part of the late Mr. Waterton, to induce the owner of the soap and vitriol-works to abate the nuisance ; but these friendly warnings failing to produce the desired effect, the Squire was most reluctantly compelled in self-defence, to resort to a court of justice for the protection of his property, when he was awarded eleven hundred pounds for the injury sustained, as well as an injunction to prohibit the continuance of the works. But no victory is to be obtained without some inconvenience. "*Patitur qui vincit.*" "He suffers who conquers." For a considerable period, many of the spruce and silver-firs, in the neighbourhood of the grotto, had the greatest difficulty to struggle through the shattered condition to which they were reduced, whilst a few of the highly ornamental ones fairly yielded to the baneful influence of this deadly poison. "*Hæret lateri lethalis arundo.*" "The fatal shaft remains fixed in her side."

Soon after the termination of this law-suit, "a hue and cry" was universally raised and most perseveringly indulged in, relative to the supposed destruction of a number of splendid trees by the Scolytus in some of the southern counties, when owners of well-wooded parks and pleasure-grounds, all over the country, were in fear and trembling, lest their ornamental scenery should be subjected to similar depredations by this beetle. Mr. Waterton, who, unfortunately for himself, had already had woeful experience, by the destruction of the trees, in consequence of the miserable plight to which many of his own were reduced, from the poisonous emanations arising from the neighbouring vitriolworks, could authoritatively assert,—"*Ærumnabilis experientia me docuit.*" "Sorrowful experience has taught me." Fortified by a practical knowledge, the Squire "took the bull by the horns," and at once boldly disputed the opinion which was then promulgated, insisting that the Scolytus was not the destroying agent of a single *healthy* tree, but that this beetle, in his boring propensities, merely took advantage of the morbid, or, I might safely say, the moribund condition already existing in trees, in which he was erroneously declared to have committed such *primary* ravages. Of course, closet naturalists, having once fairly committed themselves, by publicly arraigning the Scolytus as the destroying agent, maintained their assertion with great earnestness, and warmly vindicated their opinion with apparently unlimited confidence, although devoid of an atom of practical information on which to fight their battle ; and for a time, but for a brief period only, the more the accuracy of their judgment was questioned, ("happy in their error," "*felices errore suo*," or, as Gray has it, "where ignorance is bliss, 't is folly to be wise,") the more staunchly, nay, the more pertinaciously did they adhere to and vainly endeavour to support their previous pompously proclaimed edict.

In addition to information gleaned from careful observation antecedently made in his own park, Mr. Waterton perfected his knowledge, on this subject by a series of practical experiments, so as to unravel, with certainty, the mysteries enveloped in the wholesale accusation against this poor beetle, by immediately subjecting some of his supernumerary trees to circular "barking," or, what I should call, debarking the trunks near their roots, so as to reduce these *then* healthy trees to a moribund condition, in order to prove that a perfectly *healthy* tree was not the material in which the Scolytus would bore and deposit its eggs for a future change. So soon as the Squire succeeded in reducing healthy trees to a morbid and moribund state, then, and not until then, were the trees seductive, nay, even acceptable boring-ground for the Scolytus. I was witness to numerous experiments in the course of this interesting investigation, and still possess specimens corroborating the opinion which Mr. Waterton had

previously entertained, and which he as energetically
and successfully vindicated in a newspaper discussion.
There was always something on the very face of this
ungenerous accusation against the Scolytus, when first
promulgated, that appeared to really carry its own condemnation along with it, as we rarely, in the lower
grades of animal life, see any living creature *destroy*,
unless some future beneficial result should be obtained
in order to counterbalance in some way or other, this
destruction. If it were otherwise, it would appear to
be flagrantly inconsistent with the harmonious order
of nature in creation.

At one time, Mr. Waterton might, without much
exaggeration, have fairly enough quoted Cicero :—
"*Arbores serit diligens agricola, quarum aspiciet nun-
quam ipse baccam.*" "The industrious husbandman plants
trees, of which he himself will never see a berry." The
Squire, from an early age, took an infinity of pains
with his trees, whether isolated or in groups, all of
which have been planted with so much taste and
sound judgment, that they really are very decorative
to the hall, which, itself, can boast of little or no stone
ornamentation in an architectural point of view.

The external appearance of the house is not calculated to influence in its favour, but its singular position
being closely surrounded by deep water instigates a sort
of recommendation on its behalf.

The Grecian mansion is, without doubt, a truly substantial structure, and a really good and convenient

family-residence. The Squire might have justly said with Cicero, "that by many appliances and elegancies, he had rendered his house more commodious and convenient." "*Multis commoditatibus et elegantiis, suas ædes commodiores aptioresque fecit.*"

The mansion has three entrances, viz., a northern, a southern, and a western one. The first is the receiving entrance—the second is a more private one—whilst the third, the western entrance, is for the domestics. The front windows command a view of the four sycamores, and the flagged path-way from the entrance-door to the cast-iron bridge; on the east of which is the ruin, encompassed by a beautiful yew fence. The gable of this ruin covered with ivy, has its foundation in the lake, and upon it is a stone cross, recently substituted for a wooden one. This gable with its ancient door, forms the northern portion of the ruin.

Within the lofty yew fence stands the nesting tower for the starling, jackdaw, and white owl, which I have already described, on the top of which is an ornamental finish, in the form of a globular stone.

Between the cast-iron bridge, which is a pleasing object from the windows, and the ruin, is an entrance to the latter, which is not visible from the house. The clump of trees immediately beyond the bridge, and in a northerly direction, consists of a large number of splendid hollies, which afford a protecting and secluded retreat for our smaller British birds during an inclement winter.

At a little distance beyond, and on the left of the

LOFTY YEW FENCE, THE BRIDGE, AND FISHERMAN'S HUT, AT WALTON HALL.

ruin, is seen from the house, across the narrow portion of the lake, the very dense and compact yew tree grove, which forms the larger pheasantry.

On the right of the ruin, and on the opposite side of the lake, is the fisherman's hut, the noted Lombardy poplar, and the smaller pheasantry. Between the bridge and the carriage road leading to the stables, and surrounding the magnificent clump of hollies, there are a few ornamental and isolated fruit-trees.

On the left of the bridge is the rookery; and in the distance is seen a considerable extent of grass-land, with here and there detached oaks. The grass-land gradually ascends from the lake, is bounded by wood on both sides, and in its further prospect in front, by the horizon. This varied view is mellowed down by including an interesting portion of the lake, and much enhanced in beauty when seen from one of the two windows in the extension-staircase, inasmuch as many of the smaller objects then become conspicuous, and the visible extent of water is also very materially increased.

In the spring of the year, this scenery is made yet more interesting and attractive to all, as well as specially instructive to the ornithologist. He is then able to accurately ascertain the mode of feeding, and the character of food provided by the old birds for their offspring, and now and then, he is favoured with a sight of the parent owl silently and softly gliding into the ruin, firmly clutching a mouse, or a half-naked young rat, as a dainty delicacy for her little favourites.

The southern, and more private entrance to the house, is graced, at a distance of about twenty yards, by Boulby's beautiful sun-dial on the island—a lasting trophy of the unlettered genius : beyond which you have an expansive and beautiful view of the lower and western portion of the lake, its extreme boundary being clothed with rushes, the favourite resort of the water-hens and coots. From the edge of the water, the eye is delighted by an extensive tract of undulating pasture-land, rising to a considerable elevation above the lake, and studded with a profusion of plain and ornamental forest-trees, with the heronry and its neighbouring swamp in the fore-ground.

Close to the lake, and on its southern side, nearly opposite the heronry, the voice, when loudly spoken, resounds. "*Reparabilis adsonat echo.*" "Repeating echo resounds." This is the only relic left by Echo, the daughter of Aër and Tellus.

I cannot here refrain from introducing Ovid's beautiful description of Echo, who, he observes, has neither learned to hold her tongue after another has spoken, nor to speak first herself.

> . . . "*Quæ nec reticere loquenti,*
> *Nec prior ipsa loqui didicit.*" . . .

> "She, who in other's words her silence breaks,
> Nor speaks herself but when another speaks.
> Echo was then a maid, of speech bereft,
> Of wonted speech, for though her voice was left,
> Juno a curse did on her tongue impose,
> To sport with every sentence in the close."

The dining and drawing-room windows, numbering five and four, occupy the northern, southern, and eastern sides of the mansion, from all of which you have an excellent view of the greater portion of the lake, in the centre of which is the "little island." The lake extends, longitudinally, a considerable distance in an easterly direction from the mansion; its proximate portion having pasture-land banks, whilst its more remote one is on both sides densely wooded to its very brink, terminating in pools and swamps, which are admirably adapted for the encouragement of herons and all kinds of water-fowl.

In the midst of all his earthly cares, the Squire was always prepared to support and enjoy a little joke, if unassociated with any really mischievous intention, and the more especially, if even in the remotest degree, connected with natural history. Now, it happened on one occasion, at Walton Hall, in the absence of Mr. Waterton for a few minutes, that a swallow darted through the open window, passing so closely to me that I laid hold of the bird during its flight. At the moment, it occurred to me that an artificial "*lusus naturæ*" might be concocted, from which some pleasantry might be derived, and, therefore, having procured two white feathers, each about five inches long I tied, by a waxed thread, one to each fork of the tail, and forthwith gave the timid little creature its wished for liberty. No sooner was this trifling deception accomplished than Mr. Waterton and an intimate friend of ours made their appearance; of course, totally uncon-

scious that I had been perpetrating any treachery. To
my great delight, the Squire proposed a stroll to the
Cast-iron Bridge, to admire the rapid flight of the
swallows, then skimming the unruffled surface of the
lake, and, taking their sundry superficial dips in the water
whilst feeding on the wing.

> " .   .   .   . *Flumina libant,*
>   *Summa leves.*"

> " They lightly skim the surface of the rivers."

No sooner was our destination gained, than the hawk-
eyed naturalist immediately detected the phenomenon
performing its accustomed gyrations, apparently, not in
the slightest degree impeded by its caudal supplement.
A knowing look, *aside*, from the Squire, conveyed an
intimation to me, that *he* was not to be bamboozled, and
had not been so, but, in order to carry out the joke, he
would remain perfectly silent as to the discovery to be
made.   The singular appearance of the bird, however,
was so palpable that our friend, in an ecstacy of delight,
cried out, "Oh, Mr. Waterton, there is a foreign swallow,
did you ever see one in this country before." "Certainly not," replied the Squire, with the greatest apparent gravity, "I never saw a swallow with its tail so
attired." "Then," rejoined our friend, in great earnestness,—" I first discovered the bird, and, consequently,
it is my privilege to introduce it to the British *fauna.*"
At subsequent periods, Mr. Waterton, when in a jocular
mood, which was frequently the case, would, with a
solemn aspect of countenance, ask our old friend, if he

had recently added any ornithological discovery to the British *fauna*. But being up to the best way of getting out of a scrape of this nature, he would reply, " No, nor shall I care to look out for any, as the one I did make yet remains unacknowledged by the authorities of the present age."

In conversation with the Squire one day as to his indulging to a fault in promiscuous charity, I adduced as an instance, in support of my assertion, an incident which had occurred that day, saying, that I had been accosted at the entrance lodge by a woman soliciting alms, who had a profusion of flowers in her bonnet, and on my assigning this inconsistency as a reason for refusing her request, she replied with an air of dignity, " There is, sir, no necessity for an apology. Your appearance warranted me in the expectation of a silver penny, but my checkered life has taught me to submit to miscalculations of this character, and never to implicitly rely on outward appearances, good morning, sir." Mr. Waterton laughed so heartily, and with such a knowing look, that I thought there was something more than met the eye to be revealed ; and, therefore, invited an explanation, every syllable of which so amused me that I have no difficulty in repeating word for word his explanation of what had occurred with himself and the self same lady beggar.

The Squire observed, " I should have been strictly taciturn on this chapter of incidents, as a joke against myself, but, as we have been pretty equally dealt with by this identical damsel, it would be cowardly in me, after your frank avowal, to attempt to conceal my equally anomalous *rencontre*.   Meeting me on the Wakefield road, this gaudily bedecked butterfly checked my onward career, by really a graceful courtesy, accompanied by a rather simpering entreaty for alms.   You know my aversion to finery, even where prevailing usage sanctions such folly, but this exhibition, under such circumstances, was beyond all endurance, therefore, with some warmth, and I dare say, a countenance expressive of my inward feeling, I said, 'How dare you, bedizened about your head with such trash, assume your present position, that of a mendicant?'

"The impertinent hussey immediately cut me short, by, 'Oh, my dear sir, pray don't get into a passion. You appear to have totally mistaken my request, I did not ask your advice, nor yet to preach me a sermon. Self-preservation is the first law of nature. How am I to live without food? and how is food to be obtained without money?'

"The 'weaker vessel' did not give me time to 'turn the tables,' but rotating on a high-heeled shoe, she gracefully ejaculated, 'Adieu!' and with superciliously contemptuous affectation finally disappeared."

In the year 1861, or 1862, an application to Mr. Waterton was made to permit the celebrated Blondin to exhibit his marvellously daring powers, on a rope extended across a portion of the lake in the park, but, of course, pecuniary temptations had no influence, in such a quarter, for the purpose proposed. On the other hand, if the proposition had been, that the profits arising from such a display should be given to the poor, I am not at all sure that the Squire would have been able to resist so very seductive an inducement, notwithstanding the almost irreparable injury that would have been perpetrated, by numerous, motley, probably mischievous, and certainly ungovernable sight-seers. Undoubtedly, the lake is admirably calculated for such an exhibition, the chief part of the surrounding grounds being of so amphitheatrical a configuration, that many thousand spectators, without any inconvenience, could have easily witnessed such a display, whilst the island and the mansion would certainly have commanded as complete a view of the lake as could have been desired.

Exhibitions of every description were always at variance with the natural taste and feelings of the Squire, otherwise the adaptation of the park for such displays is unrivalled in every point of view. In addition to the very high wall surrounding these grounds, a portion of their boundary is moated by the Leeds and Barnsley Canal. Indeed, the park is entered by a narrow bridge crossing this canal, which entrance is guarded by two lodges, having a central gate-way common to both.

On passing over this viaduct, and entering within the gate, you are forcibly struck with the calm serenity and seclusion that instantaneously meet the eye in every direction.

Four lines from Virgil admirably describe this very
entrance :—

> *" Hic secura quies, et nescia fallere vita,*
> *Dives opum variarum ; hic latis otia fundis,*
> *Speluncœ, vivique lacus ; hic frigida Tempe,*
> *Mugitusque boum, mollesque sub arbore somni."*

"Here is quiet free from care, and life ignorant of
guile, rich in varied opulence; here are peaceful
retreats in ample fields, grottoes, and refreshing lakes;
here are cool valleys, and the lowing kine, and soft
slumbers beneath the tree."

Beautifully formed forest-trees attract your attention,
and few within this domain, however lofty or difficult
to swarm, but have, at some period or other, been
scaled by the Squire, in his bird-nesting propensities,
whose remarkable suppleness of limb, and elasticity
of muscle, I have often seen marvellously and most
amazingly displayed, in his eighty-first year, by a
variety of physical contortions. When Mr. Waterton
was seventy-seven years of age, I was witness to his
scratching the back part of his head with the big
toe of his right foot. He knew no fear; and in
daring enterprise, or in what is vulgarly termed
"pluck," my friend signally excelled in comparison
with the amount usually allotted to man.

When the "South American Wanderings" made
its appearance, his mounting the cayman, as stated
in that volume, was disbelieved by many; but this
denial of belief arose from two mistaken causes,

which are, I think, easy of explanation. The former misconception proceeded from a want of knowledge of the man, whose powers, activity, courage, and determination, were not sufficiently known, and had not, even by his intimate friends, been duly appreciated; the latter mistake arose from a want of coolly reflecting on the utterly powerless condition of the cayman, when mounted. When I say utterly powerless, I must explain that an immense hook, baited with raw flesh, and securely affixed to the end of a strong rope, had been swallowed by the cayman, and that the peculiarly barbed construction of this hook prevented the possibility of its being returned through the mouth—that several natives along with Mr. Waterton's own black servant, had command of the rope, by which they had drawn this saurian reptile from his natural element on to dry ground, where, of course he was neither at home nor at ease. Now, if a man perform the more difficult, and the more dangerous of two feats, we should give him credit for being able to accomplish the less difficult, and the one attended with less danger. The Squire, in reference to some doubts publicly expressed, as to his having ever mounted the cayman at all, observed to a friend, in my presence "Previously to the publication of 'The Wanderings,' it was at one time my intention to place on the first page of the work a quotation from Ovid; but I now rejoice that I did not do so, as it might have prevented those ungenerous remarks, which have evidently been disgorged from a malevolently bilious stomach, and consequently highly gratifying to those illiberal sceptics at my expense. The quotation is :—

' *Facta canam ; sed erunt qui me fixxisse loquantur.'*

' I shall sing of facts, but there will be some to say that I have invented fiction.' "

Our friend remarked, " Probably these critics have never seen .either you or a cayman." " Of course not," rejoined the Squire, " They condemn that which they do not understand," " *damnant quod non intelligunt.*" Let this, then, be the basis on which to form an opinion, and be the ground-work of our decision, as to the credibility of a feat so much questioned at the time of its publication.

I will now describe a far more daring exploit, performed by the Squire at my house, than his mounting the *then* powerless and terrified cayman. The heroic act to which I allude was witnessed by many of my professional brethren, as well as by myself.

A few years ago, a Yankee appeared in Leeds, with eight and twenty rattle-snakes, in a very large flat case, divided into four equally ·sized and separate compartments, with a hinged plate-glass lid to fit each division, so that they could be opened and closed singly, and at pleasure in a moment. Having been previously supplied by Mr. Waterton with the Woorali poison, which he had personally obtained in the year 1812 from the Macoushi Indians who prepared

EXPERIMENTS WITH RATTLE-SNAKES, AT LEEDS.

it, and having for some time desired to experiment
with it as to its efficacy by comparison with the poison of the rattle-snake, an excellent opportunity was
now afforded. I therefore engaged the American to
bring his venomous treasures to my house, and invited
about forty medical men to be present, whilst carefully testing, on animal life, the effect of the bite of
the rattle-snake, comparatively with the effect of the
insertion of the Woorali posion, by an incised punc-
ture for its introduction within the cuticle. A rare
opportunity then presented itself, and a great number
of the faculty assembled to witness and bear testimony
to the result of those extremely interesting experiments on rabbits, pigeons, and Guinea pigs.

The room, in which to conduct our operative experiments, was large and extremely well lighted from
the roof, a character and position of light admirably
adapted for the purpose specially required. Of course
the South American Wanderer was present, as the
hero of the day, and in his genial element every inch
of him. The Yankee-owner of the rattle-snakes,
also formed one of our number, but he turned out to
be a perfectly useless member of our party, openly
declaring that he would have nothing whatever to do,
"personally," with his venomous friends, and I will
do him the justice to say that he strictly adhered to
the honest declaration he had made. Indeed, several
days previously, he had at Wakefield, entreated Mr.
Waterton to make some change for him in the arrangement of his rattle-snakes, into different compartments,

which the Squire, greatly to Jonathan's horror and amazement, but much to his gratification, speedily and safely effected; but no amount of persuasion, nor of pecuniary bribe nor reward, could induce the Yankee to render the least assistance to the Squire in removing the rattle-snakes to other compartments.

At the meeting at my house, we soon discovered that in supposing we should have no difficulty in carrying out our experiments, we had "reckoned without our host," as, at the very outset, we found we had to encounter danger never previously dreamt of, and that it would require infinitely more than an ordinary amount of nerve and of a knowledge of snakes than any of us medical men possessed, to overcome the then *apparently* insurmountable stumbling-block. In truth, no man dared to hold the rabbit nor the pigeon, within the case, to be bitten by a rattle-snake, much less dare any one venture to touch the snakes. We vainly looked at each other for some solution of our hitherto unforeseen perplexity, that is, to bring the biter and the to-be-bitten into close proximity. Silence prevailed, and we were in a "stand still" position when Mr. Waterton observed, —"Gentlemen, if you, who surround the case, will be quite silent and absolutely motionless, I have no doubt about easily accomplishing all that you require." Instantaneously there was breathless silence, when the Squire, on my raising the lid of one of the compartments, in the coolest manner possible, fearlessly but gently introduced *his naked hand within the*

case, keeping his eye intently fixed on the snake
he intended to secure, and in this unprotected state,
and with the utmost composure, he gently, and yet
firmly grasped the venomous monster by the neck
immediately behind the head, and deliberately removed
him from his neighbours, which were loudly hissing
and springing the rattle all around his hand. The lid
being again closed, Mr. Waterton held the rattle-snake
in his hand, whilst it bit the pigeon, the rabbit, or
the Guinea pig, and then, on the lid being gently
re-opened, he dexterously replaced the snake among
his congeners. This dangerous game was repeatedly
played in the various compartments, but with scrupulous circumspection, on the part of Mr. Waterton
and myself, and without any mishap, until on one
occasion, whilst the Squire was withdrawing his hand
from the case, after having replaced the snake, which
had just bitten a rabbit—most unexpectedly, and to
the dismay and extreme terror of not a few, a large
and fierce looking rattle-snake angrily raised himself
into nearly an erect position, and, as quick as lightning, suddenly and rapidly darted forward, projecting
the upper half of his body over the edge of the case,
before the lid could by any possibility be closed. So
instantaneous was this hasty rush, that a moment's
earlier closing of the lid, would have caught and
retained the Squire's hand within the case, among the
snakes. I, having the guardianship of the lid, prevented the complete escape of the snake, by instantly,
and rapidly, but gently closing the lid upon the half-

protruding body of the snake, pressing upon it just sufficiently to prevent its escape, or, indeed, its further progress, until Mr. Waterton, who was as composed as if nothing particular had occurred, promptly laid hold of this enraged reptile, by deliberately grasping him round the neck, and quietly replacing him in his former quarters

> . . . . *" Fortissimus ille est*
> *Qui promptus metuenda pati, si cominus instent."*

"He is the bravest who is prepared to encounter danger on the instant."

I may add that this last scene did not diffuse any genial influence over our scientific party, as the tumult among the faculty, in apprehension of a venomous assault, was so extreme, that in the sudden determination to beat a hasty retreat at every hazard, nearly all fled from their supposed perilous position, and several not only rushed down stairs, but even into the street without their hats. During the whole of these dangerously operative experiments, when the unprotected hand was within the case, in the midst of the deadly poisonous reptiles, the Squire was as much at home as if he had been leisurely selecting the sweetest bon-bon, instead of the most vigorous rattle-snake.

Mr. Waterton insisted that all snakes attack only when provoked, and that in this instance, there was no provocation given by him, until the rattle-snake was positively within his grasp, and completely within his power, having a firm hold round its neck, and so close to the head, that it was utterly impossible for it to turn or twist its head in any direction whatever, and that it consequently was totally unable to inflict any wound on him, however anxious to do so, or however enraged it might be. He added, that so long as his fortitude did not desert him, and he was still able to maintain an unwavering determination to keep up his grasp, he was safe. But, on the contrary, if his courage had failed him, or if any unforeseen accident had occurred to liberate the snake, every man present must have taken care of himself, and even in that case, he saw no reason to be very uneasy, as self-preservation appeared to be a prevailing, and, indeed, a predominant feeling, among the majority of the faculty who were present.

Now, the man who dared to put his unprotected hand amongst a host of the most venomous snakes in existence, would not be likely to have refused a mount on a defenceless cayman, dragged by seven men, by means of a rope with a barbed hook at its extremity, and firmly fixed within the stomach of the animal. This mechanically restrained condition of the alligator, it must be admitted, rendered it totally incapable, in a physical point of view, to give battle to any creature on earth.

I may, whilst defending the Squire's fortitude and vindicating his veracity, mention another *marvellous* instance of cool courage. I allude to an occurrence in the Zoological Gardens, in London, in the year 1861, when, after much entreaty on the part of Mr. Waterton, he was permitted by the then curator, Mr. Mitchell, now deceased, to pay his personal respects to a large orang-outang, from Borneo, which was reputed to be very savage. Indeed, the keepers, one and all declared that "he would worry the Squire, and make short work of it," if he should enter his den, especially as he was just then in a horrid temper, having been recently teased by some mischievous boys. The late Mr. Mitchell, even at last, yielded to Mr. Waterton's urgent request, with great reluctance. Nothing daunted by all this badinage of the keepers, the Squire, to the very great horror of the numerous spectators, entered the palisaded enclosure with a light heart. The meeting of these two celebrities was clearly a case of "love at first sight," as the strangers embraced each other most affectionately; nay they positively hugged each other, and in their apparently uncontrollable joy, they kissed one another many times, to the great amusement of the numerous spectators.

Mr Waterton, who has written specially on the monkey tribe, had long been anxious to minutely inspect the palm of its hand during life, and was also wishful to examine the teeth of his newly-acquired friend, both of which investigations were graciously conceded to the Squire without a murmur, his fingers being freely admitted within its jaws. These little ceremonies having been accomplished on the part of

Mr. Waterton, his apeship claimed a similiar privilege, which was courteously granted. The ape, true to its natural inclinations, with great familiarity and evident satisfaction at once set to work in good earnest, after his own instinctive order, and having most carefully scrutinised every portion of Mr. Waterton's face, by pawing, as well as by the closest occular inspection, coolly commenced, to the infinite entertainment of the surrounding spectators, a careful and even critical examination of, or, probably I ought to say, an elaborate *search*, on the Squire's head.

These hazardous snake and monkey - adventures, just related, put in competition with the feat of mounting the cayman, when in its then powerless condition, must convince every reasonable person, that the latter act, (although we admit it to have been a some-what bold achievement,) really sinks into insignficance, when compared with Mr. Waterton's daring and intrepid exploits with the rattle-snakes and the oran-outang.

When Mr Waterton was chaffed about the "search" made by the ape, he observed, that reminded him of an anecdote told by a Cantab who, one day, seeing a raga-muffin-looking boy scratching his head at the door of a gentleman's house where he was begging, and, thinking to pass a joke upon him, said, "So Jack, you are picking them out, are you?" "Nah, sir," retorted the urchin, "I taks 'em as they comes."

The Squire was always delighted to hear a little of any countryman's unaffected provincialism, and especially, if of a rather pungent and pithy character, and "whilst," as he observed, "vagabondising at Scarbro'," he meditated a visit to Filey in search of sea-birds' eggs. He was, therefore, on the look-out for a man on whom he could thoroughly depend, to accompany him and assist in his egg-gathering expedition, so that they might descend the precipitous rocks alternately.

The Squire accidentally met a man, who professed, as he himself stated, to be "skilled in that line." Mr. Waterton, therefore, asked him if he thought Tom-so-and-so would answer his purpose, when, after a little consideration, the reply was, "Now, Mr. Watterton, I's a man as niver says nout as is bad a nobody, but I will say this, that chap as you name, is the biggest thief as iver God created." "Then," rejoined the Squire, "he won't do for me." "No, no," responded this knowing and benevolent subdivision of humanity, "he'll do for nobody nor for no place but the devil and the bottomless pit."

My old friend was wont to tell this anecdote with great pleasure, and frequently wound up by saying, "This tale reminds me of my old farm bailiff, who some time ago was complaining to me of the improper conduct of the stable-boy. On my hoping that he was not guilty of using improper language, 'Yes, d—n him,' he replied, 'that's wars't on it, he swears like a fighting cock, and that, you know, Squire, is very unseemly in any boy.' 'Yes,' rejoined Mr. Waterton, 'but you forget William, that what is unseemly in the boy is doubly so in you at your age.'"

In consideration of what I have stated, as to Mr.

Waterton's daring exploits, and his progress, I am tempted to quote the words of Sir Jas. Stuart Menteth, Bart. :—" Among the most choice of the variety of this collection, none are more interesting than the birds," observed the Baronet,—

> " Their plumage neither dashing shower,
> Nor blasts that shake the dripping bower,
> Shall drench again or decompose ;
> But screen'd from every storm that blows,
> It boasts a splendour ever new —
> Safe with " . . . .

The amiable wanderer, who, often at the hazard of his life, and suffering dangers by land and water, while exploring the wilds of South America, got them together.

It would be idle to attempt a description of these treasures. That delightful book, (the *Wanderings,*) which, like White's *Natural History of Selbourne*, is in almost every hand, has already rendered the reader familiar with them all ; and it has also acquainted us with many a hairbreadth escape of its author, that one ignorant of the daring resolute character of Mr. Waterton almost hesitates to believe : but those who have known him from his early youth to manhood can bear testimony to the strict veracity that has ever characterised him, and can recount not a few of his dangerous feats of prowess and of daring. Few, at his time of life, are his equals in climbing a rope or a tree : this activity of body and steadiness of nerve give him infinite advantage over most of our modern naturalists in examining the nests of many birds, placed in almost inaccessible situations, and in thereby ascertaining important facts relative to their habits and character.

During the present summer, no less than eleven times this dauntless naturalist was let down the frightful beetling precipice of Flamborough Head, whence

> "The fishermen, that walk upon the beach,
>   Appear like mice ; and yon tall anchoring bark,
>   Dimish'd to the cock ; her cock, a bouy
>   Almost too small for sight ; "

in order that he might collect the eggs of the guillemot, the puffin, and the cormorant, and likewise examine their mode of hatching and other habits.

On leaving the house, and its island, and its old ivied tower, we next enter upon the park. This piece of ground embraces almost 300 acres, surrounded by a high wall to keep out the poacher and other intruder. As no gun is ever fired within its precincts, that

> . . . "Clamour of rooks, daws, and kites,
>   The explosion of the levelled tube excites,"

is never heard, nor any dog suffered to disturb its peace, it may easily be supposed it will be the favourite resort of many kind of birds. Abounding in extensive woods and groves, and an ample space of water, every fowl can suit its own taste for a sheltering-place, for a haunt to build its nest, and rear its little brood ; all those birds which elsewhere suffer from the gamekeeper's ruthless gun and trap, and from those whom the bird-stuffer employs to take them prisoners, receive protection within the walls of Walton Park. The owl is an especial favourite. Besides our slumbering two friends, whom we left within the old ivied tower in the island, eleven pairs of others occupy holes in trees, and other comfortable dormitories, purposely contrived and fitted up for their dwelling-places. It is not a little curious to observe, that, if these "wanderers" of the night be offered an unmolested habitation, a pair are not long in finding it out, and taking possesion of it. Mr. Waterton, from his careful and accurate examination of the habits of the owl, has clearly exculpated it from the false charges and foul calumnies, aspersing its spotless reputation, of being the destroyer of young pigeons and their eggs. The same friendly turn he has done for the starling. Both these birds often are indwellers of the pigeon-cote, not from a preference of it to any other harbour, but because the destroying hand of man has left them scarce another spot to retire to, and to breed up their young. It is the rat who kills the pigeons.

CHAPTER III.

ON resuming the further description of the grounds at WALTON HALL, together with its attached objects of interest, the rookery claims special attention; and more especially so, because it engaged much of the Squire's very careful observation, in endeavouring to minutely ascertain the habits of the rook. These birds abound here, for the whole year, at some period of every successive twenty-four hours. They *roost* at the rookery at Walton Hall only during the period of building, of incubation, and of maturing their young. So soon as the young ones are ready to leave the trees which contain their nests, they, together with the old birds, enjoy their nocturnal repose in the surrounding woods until the second week in October, when both young and old finally leave the woods for Nostel Priory, the residence of Mr. Winn, situated between Wakefield and Pontefract.

At this ancient, beautiful, and extensive place, there is an avenue, surpassing all others in this part of the country, its length being upwards of a mile, and formed of magnificent trees. In this avenue, the rooks henceforward roost in congregated thousands upon thousands, there passing their nights until the 12th of March, at which time they, that is, the Walton Hall portion return, and again assemble there, for the sole purpose of incubation, after a *roosting*

absence of about nine months. During their roosting period at Nostel Priory, they invariably call at
Walton Hall every evening on their return to the
priory. Punctuality is a marked feature in all their
movements, and consequently, their evening-call may
be calculated upon to a very few minutes each successive day; in proof of which, I have frequently
seen Mr. Waterton standing with watch in hand, and
heard him say, "the rooks will be here in two or
three minutes, or at all events, in not more than
five;" and it was a rare occurrence that the Squire
had to complain of a want of punctuality on the
part of the rook.

The poor rook has few friends, but many foes.
Now this bird is either injurious or he is beneficial
to the interests of man, as there is no third party
willing to sanction his neutrality. If he be injurious,
it would appear that he is so to the farmer only, as
no other interest complains. Let us endeavour, if we
possibly can without prejudice, to carefully examine
into the murmuring and discontented representations,
or probably, misrepresentations of the farmer, ascertaining how far his multitudinous accusations against
the poor rook are correct, and, as far as we are able
with our present knowledge of the rook and its habits,
determine how the debtor and creditor account really
stands between the farmer and the rook, and how it
might appear by a little forethought, a little care, and
the expenditure of a very little money.

G

A portion of the seed which the farmer sows, is doubtless pilfered by the wily rook—the farmer stoutly contends that his yonng turnips are occasionally destroyed — that his potatoes are now and then, in a trifling degree, purloined by means of the rook boring into the ridges with his pointed and powerful bill; and, in addition, the farmer declares that large patches of his grass-land are destroyed and laid waste by the rook pulling up tuft after tuft of his grass, and leaving them on the surface of the ground, a manifest evidence he asserts, of their mischievous propensities, and of the serious amount of damage sustained by their mortifying depredations. Here we have four distinct, plausible accusations, ostentatiously paraded. I at once freely admit, that whatever amount of grain the rooks steal from recently sown land, is abstractedly, a positive loss to the farmer; and if this robbery, during seed-time, be of such extent as to lessen in any appreciable degree, the amount of yield on reaping the crop in harvest, which is at all times very questionable, I also admit that this must be deemed an absolute loss.

If these losses complained of by the farmer actually exist, there being no remedy within reasonable reach, the farmer is fully justified in his accusation against the rook; but if preventive means are easily available and are not resorted to by the farmer, the aspect of his complaint is changed, and I contend, that if by a little forethought and at a trifling cost he has an attainable remedy, he is himself culpable if he do not put it into execution—that he deserves no commiseration, but, on the contrary, merits a severe censure which is not generally awarded to him. Two or three boys hired at a very trifling cost during "seed-time," in order to what is termed "tent" the recently sown ground, would unequivocally prevent any loss of seed, and, *consequently*, any diminution of yield in the crop; hence, two of the farmer's assumed losses might easily be avoided. But another simple, efficacious, and cheap mode may be adopted, really with wonderful advantage, which is by boiling equal parts by measure, of train oil, turpentine, and bruised gunpowder, and by dipping pieces of rag in this mixture when hot, and fixing them on sticks stuck into the ground in different parts of the field, say four or five to the acre.

The next accusation brought against the rook is its wholesale destruction of the young turnip-crop. This would be a grievous one if correct, but it is not so. Even if correct, the same remedy which would effectually preserve the cereal crops during "seed-time" viz., "tenting," would protect the turnip. But I contend that the rook never pulls up a single healthy turnip-plant, unless by accident, or unless it be so closely adhering to a dead or dying one, that the living and the dead are inseparable. The turnip-plant is no food for the rook. He has no relish for plants of any kind. It is the worm at the root of the plant which he is in quest of. That he pulls up sickly and decayed plants I readily admit; and that he can detect a morbid condition of any plant, at whose root the wire-worm rests, long before the farmer can, I am thoroughly convinced. The rook in this instance, seeks not to destroy the farmer's property but to gratify his own appetite, in doing which, he in reality destroys the farmer's enemy. Then, as to the miserable imputation of "cribbing" a few potatoes, the theft is generally so trifling in amount, and so rare in occurrence, that it really would be a waste of time to further allude to it.

Lastly, the prevailing opinion among ignorant farmers, that rooks destroy grass, is a totally unfounded charge. "*Audi alteram partem.*" "Hear the other side." The rook never wilfully destroys a single blade of grass, but he readily and gladly distinguishes the dead or even sickly tufts, and hesitates not a moment to draw them, in order that he may obtain his delicate and favourite morsel, the wire-worm at their roots.

It is evident that the farmer has but a trifling bill against the rook for damages sustained, and it is equally manifest that if a balance should be struck, John Bull would have an infinitely larger sum to pay to the rook for his sedulous labours in the destruction of the wire-worm, than any trifling amount he might be fairly entitled to as cost of "tenting," for the protection of his crops against the rook.

It is surprisingly strange that so many of the farmers of the present far-seeing age, should be so callously insensible as regards the benefit they derive from this bird. They are lynx-eyed to its supposed destructive propensities, but perversely, nay, spitefully blind to its meritorious ones. If the rook deprive the farmers of pence, I am thoroughly satisfied that he rewards them with pounds, but it seems next to an impossibility to convince the agriculturalists of this as a reality. If they could, however, be persuaded to fairly take both sides of this question into their cool and deliberate consideration, laying aside all prejudice and preconceived impressions, and be determined to ascertain the truth, and honestly keep a debtor and creditor account of the estimated damage and profit, their countenances would be brighter, their crops heavier, and their pockets fuller. The farmers, along with the extensive woodland proprietors, would be speedily and thoroughly convinced, that where the wireworm and the caterpillar abound, there will be the rooks. " *Ubi mel, ibi apes.*" "Where the honey is, there will the bees be."

Were it not, indeed, for these birds, which daily scour the country by thousands upon thousands, the devouring coleopterous insects to which I have alluded, would injure the oaks at all ages, to a much greater extent than they do at present. Would that I could prevail upon the farmer and the woodman, before coming to any positive decision, not to blindly yield their judgment to an opinion without due examination of the facts necessary to be known. The result of such an examination would be the happy means of defending the poor rook, by exposing the ignorance of those who so erroneously advocate its extermination.

Since publishing the first edition of this volume, I

have been much pleased by some remarks in a pamphlet
written by Sir James Stuart Menteth, Bart., which exactly
coincide with my views. I am also delighted to have had
permission from so eminent an authority to make any
quotations therefrom that I may wish. Sir James says
in his publication, " Farmers *versus* Rooks " :—

" No bird has a nicer discernment of the approach of
Spring than the rook. As soon as the snow-drop
peeps its head above ground, and long before the
violet and primrose appear, the building operations of
the rookery have commenced. These operations of
nesting begin often in February, when the season is
mild.

" Notwithstanding the prejudice of farmers against rooks,
arising from a belief that they feed exclusively upon grain
and root crops, and consequently are detrimental to their
fields, there can be no doubt that the services which
they perform are infinitely greater than any injury which
they occasion. The rook is to be considered as a bird
that feeds upon insects rather than upon grain. It pre-
fers at all times various kinds of worms, grubs, slugs,
caterpillars, and other insect food, to roots or grain, or
any other vegetable production. It will be found that it
is only in moments of necessity that it preys on grain
or roots. Occasionally in the latter part of Spring, when
the dryness of the ground prevents the rook from digging
for worms, grubs, and caterpillars, it may take a little of
our sown grain and potatoes. But to show how reluctantly rooks take to grain and root food, when within

reach of the sea coast, at those seasons of the year when the earth is bound up by long-continued dry weather, flocks of them frequent the beach; and they may be observed feeding upon the sea wilks and other marine animals. The rook, therefore, resorts to a grain diet with reluctance, and abandons it as soon as rain has moistened the earth, and rendered it pervious to its bill. Though it has to supply its clamorous offspring with food, we are certain that it never feeds them with either root or grain food, but always with insects, worms, grubs, slugs, or caterpillars. Were the contents of the stomachs of these birds, after they have been killed, to be oftener examined than they are, it would be found that they are filled with insects, and not with grain. When the labours of the husbandman in Spring are going on, it cannot have escaped the notice of the most inattentive observer, that the track of the plough is followed by flocks of rooks, greedily picking up the worms, grubs, maggots, slugs, and caterpillars, from the newly turned furrow. Thus, these birds ensure to the farmer a harvest from the seed he has sown, by removing myriads of noxious insects from his fields; and to be convinced of this, we have only to enumerate a few of these most destructive insects, all of which are the favourite food of the rook.

"Among those insects that occasion most mischief to the husbandman's crops are—the turnip fly, or *tenthredo;* the cockchafer beetle, *melolontha vulgaris*, both in the grub and winged state; the long legged crane-fly, *tipula oleracœa;* the wire-worm beetle, *elater segetis;* the slug, *limax agrestis*.

" As soon as the turnip plants have thrown out three
or four rough leaves, the caterpillar of a Saw Fly,
tenthredo, begins to attack them. These caterpillars have
been known, (as in 1783) to have destroyed many thousand
acres of this root. The rooks, jackdaws, and magpies,
seek after these caterpillars with such avidity, that
those farmers, whose good sense has led them not to
destroy, but rather to encourage these useful birds, need
not fear any great damage from this insect.

" No insect is more destructive to the hopes of the
farmer than the grub of the Cockchafer Beetle, *melolontha vulgaris*, which is known under a variety of
names in different districts, as the brown tree-beetle,
the May-bug, the brown clock, &c. The eggs of this
insect are white, and laid in the ground, where they
soon appear as a soft whitish grub wtth a red head,
and about an inch and a half long. In this state it
continues about four years, during which time it commits
most destructive ravages on the roots not only of grass
but of all other plants and young trees. After this grub
has lived its due time under the turf, it issues forth
in its winged state from the ground, and commences
to devour the leaves of all kinds of trees, but more
particularly those of the oak. And it is to prey upon
these winged beetles that the young rooks and their
parents assemble in such large flocks in June and July
in our oak woods. Those fields also, which are infested
by this grub, attract these birds, with several companions, such as the jay, the magpie, and the jackdaw,
to feed upon it. For nearly three months in the Spring,

almost the sole employment of the rooks and the above-named birds, is to search for insects of this sort; and the destruction they cause among them is beyond all calculation.

"The grub of a small beetle, called the Wireworm, *(elater segetis)* derives its name from its slender form and uncommon hardness. It lives in the grub state nearly five years. During which time it devours the roots of wheat, rye, oats, and every variety of grass, which it attacks indiscriminately, and causes yearly a great loss of produce. It abounds chiefly in newly broken-up land, and is particularly destructive in gardens recently converted from pasture land. The wireworm is a favourite food of the rooks, and of the birds of the crow family."

How singular that farmers are so short-sighted as not to readily take hold of such valid and substantial arguments and information, for their advantage, expressed in such lucid and convincing language that he who runs may read. Mr. Waterton not only agreed to the fullest extent with the opinions expressed by Sir J. S. Menteth, but strenuously advocated the protection and preservation of the sparrow. Of course, in the present destructive age, it would be untenable ground on which to say a word in favour of the sparrow.

Inasmuch, however, as every question has two sides, it is but fair to hear both, especially on such subtle points as these disputed ones connected with the rook and the sparrow, and more particularly so, because the *injury* sustained is direct, visible, and immediate, whereas the *benefit* derived is indirect, and frequently remote.

I have already given my own reasons relative to the rook, but will state those in favour of the sparrow, by quoting the President of the Naturalist-Field-Club, at a meeting of the Gateshead Club. The President observed "That he had been calculating the number of caterpillars which the 6,000 sparrows killed by a member of the sparrow club in Essex, and for which he had actually received a prize of ten shillings, would have eaten. The amount was 6,307,000,000. Whilst the clodhoppers of Essex are killing sparrows by the thousands, the Australian colonists are importing them at a considerable expense from England to act the part of protectors of their crops, and thereby of promoters of the comforts of the people."

On the south side of the rookery, and close to, or within a little circular clump of trees, where stone for building-purposes has been, at some former period, excavated, and about fifty or sixty yards from the lake, was interred the great-grandfather of the "South American Wanderer." This was stated to me as a fact by the Squire himself, but whether it has been recorded in writing, or has simply passed by oral tradition from father to son, I know not.

On the western side of the rookery, and at a short distance from the well-arranged dog-kennel, stands a

Scotch fir closely embraced by a profusion of ivy, which in 1860 contained in a cleft branch, the nest of a pea-hen, at an elevation of twenty-four feet from the ground. This was an unnatural position for a pea-fowl to occupy, and it seldom happens that any thing ultimately thrives, when diverted from nature's usual course. At any rate the poor bird, notwithstanding her lofty pretensions, cut a sorry figure in this instance, hatching only two young ones, and even these were prematurely cut off, by their unlucky descent from the nest. Whether, on reflection, she imagined that her efforts had been rendered abortive in consequence of this foolish and fanciful freak, I know not,—she, however, acted more humbly and wisely afterwards, and was more successful in her future incubations. In a letter from Mr. Waterton at the time the pea-hen was entertaining her aspiring notions, he observes,—"In a jackdaw's nest, half way up a Scoth fir well clothed with ivy, the pea-hen is sitting on three eggs, and the male bird often ascends to her nest and sits by her for company."

Within fifty yards of this tree, is a large and excellently arranged farm-yard, in the centre of which is erected a noble dove-cote, very lofty and having a cross on its summit. This cote is capacious within, admirably ventilated, and agreeably aired by a stove in a room underneath it. It is so fitted up, that any particular pigeon-hole can be examined without difficulty, and, what is most important to the owner, this cote is now really thief-proof, which cannot be said of any other in the neighbourhood.

Within a short distance of the western extremity of the lake, in a position concealed from the hall, in consequence of a sudden and acutely angular turn of the water, there is a creek leading into the wood on the eastern side of this portion of the lake. A boat can easily ply up this narrow channel, under a small obtusely arched bridge.

At the extreme end of this creek a fine old willow was cut down in 1812, and from its stump have sprung twelve separate stems, each of which has now grown to a considerable height and circumference. One of these has been, for a long period, in a disabled condition, having been very detrimentally influenced by a severe storm, but has been by the Squire ingeniously repaired to a considerable extent, by hoops and iron bolts. These twelve willows were designated by Mr. Waterton, the "Twelve Apostles," the disabled one being always called Judas; which, although so restored as to live, nevertheless, has, when under the influence of a boisterous day, a mournful and groaning creak, as if in misery because of its previously mutilated state.

In their ancient stateliness, and within a few yards of the creek, stand two veteran oaks on the very brink of the lake; in a cleft branch of one of which, twelve feet from the ground, a wild duck nested and hatched her young in the year 1832. She was peculiarly fortunate in landing her whole brood safely on the grassy surface. So capricious a freak on her part was the more singular, because, as if in very defiance

THE SEPULCHRAL RESTING-PLACE OF THE LATE MR. WATERTON, AT WALTON HALL.

of nature's more prudent suggestions, there was a vast abundance of the choicest nesting-ground in the immediate neighbourhood of the very tree she selected. At this spot has recently been erected a Mausoleum for the remains of the late Mr. Waterton, which were there interred on Saturday, June 3rd, 1865, the very day on which he completed his eighty-third year. Time was, when Mr. Waterton and I in his little sailing craft, slowly drifting along the margin of the upper portion of the lake, rarely passed the two Oaks forming the boundary-line of that limited recess now revered from its being the final depository of the ashes of the dead, without indulging in admiration of those patriarchal looking trees, and hovering opposite that spot which, singularly enough, is now the resting place of the "wearied bones" of the good old man.

There was *even then* a somewhat sombre, yet a pleasing and really soothing solemnity in the scenery around and in close proximity with the manifestly time-honoured antiquity and pre-adamite character of those two Oaks, but now, a survey of the spot which contains what the Squire during life, designated the dreary tomb, could not fail to bring to mind Milton's epitaph on Shakespeare

> " Thou so sepulchr'd, in such dost lie,
> That Kings for such a tomb would wish to die."

The absolute and unequivocal attachment which Mr. Waterton entertained up to the close of life, for the location of his nativity, for the habitation of his ancestors, for the abode of a parent whose memory he venerated, nay, idolised, impregnated him with such a simple-minded affection for that limited space of earthly tenure on which the legitimate and rational pleasures of life had been enjoyed, that he could never endure the idea that his bones, even after death, should be separated and dispersed from the spot where innumerable mercies and the duration of life itself had been so lavishly granted to him.

The Squire always encouraged, by strongly expressed feelings, the conviction that his bones had a special claim of sepulture by birth-right within the grounds of his forefathers.

The solitary heron, by its presence in the foreground, seems to consistently add its mite of mourning to the melancholy yet tranquillizing scenery, whilst the *tout-ensemble* of the aspect so harmonises with impressions of regret for the loss of our friend, that the partially healed wound is again torn asunder, and we deplore afresh the deprivation of one which no human power can replace.

> " His friends and people, to his future praise,
> A marble tomb and pyramid shall raise,
> And lasting honour to his ashes give.
> His fame ('tis all the dead can have) shall live."

This part of the lake being narrow, is conveniently under the influence of the net, when immense draughts of pike, carp, tench, perch, roach, dace, and gudgeon, are brought to land. The pike taken here, have the reputation of being very superior in flavour. Eels, which are caught without difficulty by bait, are certainly excellent, and are now and then large. Securing a pike by his bow and arrow, was at one time, a favourite amusement with the Squire on "a fish day," when frequently at the last moment, the lake had to yield a portion of its finny contents, as a scanty provision for the approaching dinner. Latterly, however, since the principal part of the weeds has been dragged out, the water is seldom sufficiently transparent for this really amusing mode of warfare.

Recently, the absence of any material quantity of weed in the water has unquestionably had its detrimental influence, as regards natural history pursuits, inasmuch as the coots, being in a great measure deprived of their choicest food, do not now assemble and breed in such numbers as they formerly did. As the time of nesting, incubation, and maturing their young, is the most interesting, as well as the most instructive to the ornithologist, it is desirable to render these periods as agreeable and as tempting as possible to the birds themselves, in order to incite and to induce them to select the park as their breeding ground, where they would be in a position to delight all, and furnish genuine and practical information, to those who would take the *trouble* to diligently look out for it, in order to acquire a thorough knowledge of natural history, as, "without perspiration and labour, no work is perfected."

"Absque sudore et labore nullum opus perfectum est."

In the year 1860, a pair of coots built their nest

on the extreme end of a branch of a large willow,
closely overhanging the water, on the northern side of
the lake. This branch, extending three or four yards
on to the lake, and being of considerable magnitude,
had the appearance of being entirely independent of the
neighbouring bank. Notwithstanding its inherent power,
yet, from its great length, its leverage, and the pliant
nature of the willow, its apicial extremity was easily
under the influence of the wind, or of the rising and
falling waves underneath it; or even of the additional
weight of the male bird, when the nest was completed,
and when he now and then called to pay his respects to
his mate whilst discharging her solitary duty. During
the original formation of their temporary domicile, as the
birds added weight to the branch by furnishing more and
more materials upon its very extremity in order to perfect
the nest, the branch of course gradually descended, until its
exterior base actually rested on the surface of the water,
so that when there was a tolerably perceptible ripple
on the lake, the supernatant nest and its contents
were continually rising and falling in unison with the
motion of the waves.

This pleasing object, for such it really was to the
naturalist, was within a very trifling distance of the
mansion, so that the powerful telescope in the drawing-
room, when put in requisition, at all times revealed any
peculiarities or interesting habits, of this species of
bird. You were enabled, through this trustworthy
medium, to judge of the absolute amount of labour
performed by each bird, whilst constructing their simple

and temporary fabrication. You could be convinced by ocular and unmistakeable evidence, that the male, as a general rule, sought for and procured the building materials that were required, and that he managed this portion of the labour allotted to him with great energy and with unceasing industry; and that the female, with equal anxiety and ability, attended as diligently to her special department, viz., the *construction* of the edifice. The male bird would frequently show his expertness in obtaining materials for building purposes, by diving to the bottom of the lake for twigs which had fallen from the over-hanging willow in which the nest was built, and also to select from the same source, the smaller, more pliable, and more fibrous roots, as a softer and less pervious investing finish, with which to line the interior of the nest; and, having brought them up to the surface of the water, evidently delighted with the possession of his booty, he lost not a moment in conveying them to his lady-love. You could frequently see quick and repeated declinations of the head, which appeared to be consultations between the two relative to the mode of construction of their nest, or which might be congratulations as the work progressed in having accomplished certain portions, when great harmony and satisfaction invariably appeared to prevail. If the lady had finally fixed within the nest the last twig furnished by the male previously to his return with another, she, apparently spurning an idle life, instantly set off herself, in search of additional building-stores. You could witness the affectionate gallantry

H

and sedulous attentions of the male bird, in rendering
to his better half the services of temporary incubation;
a domestic and usually a feminine duty, but one which he
evidently did not consider derogatory nor humiliating
to perform, whilst his dearly beloved washed, fed, and
plumed herself. Indeed, you could always, from the
drawing-room windows at Walton Hall, examine minutely
and quite at your leisure, all the land and water-fowl
within view. You could carefully scrutinise their form,
their colour, their plumage, the colour of their legs, the
accurate form and precise colour of their mandibles, and
not unfrequently, even the colour of the iris* of the
eye; also, their mode of walking, swimming, and
resting. You could distinctly ascertain the various
kinds of food on which they lived and fed their young,
and thus become thoroughly acquainted with the habits
of each species. It was truly delightful to see the
peaceful harmony that prevailed, notwithstanding the
numerous varieties now and then congregated in so
small a space. You could see the herons, water-hens,
coots, Egyptian and Canada geese, carrion-crows, magpies,
ring-doves, (occasionally on their nests,) wild· duck, teal,
and widgeon at one glance. You could, with infinite
satisfaction, be convinced of the care they bestowed on
their eggs, and also of their parental kindness and
persevering attention, as regarded the management and
anxious protection of their young.

Having alluded to the construction of the coot's nest,
I may add, that long before her first brood are able
to take care of themselves, they are taken charge of

by the male bird, who provides for them while the female incubates a second brood.

Very frequently you could be gratified by seeing, in all their beauty and extreme richness of plumage, an assemblage of from twenty to thirty herons at the same moment, and in the limited space of a few yards on the banks of the lake, all quietly and confidentially enjoying their calm and undisturbed repose after a laborious night's fishing, and probably, a wind opposing their flight on returning to their usual quarters. An assemblage of from twenty to thirty herons, whether regarded as a group or as isolated objects, form a rare as well as a most interesting and instructive picture to the ornithologist, when leisurely and carefully examined through the medium of the telescope.

The figure of the heron in outline, is very peculiar. His walk is slow, graceful and stately, whilst his physical position and attitude, when free from fear and entirely at rest, is extremely singular and even fantastic. Each heron "standing on one leg," "*stans pede in uno*," under his accurately balanced centre of gravity, remains, sometimes for hours in succession, as motionless as death, on his long, erect, and jointless-looking leg; its fellow together with its foot, being concealed within his abdominal feathers, whilst his head is gracefully buried under one of his wings. Occasionally, instead of one leg and foot being hidden by the abdominal feathers, the bird stretches the entire limb in a direct line backward and horizontally.

The telescope in use at Walton Hall, was a large and a very excellent one. This admirable acquisition to the drawing-room was mounted on a light and moveable table or stand, which smoothly glided on castors. You could, with perfect ease, even whilst in conversation with a friend and enjoying your arm-chair, change its direction in a single moment, in order to examine objects on any part of the lake or landscape, within view.

A finished field-ornithologist is generally considered to be a man who has carefully, perseveringly, and judiciously, gathered his information practically, by an infinite amount of laborious voyage and travel, and that, frequently of a dangerous character; who has spent nights as well as days on the ocean, on fresh-water lakes, on the precipitous and rugged mountains, in the unwholesome morasses, and on the arid plains, also during frost and snow, so as to secure an intimate knowledge of the almost endless variety of the feathered race. All this the Squire had already done to an extent seldom or never equalled by one individual, and had realised an additional acquisition to the science by the persevering and well-handled use of the microscope.

In possession of such very rare and advantageous privileges as were in existence at Walton Hall, it is not surprising that Mr. Waterton, with his inherent taste for natural history — that he, who had laboured hard and unceasingly, during a long and harassing life, to attempt to unravel the interesting and secret

mysteries in the various branches of this science—
that he, who with lengthened and extensive experience
in various climes, from infancy to the hale man at
eighty — that he, who with the knowledge acquired
by travel and by unequalled opportunities to gain the
practical information of *field*-ornithology, absolutely at
his own fireside—I say it is not surprising, that such
a man should have stood unrivalled in this engaging
and seductive science.

" Non cuivis homini contingit adire Corinthum."

" It is not the lot of every man to visit Corinth."

With such a host of substantial and unequivocally
admitted foundations, on which to build a knowledge
of natural history, we may fairly claim Charles Waterton to have been a beacon to guide us through many
of the diversified labyrinths and hidden intricacies
of nature, and may conclude without fear of contradiction from the unprejudiced, that with all these united
aids, which were supported by vigorous health—by an
active and powerfully physical frame—by great mental
energy and resolute determination, coupled with sound
and extensive learning—Mr. Waterton has stood prominently out for many years as a giant in natural history.

" Tu mihi magnus Apollo."

"Thou shalt be my great Apollo."

As Apollo's power was universally acknowledged
in every country, so has Mr. Waterton's superiority in

taxidermy been admitted. As Apollo's oracle at Delphi was consulted by all nations in that age, so was the Squire consulted, during his life, by all countries. And as Apollo's statue, which graced Mount Actium as a pharos to caution the mariners from danger, so has Mr. Waterton stood out as a beacon to guard ornithologists from error.

The fraternization of Mr. Waterton and myself, which was, for many years, widely known to be so close and intimate was, now and then unworthily, nay, in some instances dishonourably taken advantage of; in one case especially so, and in a way certainly not reflecting much credit on the vulgar perpetrators of a most disingenuous imposition.

A party of three, in the instance to which I have alluded, proceeded from Leeds by rail to Wakefield; and *hiring* a conveyance in the latter place, they presumptuously drove over to Walton Hall, stating that they "had driven their own horse and carriage from Leeds."

"One individual of this party," said the Squire, "evidently invested in his Sunday-trappings for this special occasion, was the principal spokesman on their arrival at the hall, and he was manifestly not wanting in either assurance, or effrontery, whilst he coolly represented himself as an 'intimate friend of Doctor Hobson's,' whose name as he doubtless well knew, was a welcome passport in all seasons at Walton Hall."

On their *entrée* to the mansion, the Squire, of

course, believing that this gentleman had actually
driven his own horse fourteen miles, and that he
really was " an intimate friend " of mine, and having
had no opportunity to measure his mental capacity,
was immediately anxious to shower down the blessings of the house upon a leash of men he *then*
considered meritorious, but who, after a further acquaintance, he designated " a misrepresenting assemblage of clownish mushrooms."

When the Squire had good-naturedly lionised them
through the natural history in the staircase, he not only
very kindly invited them to take tea, (a proposition
which, it would appear, they rather voraciously accepted,)
but he actually urged them to come some future day
to dine and to bring their "better-halves" with them.

Mr. Waterton afterwards, however, observed, " So
soon as I had a fair opportunity of 'taking stock' of
this trio, I felt that I could not congratulate the
Doctor on the acquisition of his 'intimate friend,'
and my suspicions of fraud began to increase in consequence of the evidently shallow and superficial attainments of these intrusive curiosity-mongers."

On taking their final departure after the hospitable reception they had so undeservedly met with,
Mr. Waterton cast his keen eye on the horse which
he thought he recognised as a Wakefield hack, and,
anon, around the dog-cart, on which he fancied that
he caught a glimpse of the name of a Wakefield
livery-stable keeper, but was not so certain as to consider himself in possession of evidence sufficient for

absolute conviction, or, as he observed, "these exqui-
sites should have had the reward of their merits duly
meted out to them free of discount, and by a species
of electricity which would have astounded them."

"The leader of the clan, whom I shall, for distinction's sake, call the insolent 'beau,'" said the
Squire, "is *now* known to me by name, but I shall
not enlighten you as to his *sobriquet*, because it might
create a disagreeable feeling against these worthies.
By the way, one of the three, an ungainly animal
in formation, and rejoicing in broad Yorkshire ver-
nacularism professed to be indisposed, and was therefore put to bed; whether this was a *ruse* in order
to conceal his slaughter of the queen's English I
know not, but, from certain telegraphic symbols passing between them my suspicions were aroused. I
must confess that I did not like his being in a room
alone, as there were many little tempting trifles unat-
tached to the walls, whilst he was big enough to
have taken a feather-bed home with him, if he had
only had a fair chance.

"You may think me rather spiteful, but of all
vices I thoroughly despise deception, and excessively
dislike being myself so meanly victimised.

"The following day I called at the livery-stable
in Wakefield, to ascertain if some Leeds gentlemen
had the previous day, hired a conveyance to take them
to Walton Hall, and if the vainglorious leader of the
leash had represented himself as 'an intimate friend
of Doctor Hobson's.' 'Sure enough,' quoth the

master of the horse, 'some Leeds shopkeepers did yesterday hire a conveyance, but the gaudy-got-up-leader knew better than try to gammon me with any of his nonpariel. No, no, he knew that his fabrications would not go down here. Never trouble your head Squire about that macaroni, he has more cheek than brains, indeed, them as knows him, tells me he has not as many as would bait a mouse-trap."

"Now, so far as I had an opportunity of judging, the third individual conducted himself like a gentleman; but inasmuch as he was a '*particeps criminis*' in the deceitful transaction, if the fop and the giant should be transported, their more gentlemanly companion should, most assuredly, not go scot-free.

"If the leader in the team should ever hazard a second visit to Walton Hall, you shall hear the sequel, and you shall then know his name, which, however, I will not reveal—even to you—unless this lord paramount should again break the bonds of propriety and of truth. Let him rest in, I suspect, his obscurity. He told me he kept his carriage and resided in the suburban district of Leeds, on this allegation I am sceptical, yet I have charity enough left to forgive him."

On subsequently pressing Mr. Waterton to give the name of the Leeds swell, he replied, "I will never do that; but I will admit that I have my suspicions he is of Israelitish descent, as he turned up his nose at a piece of fat bacon on the tea-table as if he had some Hebrew blood in his veins."

CHAPTER IV.

THE park at Walton Hall is a favorite resort, and probably I might fairly add retreat for the carrion-crow, and has afforded most satisfactory information relative to the long-disputed question at issue as to the gregariousness of this species.

Mr Thompson in his admirably written "Natural History of Ireland," admits that a dozen carrion-crows had been seen congregated in the evening at Rammerscales in Dumfrieshire. On the other hand, the Rev. F. O. Morris says, "These birds keep in pairs the whole year, and are believed to unite for life, and that more than two or three are seldom seen in company."

Another author says, "The brood remains with the parents till near breeding-time, and though carrion-crows collect in small flocks during the winter, they seem to do so rather from an accidental meeting in quest of food, than from any principle or instinct of a solid nature."

Montague observes, "These birds keep in pairs all the year, seldom congregate but to regale on some carrion, or in winter to roost."

Yarrell's remark is "The carrion-crows keep in pairs all the year, and more than two are seldom seen together, unless assembled over a carcass."

The observant Gilbert White says, "Carrion-crows go in pairs the whole year, it is therefore probable that they, like ravens, pair for life."

Macgillivray quotes Mr. Haslay, who says, "In the neighbourhood of Leicester, I have seen the carrion-crows in little groups of fours and fives, perhaps so many families which had not broken up their brotherhood."

Mayer says, "Carrion-crows, although not gregarious, appear more sociably to consort with other members of the *corridæ* in general than the raven does."

In Wilson's American ornithology it is stated that "the American crow agrees so nearly with the European species as to satisfy me that they are the same," and the only allusion made by him as to their being gregarious is this, "towards the close of summer, the parent crows with their families, forsaking their solitary lodgings collect together, as if by previous agreement when evening approaches."

Selby observes "Carrion-crows seldom associate in numbers, but generally remain in pairs through the year."

It is evident from the extracts of the various authors from whom I have quoted, that up to this period, the question of gregariousness has not been finally determined, but, in the park, at Walton Hall, this embarrassing and disputed subject of inquiry has been definitely settled. In the winter, and in the early spring months, it has not been unusual to see from forty to fifty, and occasionally, upwards of eighty of these birds in a single flock, — a sufficiently valid testimony of

nature's laws, where the agency of non-intervention has
been effectually carried out, and a convincing proof that
the wily carrion-crow, not only knows where he is cared
for, but is sagacious enough, and also desirous to take
advantage of the laws of protection.   Many ornithologists
of celebrity have pooh-poohed the idea of the carrion-
crow being gregarious; but how do they get rid of the
awkward evidence of large flocks of this species
congregating for months in succession, where and when
they have an opportunity to do so?   The Squire and I
have repeatedly counted upwards of eighty of these
birds, in both December and January in one distinct
flock, before their deserting the park, whilst a few remained
to nest and nature their young yearly within the walls.

There has been another controversy relative to the
carrion-crow which has held a doubtful position, and
probably with good reason, viz., whether the female
covers her eggs previously to temporary absence from
her nest.

Mr. Waterton and I have repeatedly had opportunities
of examination, and never on any occasion found the
eggs covered, but frequently observed a marked difference in form, size, and colour.   Men of equal and
undoubted authority and veracity have found the eggs
of the carrion-crow covered and uncovered.   "When
doctors differ, who shall decide?"

My opinion is, that if the carrion-crow is leaving her
nest to feed, and in no way hurried in making her
necessary arrangements, she will cover her eggs, but
if disturbed, and leaving her nest from fear of some

intrusion, I think it then very probable, that in the hurry of the moment, she will speedily fly from her nest without covering them.

At one period, there was, in this park, another instance of rare occurrence, indeed, probably, the only similar one on record. You could daily see a purely white common goose having become a monogamist, being paired with a Canada male bird, taking her lofty aerial flights in company with her foreign mate, forgetting her former, and her naturally domestic habits, appearing now as an espoused partner, and assuming in all her nuptial felicity, the varied habits of her wild paramour.

Here, the nightingale pays its annual and cordially welcome visit, and is listened to at the hall, evening after evening, with infinite pleasure, melodiously warbling its charming song in its silent and secure retreat.

> " Whence is it, that amaz'd I hear
>   From yonder wither'd spray,
> This foremost morn of all the year.
>   The melody of May !
>
> " But thee no wintry skies can harm,
>   Who only need'st to sing,
> To make e'en January charm,
>   And every season Spring."

The "packing" of carrion-crows, in this park, is a remarkable and a convincing proof of the validity of protection among the feathered tribes, when efficiently used in order to secure the ends desired to be obtained by the naturalist. It is, however, scarcely possible to conceive a place better adapted for this object, and for the study and elucidation of the mysteries in nature, than the park at Walton Hall; especially for that section which may be deemed minute ornithology, and which, in later years has been so marvellously revealed by the extraordinary powers of the telescope.

In this park, it seemed as if all nature had been formed to meet the wishes of the Squire. There is an abundance of wood, underwood, water, and undulating ground, whilst the extent of the park is sufficiently large to allow of portions being devoted entirely to absolute seclusion for those birds which are naturally disposed to avoid the haunts of man.

The upper two-thirds of the lake with its adjacent wood and pasture land, are kept altogether free from any intrusion whatever, for six successive months every year. Even visitors at the house of whatever rank they might be, were always " warned off" those portions specially set apart for natural history purposes. There was never any favour shown to either rank or sex, if it happened to clash with any part of natural history which taught to distinguish, to better comprehend, or to more accurately ascertain and describe the objects of nature. Even during the whole breeding-season, the heronry district was strictly forbidden ground, unless in case of accident to a young heron by falling from its nest—in which case aid would be immediately afforded.

Mr. Waterton was in the habit of registering *memoranda* as to dates and names of birds as *occasional* visitors in the park for upwards of thirty years, with which information he kindly furnished me, in order that all my statements should be of unquestionable accuracy.

From the following list carefully examined, and from his own recollection, it appeared that all the birds of which record is made in the annexed catalogue had at one time, or another, sojourned or, at all events, been seen within the park at Walton Hall. I may add, that I have myself very frequently seen a great majority of those here named on the lake, or in the grounds; and many of them to the greatest possible advantage by means of the telescope, which I seldom omitted using on my oft-repeated visits to the Squire.

Birds seen in the Grounds of Walton Hall.

Osprey.	Rook.	Spotted woodpecker.
Peregrine.	Jackdaw.	Lesser woodpecker.
Kestrel.	Magpie.	Creeper.
Sparrow-hawk.	Jay.	Crossbill.
Hobby.	Missel thrush.	Grossbeak.
Merlin.	Song thrush.	Bullfinch.
Wood owl.	Fieldfare.	Goldfinch.
Larn owl.	Redwing	Yellowhammer.
Bong-eared owl.	Blackbird.	Common bunting.
Little earless owl.	Skylark.	Black-headed ditto.
Woodcock owl.	Titlark.	House sparrow.
Raven.	Starling.	Mountain sparrow.
Carrion-crow.	Cuckoo.	Chaffinch.
Hooded crow.	Green woodpecker.	Brambling.

Siskin.
Brown linnet.
Green linnet.
Lesser redpole.
Pied flycatcher.
Common flycatcher.
Nightingale.
Robin.
Redstart.
Hedge sparrow.
Reed sparrow.
Blackcap.
Willow wren.
Golden crested wren.
Common wren.
Wheatear.
Whinchat.
Stonechat.
Oxeye titmouse.
Blue ditto.
Cole ditto.
Long-tailed ditto.
Bearded ditto.
Nuthatch.
Yellow wagtail.
Pied wagtail.

Grey wagtail.
Chimney swallow.
Sand martin.
House martin.
Swift.
Kingfisher.
Nightjar.
Ringdove.
Stockdove.
Turtledove.
Pheasant.
Partridge.
Snipe.
Quail.
Land-rail.
Water-rail.
Lesser rail.
Little land-rail.
Thick-kneed plover.
Lapwing.
Golden plover.

Wild swan.
Common swan.
Mallard.
Shoveller.

Widgeon.
Teal.
Tufted duck.
Pochard,
Golden eye.
Chestnut duck.
Common scoter.
Velvet scoter.
Dabchick.
Dusky grebe.
Eared grebe.
Canada goose.
Egyptian goose.
Barnacle goose.
Cape goose.
Goosander.
Smew.
Garganey.
Cormorant.
Coot.
Water-hen.
Heron.
Common sandpiper.
Four of the gull tribe.
Common tern.
Black tern.

Apart from the breeding-season, coots are very numerous at Walton Hall. They are continually feeding and sporting on the lake within a short distance from the windows of the house, together with countless thousands of a great variety of water-fowl. During the severe winter months, when the whole lake is one sheet of ice, its appearance would, now and then, astound an old and even travelled ornithologist, as it not unfrequently occurs, that you may see nearly the whole frozen lake literally covered by a startling variety of water-fowl. This multitude of visitors on the lake in winter, consists (and frequently at the same time,) of cormorants, teal, tufted ducks, pochards, widgeons, the garganey, smew, shoveller, and now and then of the velvet and common scoters, together with extraordinary numbers of wild duck. Thousands, especially of the latter, rest in such close proximity to each other, as sometimes to conceal even any appearance of ice. They will thus silently congregate for hours in succession, in a perfectly quiescent state when sitting on the ice. You will see the Egyptian and the Canada geese, which are permanent residents in these grounds wandering here and there in vain and anxious search for water, whilst the apparently indolent and listless herons then stand out on the banks of the frozen lake, isolated and prominently interesting objects, gracefully beautifying and perfecting this enchanting scene of natural history. The stillness and complete quietude on the icy surface of the lake and its immediate environs, evidently inspire the birds with a relying confidence and an assurance of safety, which you do not meet with elsewhere. All living nature, as if grateful for the Squire's protection, appears to have formed a positive attachment to this special locality. That birds, however, should prefer this to other land and water resorts is not surprising, when we know that in other places they are generally surrounded by enemies, and consequently, in perpetual fear; whereas here they are

I

fostered and protected on every side, and live in peace and happiness.

> " Those Christians best deserve the name,
> Who studiously make peace their aim ;
> Peace, both the duty and the prize
> Of him that creeps, and him that flies.''

In speaking of the attachments of birds to particular objects or to peculiar localities, it may not be out of place to allude to a singular instance bearing on this question, which occurred in the lake at Walton Hall in the year 1858. A pair of coots formed their nest on some material which they doubtless believed to be an immoveable foundation ; but the wind came and the storm arose and mercilessly detached the rushy turf on which the nest rested, leaving the entire fabric with the female and her fondly cherished eggs in its centre, a floating mass, and drifting at the tender mercy of the uncontrollable tempest. As the fickle breeze veered to the different points of the compass, so the patiently submissive and powerless coot with her buoyant edifice, altered her direction, and unwittingly changed her locality. Notwithstanding her uncertain tenure of ubiety, and possibly, even of house and home for the next moment, she patiently yielded to her lot. Here to-day, elsewhere to-morrow, but wherever her destiny cast her, whether buffeted on the open water or driven amid the reeds and the rushes, there was she always faithfully supported, cheered and comforted, by the partner of her weals and her woes. Ovid has beautifully expressed the feeling that must have animated this constancy in the male bird,

> " *Hanc cupit, hanc optat ; sola suspirat in illâ ;*
> *Signaque dat nutu, solicitatque notis.*"

> "Her he desires, for her he longs, for her alone he sighs ;
> He makes signs to her by nods, and courts her by gestures."

His warm and abiding affection knew no change in their hitherto wretched uncertainty. Throughout this long and anxious trial of attachment, he never once forsook her, nor was this noble-hearted bird freed from his painful state of solicitude until that period had at length arrived when they could mutually congratulate each other on their abiding and unbroken constancy prompted by nature, which rewarded these two immutably attached coots with a progeny to amply repay the anxiety and care they had never failed to bestow on each other, and upon the contents of their previously fragile and floating capital.

We have this generally corroborated by Col. Montague, who having described their nests and attachments, says " In this buoyant state a sudden gale of wind has been known to draw them from their slender moorings, and we are assured that the nests have been seen floating on the surface of the water with the birds upon them."

To which confirmation Selby adds. " From the nature of the materials comprising the nest and the situation in which it is built, it sometimes happens that it is torn from its moorings by a flood, and afterwards floated at random on the surface of the water, without destroying the eggs or preventing the female from continuing her incubation."

Independent of the rigid protection of the feathered tribes within these walls, every part of the park seems to be, somehow endowed with a congeniality favourable to the existence and propagation of birds, and therefore, singularly conducive to all ornithological pursuits. Unless the white owl felt herself perfectly at home, and entirely free from any thing like danger, she would not be seen frequently during the day in the month of June, fearlessly pursuing her mousing avocations. Her attachment to this protected place where she is exempt from every molestation, renders her so happy and confident, that she generally contrives to hatch two broods, yearly; and, as there is nothing to incommode nor disturb her offspring, nor to prevent their reaching maturity, this park must largely contribute towards the prevention of the entire extinction of the white owl.

The ivy-covered ruin on the island has long been a favourite nesting-resort for the owl ; but the recently severe winters have destroyed much of its luxuriant growth and foliage, which previously, whilst adorning the ruin, afforded to the owl a tempting retirement for incubation. Indeed, if these saving retreats had not here existed for the propagation of this very useful bird to the farmer, in which to mature its offspring for future years, the neighbouring district would have been deprived altogether of a bird, which probably destroys more rats and mice for the farmer than all his cats do which he so much prizes. And yet the farmers seldom care for the preservation of a friend who is always on the watch for their interests.

I may add, that two or three pairs of the *brown* owl were always fortunate enough to yearly hatch and mature their young in the wood adjoining the grotto.

I would that an admonition, from that luxuriantly cultivated district, East Lothian, could influence our English farmers to endeavour to multiply the white owl, but they have hitherto turned a deaf ear to all remonstrance or persuasion of this nature.

Mr. Hepburn, from that elysium of agricultural cultivation, says :—" Shortly before sunset the white owl leaves its retreat, skims along the hedge-rows, hunts over the meadows and corn fields like a spaniel, and drops suddenly on its quarry.

You see her approach the homestead on noiseless wing, threading the labyrinth of stacks. She now enters the outhouses or the barn, and speedily re-appears with a mouse in her claws.

Perching on the top of a stack, she devours her prey, preens her feathers, and shrieks. Should plenty of food occur she will remain all night and visit the place very frequently.

It is at this time, especially if the weather be fine, that mice betake themselves to the outside of the stacks, where, all night long, they sport amongst the extremities of the sheaves and, doubtless, drink the crystal dew-drops in their season. From her watch-tower, this owl swoops down among them or nimbly seizes them as she slides between the stacks.

A sorry adept indeed she must be if she do not secure one with each foot at a time. Nor must we forget the

owl's services in the meadow and corn-field. With such
facts before his eyes, where is the man who has the
least interest in the cultivation of the soil, that will not
protect this beautiful and highly useful bird ? "

In 1815, the late George Rennie, Esq., of Phantassie,
in East Lothian, had the late Sir John Sinclair, Bart.
staying a few days with him whilst I was also a visitor
in the house, and I shall never forget the very interesting discussion they had on the destruction of mice and
young rats by the white owl.

Like Mr. Waterton, they had counted the number of
these vermin which had been taken by a pair of white
owls to their offspring during one night.   Although I
do not remember the number, yet I well recollect that
it was enormous, and that they agreed to write to the late
Mr. Curwen of Workington Hall, then M.P. for the
county of Cumberland, asking him to unite with them
in publishing the result of their determinations on this
subject, and as these three gentlemen were the great
agricultural luminaries at that day, such a document
would have been likely to have had weighty influence
throughout the United Kingdom.

On appearing at breakfast one morning, Sir John, with
a countenance pleasantly lighted up observed, "Rennie,
a happy thought occurred to me during the night,
conceived, and I dare say, hatched by the influence of
your excellent toddy."

"Well, Sir John, as my toddy has aided in developing

the happy thought,' we should share the honour," replied Mr. Rennie.

" With all my heart," rejoined Sir John.

" As the germ has its origin in only one end of the grain of wheat, I have been calculating what an immense saving might be secured nationally, by employing old women beyond the age of physical labour, to cut each grain transversely into two parts with a pair of scissors. One half of the seed sown would thus be economised as a clear gain for the common weal."

" What would the 'common weal' have to pay for the 'clear gain?' retorted the intelligent and sharp-sighted Rennie.

A moment's reflection was sufficient to convince Sir John of the absurdity of his proposition, and to induce him to instantly acknowledge that he began to doubt— whether he was a native of Scotland, as it was so totally unlike a genuine Scotchman to estimate the gain without counting the cost.   He laughed heartily at his abortive " happy thought," and addressing himself to me, as an Englishman, playfully remarked, " What would your friend, Curwen say to this *ignis fatuus* of mine.   Pray tell it not in Gath."

On the lake at Walton Hall there have been Canada geese for very many years, a few of which are always kept pinioned so as to induce those that are not pinioned to remain along with them on the water, and also to secure, at all times, a certain number on the lake or on its surrounding banks in order to enrich the natural history scenery and add beauty to the landscape. The process of pinioning should be had recourse to when they are goslings, and consequently, unable to fly; but should this opportunity have been accidentally omitted, the keeper always managed this trifling operation upon the old birds between the 12th and 24th of July, as, a little after the summer solstice they invariably shed their wing-feathers, and are therefore totally unable to fly for a few days; consequently, by a little manœuvring at that time, they are easily laid hold of, provided the capturing parties thoroughly understand how to go about their business. During this period however, the Canadians seem to be quite conscious of their inability to escape by flight and are therefore extremely cautious not to trust themselves at such a distance from the lake as to encounter any difficulty on their part, in again reaching the water before you could intercept them on land. Indeed, you have to slily watch for a feasible chance to accomplish your object, and even then, it sometimes requires very considerable physical ability to secure your intended captives. I may here state, that if the cunning Canadians once escape being captured by your incautiously permitting them to reach the lake before you are able to intercept them, they will never, so long as they are unable to fly, give you another chance *on land.*

These birds breed here, but seldom prolifically. If their eggs were entrusted to the common domestic hen, I believe that the fecundity of the Canada as well as of the Egyptian geese would be materially increased. We all know that the barn-yard hen will hatch, diligently attend to, and mature the web-footed duck, but it must be remembered that we and not the hen, supply the young broods with *suitable* food; and of course, the young of the Canada and Egyptian geese would need to be supplied with that peculiar character of food, specially applicable to their *natural* requirements.

Instinct inspires the cuckoo with an unerring knowledge, to discriminate into what bird's nest to deposit her egg, so that the character of food of its future foster-parent may be *naturally* adapted to the young cuckoo which she will have to feed and protect; but instinct ceases to inspire when different species clash with each other. The Squire, on one occasion, to a certain but limited extent disregarding instinct, placed the eggs of the magpie under the jackdaw and those of the jackdaw under the magpie; and he placed the carrion-crow's eggs under the rook and those of the rook under the carrion-crow. So far as this trifling deviation from nature extended, the result was, as it was anticipated it would be. They each incubated, hatched, and matured their spurious offspring, but, in all human probability, if Mr. Waterton had diversified the distinction of the species a little more widely, he would have met with a reverse of his former success.

When occasionally indulging in an idle hour, seated on the favourite rock in the grotto, I have frequently been surprised by Mr. Waterton's immediate and never failing *discrimination* of the song or even of the chirp of *any* bird in the fir-grove. Their variety of notes, confusion to me, was to the Squire simply the mingling of so many languages, in the knowledge of which he had been perfected.

> " Hark ! on every bough,
> In lulling strains the feather'd warblers woo."

And yet, although two or three songsters of different species were warbling simultaneously, Mr. Waterton would distinguish by name the various birds without any apparent difficulty.

On one occasion however, the Squire was "fairly floored" according to his own admission, by a wonderfully clever vocal imitation, but certainly not of a warbling character, and I am delighted to have it in my power to furnish the identical anecdote to which I allude from its original source.

The annexed letter written to me the other day by my friend, Mr. Salvin, the author of that eminently standard work, entitled " Falconry in the British Isles," needs no preparatory observation from me.

" WHITMOOR HOUSE, GUILDFORD,

" *October* 20*th*, 1866.

"Dear Dr. Hobson,

"Perhaps two little anecdotes relating to our old friend the late Mr. Waterton, (who was certainly the most wonderful man I have ever seen,) may be considered worthy of a place in your excellent work which I am delighted to see is so well received.

"I will begin with my first introduction to the old Squire, for it was so ridiculous and characteristic that I shall never forget it. One fine Sunday morning in spring, my brother M. C. and I drove over from Leeds to Wakefield and thence to Walton Hall, but before arriving there adventure the first befel us. At that time the Squire went to Wakefield on Sundays to attend divine service. We had also been to the same chapel and knew his carriage, which to our dismay we now saw before us, so we held a council of war when it was decided that as he (the Squire) was only acquainted with our family &c., and not with ourselves individually, it would be awkward to pass him and arrive before him, so we determined to pull up and to let the carriage get well a-head. Having given him plenty of law, we proceeded, and passed the first barrier by telling the lodge-keeper some plausible tale, upon which she let us through, and we arrived at the iron bridge before the house. Here I held the horse, whilst my brother sought admission to see the collection, of the butler who came to the front door with copper coal-scuttle and brush in hand. "I am sorry, Sir, said the faithful looking servant, master never allows the collection nor the grounds to be seen on Sundays." Well, said my brother, we have come a long way, and indeed if Mr. Waterton knew who we were, for he was at school at Tudal, with our Uncle Bryan Salvin, all would be right. No sooner was this said than the brush went into the applicant's ribs, and with a hearty

good shake of the hand the Squire owned to have been
"doing the butler" and welcomed us both in. We
remained until the evening, being well entertained with
the Wanderer's charming stories of his travels and the
many curious and interesting facts in natural history which
he pointed out. My father had acquired a taste for
natural history from Mr. Tunstal of Wycliffe, the last
of that family, who at that time had one of the finest
private collections in the north, and with whom the
famous Bewick was constantly staying. I may therefore,
almost say that I inherited a taste for natural history,
which was greatly increased after this delighful visit. It
also taught me that many writers on this subject were
mere copyists, and so keep handing down errors which
are a disgrace to the age, instead of studying it for them.
selves in the ample field of nature.

"I had the pleasure after this of frequently visiting
Walton, and upon one occasion I had the honour of
assisting the Squire in arranging his splendid collection,
and I well remember having the misfortune of breaking
the glass belonging to "the nondescript," which mishap
was most good-naturedly forgiven.

"It was not often that the Squire was "done," but your
humble servant once took him in, even in natural history.
Some people have the gift of imitating animals, and I
believe I can boast of the elegant accomplishment of
"doing the pig" and one evening I slipped out upon the
lawn and standing near the window I did my part so
effectually (being in particularly good tune) that out came
mine host armed with a broom, in the greatest state of

excitement, fully believing that the pigs had got out, that some one had left the gates open on the bridge, and that they were hard at work rooting up the beautifully mown grass. Upon finding out his mistake he was greatly amused.

"Believe me, very truly yours,

"F. H. SALVIN."

I have previously observed that Mr. Waterton always entertained an antipathy to the rat, and that it was the only animal at Walton Hall to which he gave no quarter. His hostile feeling against the "Hanoverian," and his ingenuity how to quit him were, several years ago, productive of means so unique and so instantaneously effective, that they certainly merit a passing notice. On the Squire's return home, after a somewhat lengthened period in the desert-forests in South America, he found Walton Hall so infested with rats that the whole house was overrun with them. He therefore immediately set his wits to work, in order to devise some plan that would speedily free him from the "Hanoverians;" and at once designed his mode of action, which proved on execution, as successful as it was unprecedented. He caught a fine old rat in a "harmless trap," which, of course, was not in the slightest degree injured, and when all the household had retired to rest for the night, he carefully smeared this rat all over with tar, and then set him at liberty in one of his principal runs. Doubtless, this recently liberated prisoner highly scented and well "tarred" but not "feathered," would, on his unexpected escape, lose no time in reconnoitring every available avenue within his reach. In fact he would, simply from fear of himself now that he was so highly perfumed, scour the ins and outs of what might be fairly termed his own country in double quick time, by which means he would impregnate every underground burrow with an odour that is said of all others to be the most offensive to the rat. Even his own fraternity seem to have been so terrified by the unequivocally disagreeable odour of this scented "Hanoverian," that they fled by wholesale during the night across the narrow portion of the lake; and the Squire, at day-break on the following morning, found the whole house entirely freed from his hitherto unwelcome visitors. When Mr. Waterton named this laughable circumstance to me, he, at the same time, told me that he had repeatedly "scarred away" rats by mixing tar with finely chopped garlick, and leaving a small portion here and there in their "runs."

On the outside of the Cromwell doors in the old ruin there is a broad stone step nearly on a level with the threshold, but overhanging the water. It is always perfectly dry on its upper surface, and furnishes a good and accessible foundation for the visitors to stand upon whilst examining the antique doors, which are really objects of deep interest from their peculiar style of architecture, and from their attached

rude and heavy appendages then thought necessary
for the protection of the mansion, together with portions pierced by Cromwell's bullets. If these ancient
doors are closed whilst you are standing on this step,
you are then placed between them and a very deep
part of the lake with no chance of escape; — even if
you jump into the lake, you have no means of reaching
a place of safety except by swimming at least one
hundred and fifty yards,—in fact you are immured in
a most perfect "lock-up." Now, it accidentally occurred,
that a poacher who had long been very notorious in
his way, and who had for a lengthened period, been what
is termed "wanted," having committed sundry depredations on Mr. Waterton's manor, by stealing pheasants'
eggs, &c., &c., was, by a manœuvre, when in front of the
house, tempted on to the island where the Squire
happened to be at the moment.

The poacher, who was a well-known character for his
evil ways, had been, for some time, in jest, nick-named
"*fur*;" Mr. Waterton, when in a jocular mood, having
previously given him that opprobrious appellation, in
consequence of his being a well-known thief. The
keepers, and indeed the whole household, somehow or
other, soon got to know that "*fur*" was the Latin word
for thief, and, therefore, more frequently honoured the
poacher by his Latin than by his real and English name.
Now this "man of three letters," "*homo trium literarum*,"
was disposed to be facetiously impertinent; the Squire
therefore, was determined, before liberating the poacher,
to accommodate him with "a Rowland for an Oliver,"

and whilst quietly remonstrating with him in great
apparent simplicity and kindness, as if his insolence had
been forgotton or forgiven, was at the same time,
ingeniously contriving ample punishment for him, by
cajoling him, unsuspectingly on to the fatal stone step in
the "lock-up."

No sooner was the poacher "placed," than the Squire,
at once adroitly closed the doors, leaving his saucy
captive in the solitary "lock-up," to deliberate on his
past conduct. On this fellow, in a whimpering strain,
threatening to drown himself unless immediately released, the keepers cordially encored the sentiment of
their lachrymose prisoner. He then became, but not
before some hours had elapsed, an apparent penitent,
and on that ground, was freed from "durance vile."
From that time forward, he was never known to poach
on the Squire's manor, and was always ready to do
him a "good turn," at least, so said the poacher himself,
and the Squire believed him; but the wilful destruction
of eggs, which was the primary offence in this case,
always annoyed Mr. Waterton more than the slaughter
of the birds themselves. In this instance the Squire did
not recognise the old proverb, that "a bird in the hand
is worth two in the bush."

In years gone by, the Squire was a strict and determined preserver of game on his own estate. He then
like his neighbours, had a great abundance of hares,
partridges, and pheasants, and hesitated not to go to
a considerable expense for their preservation; but that

THE POACHER ENTRAPPED INTO THE LOCK-UP BY MR. WATERTON.

reckless character of population, which in the present
age almost bids defiance to the protection of property
in some districts, has latterly increased so rapidly and
so extensively in some of the neighbouring villages, that
an enormous amount of money is required to effectually
carry out the spirit of protection as regards the rigorous
preservation of game; hence it is literally beyond the
means of many country gentlemen, unless by a ruinous
expense, or at all events, by inconveniently infringing on
their income—a folly which they are not generally prone
to commit. "If gentlemen do," observed Mr. Waterton,
"indiscreetly yield to this alluring extravagance, other
miseries beyond pecuniary loss frequently await them,
as now and then, a melancholy loss of life is also
entailed by this rigid yet lawful protection of game."
The natural feelings and disposition of the Squire were
always so humane and so utterly antagonistic to every
thing which could, in the slightest degree expose any
party to the chance of sustaining injury, or of jeopardising
the life of a fellow-creature, that I am sure he would
have infinitely preferred the entire deprivation of game,
rather than have hazarded the possibility of injuring
any human being, more especially a poor man.

These remarks will sufficiently explain to my readers
why there has been no superabundance of game at
Walton Hall for many years.   Recently indeed, the
encouragement for its preservation has been so little
observed, that the temptation held out to poachers
has not been at all adequate to the expense, toil, and
risk they would have had to run.

Latterly, there have been no poachers with the solitary exception of one of the Squire's own household, viz, a very beautiful and enormously large cat, which in 1863, weighed upwards of sixteen pounds. "Whitty," for such was its name, an abreviation of Whittington, now and then took a marauding freak and occasionally on the sly, picked up a stray leveret; but he was so special a favourite with the whole household, that the sternest rebuke he ever received from his master was a smile of forgiveness. "Whitty" numbered several years at the hall, being brought from Scarbro' as a kitten in 1855, during which period he acquired a vast amount of cunning, and indulged in a considerable degree of familiarity with the domestics generally. He would jump on to and familiarly sit upon Mr. Waterton's shoulder during dinner, if his own "allowance" had been forgotten, or if the butler had not precisely suited his palate by the plate provided for him.

Notwithstanding "Whitty's" love of game, there were always pheasants in the neighbourhood of the grotto sufficiently numerous to please and amuse the naturalist by their crowing, and also to prove and instruct the inexperienced how the crowing of the cock-pheasant differs from that of the game-cock, not merely in tone and in character, but otherwise. The game-cock claps his wings and crows, whereas the pheasant crows and claps his wings. These birds never make a mistake in reversing the order of these acts. They strictly adhere to nature's instinct.

I am here reminded of an amusing description of pheasant-shooting by a Mr. Jonathan Higgins in 1837, who could, it must be fairly admitted, lay no great claim to the ordinary attainments of an English sportsman of the present age. Mr. Higgins writes :—" Heard some pheasants crowing by the side of a plantation— got within gunshot of two of the birds, vich Higgins said they vos two game-cocks, but Hicks who had often been at Vestminster Pit, said, no sich thing, as game-cocks had got short square tails and smooth necks, and long military spurs. Shot at 'em as pheasants, and believe ve killed 'em both ; but hearing some orrid screams come out of the plantation immediately after ve all took to our eels and ran away vithout stopping to pick either of 'em up. At the end of a mile came suddenly upon a strange sort of bird, vich Hicks declared to be the 'cock of the woods.' Sneaked behind him and killed him. Turned out to be a peacock."

I have previously hinted at a suspicion existing as to the destruction of foxes by the late Mr. Waterton. Now that is a subject which the Squire and I have freely discussed, and he solemnly assured me that it was a most unjust accusation, being entirely devoid of truth, adding, "In my youth, no one rejoiced more in hounds than I did, and no keen sportsman had greater enjoyment in, nor was more delighted with an "across country" run than I was. And I can feelingly and with great truth yet say, an old sportsman likes the crack of the whip. The very party who originated that foul falsehood did it merely from a petty spite, and at the moment I had it in my power to have crushed him when busily propagating so base a fabrication. I could have traced the lie to the originator, but I abominably detest all squabbles, and would have had to sacrifice a quiet and worthy neighbour in order to bring home and expose the prime mover of the scandal.

"Those gentlemen who really know me will not give credence to such a report, and if any-there be who do me such injustice, I may say with the old proverb, '*Latrantem curatne alta Diana canem?*' 'Does Diana on high care for the dog that bays her?'

"If the Badsworth hunt expect that I should encourage sly reynard to take up his quarters within my park walls, and by way of his securing a *bonne-bouche*, lunch on a wild duck, a pheasant, or a Canada goose, and enjoy a late and hearty dinner from my poultry roost, they must labour under a strange misconception; but I have no faith in that improbable scandal on the hunt. If I ever find a fox in the park, he shall assuredly be honourably excommunicated, and take his brush along with him *a-la-mode*."

Several years ago, a party of officers from some neighbouring barracks who were disposed to have a lark, rode over to Walton Hall, and sent in their cards with a request to see the interior of the mansion. Mr. Waterton received them very graciously. Young, indiscreet, and professing to have a scientific knowledge of painting which they did not in the slightest degree possess, they soon betrayed their entire ignorance of the art, by foolishly pointing out supposed imperfections where none existed, and by absurdly praising those very portions of paintings which were really defective. Mr. Waterton, conquently, soon ceased to have any pleasing interest in explaining the pictures under examination.

At this juncture, the Squire felt disposed to treat them simply with pity; but when his quick eye caught the whole party actually ridiculing him, and indulging in rude and personal remarks, notwithstanding his extreme kindness to them, he became somewhat irate, but silently so, excepting that he took an opportunity to state that there were some very splendid paintings at a house in the neighbourhood, with which they would be highly delighted. "The gentleman himself" the Squire observed, "was then from home but that an odd and eccentric old fellow who lived in the house, was a man of remarkable ability and invariably showed the paintings,—that he was the best judge, and had the most knowledge on these subjects of any man in the county." The bait was greedily swallowed by the officers. They would go at once, if it was only to have a glance at this extraordinary bit of mortality.

The Squire whispered to his butler to instantly forward to the gentleman's house where the paintings were, a disguise-suit for himself, which he had recently had prepared for another purpose, but this was too tempting a chance to be deprived of without trying the fictitious apparel. The carriage-road was rather distant for the officers, but a short footpath along the fields, allowed Mr. Waterton to himself anticipate their arrival, and give him sufficient time to put on his disguise-suit, in order that he might be properly equipped to receive the military critics. Mr. Waterton's counterfeited appearance succeeded admirably. His disguise consisted of a faded red wig—an old green shade over one eye—an eye-glass over the other—a thread-bare coat so stuffed as to give to his figure the appearance of a hunch-back—drab-coloured smalls with white stockings—and a crutch used to relieve an *apparently* crippled limb.

In this anomalous-looking costume, he supported the singularity of character which he himself had previously drawn and represented to the officers at Walton Hall, receiving them at his friend's residence in the already stated absence of the master of the house. In describing and descanting upon this exquisite collection of paintings, the Squire now and then indulged in what he ironically termed a venial blunder, such as substituting a modern for an ancient master, and *vice versa*. He also highly eulogised portions which were obviously defective, without a single objection being made by the military coxcombs.

During the whole of this time, the officers amused themselves by unmercifully and ungratefully abusing "that old devil Waterton," insisting upon it "that he had not a painting worth a rush in his whole house, and that he was thoroughly and indeed glaringly ignorant of this branch of the fine arts." These warriors had not the remotest idea that it was Mr. Waterton who was lionising them, having no conception that they had been so thoroughly duped and had really made such simpletons of themselves.

When the Squire thought that he had sufficiently gulled the would-be proficients, and reduced them to a self-evident conviction of their ignorance, he quietly, yet in a moment dismantled himself of his counterfeit habilments in their presence, making a respectful bow in his own peculiar way to the censuring critics, with the addition, your "humble servant, Charles Waterton." Their apologies, to their credit, were abject, and the verbal castigation they received from the Squire was as severe as it was merited, inducing those brave warriors to hang out the white flag and humbly sue for mercy. These gentlemen ever afterward preserved a solemn, and probably sulky silence as regarded the Squire; never, of course, acknowledging his acquaintance.

Mr. Waterton was one of the most hospitable and kind-hearted men in existence. The cordial welcome I invariably received at Walton Hall prompted me to face many a stormy day, and on my return, many a bitterly cold night.

On one occasion, when meeting on my arrival at the cast-iron bridge, he observed " we have killed the fatted calf for you, which induces me to do a little on the tiptoe," adding,

> . . . . " *Recepto,*
> *Dulce mihi furere est, amico.*'

"It is delightful to launch out on receiving my friend." His launching out, I discovered, was in reference to there being a roasted pea-fowl for dinner on that day; and a dainty dish it was when it came to be discussed. There is nothing however, very striking in the flavour of a pea-fowl; for instance, if blindfold, it would require an extraordinarly nice, discriminating palate to distinguish a roasted pea-fowl from a roasted young turkey. The pea-fowl's gay plumage, I admit, takes the shine out of the plain turkey, when on the table as well as in the farm-yard,, or admiring himself in the reflecting window.

A few extracts from some of Mr. Waterton's Letters will convince the reader of his hospitality more effectually than any simple assertions of mine. He writes,

"My dear Sir,—Last Saturday night I sang

'Cease rude boreas, blustering railer,'

and called most lustily upon that frigid God to relax his terrors and thus afford to our dear Doctor Hobson a safe highway from Leeds to Walton Hall. I have just been saying, that I was in possession of a bait to coax you over here. We have two fine cormorants, which daily swim on the lake within a stone's throw of the drawing-room windows; and I know that you would rather gaze on a cormorant in such a position, than come to enjoy all the good

things we can offer you for dinner; hence, I offer
my tempting bait. We have also, just now, great
numbers of widgeon, and some grebe and teal. '*Hoc
scripsi non otii abundantia, sed amoris erga te*'.
'I have written this not from having an abundance
of leisure, but of love for you.'

"Ever sincerely,

"CHARLES WATERTON."

Again Mr. Waterton writes,

"My dear Sir,—We have just been speculating
on your putting in appearance here to-morrow. The
Doctor is always welcome, always puts us in
good humour, and makes us enjoy our dinner. I
am not yet free from the padlock on my grinders.
You ask how we got on at Aix la Chapelle, and if
I spent my time happily? Well, we got on charmingly. We are never perfectly happy, but I can
say, '*Excepto quod non simul esses, cætera lætus.*'
'Except that you were not with me, I was, in other
respects, happy.'

"I am fettered and disabled from driving over to
Park Place myself. I hope most fervently to see you
here to-morrow. If the fish are in the mud now that
the lake is being emptied it is somewhat singular,
as we cannot find one. Possibly your quick-sighted
D.D. at Leeds might be able to draw some out.
Yet, when I call to mind the professional engagements of that celebrated divine, I am inclined to conclude that he is more in the *shearing* than in the

fishing line. Now, I think I hear you say,—What a fellow that Waterton is; he can never write nor talk about our most ‘ excellent parliamentary pastors, without giving them a slap.

"Bishop ———, the Catholic prelate at ———, is here now and will say mass for us to-morrow. Now would be your time to gain orthodox information as to extreme unction about which we had conversation the other day. When I tell you that there are now even more wild ducks on the water than last week; that the six strangers are not yet made out; and that we want your ornithological eye to determine what they are, you will surely come.

"Adieu, ever sincerely,

CHARLES WATERTON."

The grotto was the luring place for a naturalist, and where the Squire and I had our unreserved intercourse and confidential conversation. It was always a favourite resort for us. This artificial and ornamental excavation in the rock was beautiful in scenery; it was charming in aspect; it was all that could be desired in privacy; and, finally, it was what the ladies call a sweet and fascinating spot.

> " Creatures that liv'd and moved, and walk'd, or flew,
>   Birds on the branches warbling, all things smil'd."

In this position, free from every intrusion, of the rational or animal creation, did we watch, contemplate, and admire the spontaneous and unbiassed acts, operations, and labours relatively due to, and performed by each species of the feathered tribe. Immediately in front, with an extended right and left view horizontally lower than our organs of vision by some fifteen or twenty feet, was nature's repast for the birds lavishly spread in the various forms of earth-worms, grubs, slugs, beetles, and caterpillars, on the grassy surface, whilst the numerous trees, shrubs, and flowers in profusion furnished their portion of food, peculiar to the character of tree or shrub favourable to their natural nidus.

Along the centre of this little valley, glided longitudinally a gurgling stream, over which and near its surface, hovered myriads of the insect families having undergone their varied metamorphoses, and now become tempting food for the insectivorous swallow. Our position might in reality, be said to be one of repose as without moving hand or foot we had a near approach and ample view of an immense diversity of "the fowls of the air," and consequently every possible facility to gain a thorough knowledge of their habits as regarded the food on which they lived and fed their young,— as regarded their time and mode of preening,—the manner of building their own dwellings, the materials used for that purpose, and of course, with this view in the fore-ground, we soon became acquainted with, and got into the secrets of their sundry little gallantries resorted to during the interesting and evidently very agreeable period of wooing, in order to obtain and secure the affections of their favourites. The delicate and alluring attentions bestowed by the male upon the softer sex by repeated offerings of a *tid-bit* as a *bonne bouche*, were always as gracefully made as they were coyly and modestly accepted by a decorous and well-mannered acknowledgment on her part.

Trifling flirtations, I admit, did occasionally betray the mutability of attachment in both sexes, but these grievances were seldom of long duration, and rarely did jealousy with her jaundiced eye succeed in stirring up absolute war to the spur, with the exception of the pugnacious sparrow and the robin, who always fought with their own species. The irascibility of these little birds sometimes induced them to continue their splenetic contest until we have, more than once had to separate them from what appeared likely to be a last and fatal embrace.

In this pleasing and temporary seclusion, some years ago, Mr. Waterton frequently alluded to our earthly separation, and now and then to a future state, adding in a grave and serious tone, "when I die, I hope that my bones will be laid at the foot of this cross," adverting to the one that was, as he had previously stated, first publicly erected in England after the Reformation. On my replying, "No, no, Mr. Waterton, let your bones be deposited in your own parish, and at Sandal Church, in consecrated ground, along with those of your ancestors;" his rejoinder was invariably to this effect,— "It is in reality, of trifling importance, having finished my earthly career, where my bones may be laid, but notwithstanding, I intend them to rest in peace at the foot of this cross, with this inscription to mark the spot :—

> " Orate
> Pro anima CAROLI WATERTON,
> Viatoris ;
> Cujus jam fessa,
> Juxta hanc crucem
> Hic sepeliuntur ossa."

" Pray for the soul of Charles Waterton, the Wanderer, whose wearied bones are now buried here near to this cross."

The Squire's bones had precious little rest during a long and eventful life. "Waterton's Wanderings" alone display a persevering and well-trained labour which establishes the fact. Its earlier portion must have been both mentally and physically a very anxious, an extremely harassing, and a hazardous one. If we take a calm and retrospective view of his middle life and are open to conviction, we must admit that his series of Essays evince one of vast and diligent observation, and of a laboriously inquiring research up to a comparatively recent period. Indeed, even in his eightieth year, his mind was as active, as disposed for investigation, and as clear on the subject of natural history,— as much alive in doing good to his fellow creatures,— and as anxious, and as persevering as regards improving and ornamenting his estate, as most men's minds are at five and twenty.

The vast and judiciously arranged and substantially executed improvements at Walton Hall during Mr.

Waterton's life, were such, that he might with equal truth have said of Walton Hall as Augustus said of Rome :—" *Urbem lateritiam invenit, marmoream, reliquit.*" " He found a city of bricks, he left a city of marble." And I may with equal justice to the memory of my old friend add, " *Nullum quod tetigit non ornavit.*" " He attempted nothing that he did not embellish."

As to physical capability, his activity and power at his period of life, were extraordinary, and probably unequalled by any other man of the same years. For instance, in the summer of 1861, when in his seventy-ninth year, Mr. Waterton, in one of his jocose moods by a run of fifteen yards, bounded over a stout wire fence, without touching it with either hand or foot, and this I very carefully measured to three feet six inches in height,—a calisthenic feat which, probably, not one person in ten thousand could accomplish at so advanced an age.

I have frequently, in painful suspense and much against my own inclination, seen the Squire, when beyond seventy years of age, hop on one leg along the brink of a rock forming the highest terrace in the grotto, whilst the other leg was dangling over the chasm below ; and, when thus hopping at a rapid rate, he would whirl himself entirely round in the air, and dropping on the other foot, would return again by hopping back on the contrary leg. On cautioning him, he would reply,—" *Non de ponte cadit qui cum sapientia vadit.*" " He falls not from the bridge who walks with prudence." I have said to him, when painfully affected by his uncalled-for freaks and thus exposing himself to danger, "Some of these follies will be the death of you; pray do not commit suicide in my presence;" when he replied, "Dont be alarmed, there is no fear that you would be accused of being my murderer; our friendship is too notorious for a supposition of that sort, even in the present corrupt and destructive age."

I have seen the Squire repeatedly sitting on the grass or on the carpet cross-legged, as tailors sit on their work-boards, when he would, to the astonishment and great delight of any surrounding friends, rise up into an erect position, without touching the ground with either hand. His power and consequent agility in the lower limbs were marvellous, having the best formed leg and the finest muscular development I ever saw, whilst the transverse capacity of the chest was somewhat defective; at all events, it was not proportionate with the lower extremities, which were enormous, but beautifully formed.

On the Squire casually consulting me relative to what he termed "an unseemly swelling of the ankles in a gentleman in the prime of life, and on the look-out for a buxom widow, or a fat, fair, and forty-five lady," I observed that the calf being so enormously brawny rendered the ankles less unseemly than they otherwise would have been, when immediately he facetiously rejoined.

> "Harry, I cannot think," says Dick,
>   What makes my ankles grow so thick."
> "You do not recollect says Harry,
>   How great a calf they have to carry."

I immediately asked the Squire to give me a copy, which he did at the moment, written in pencil on the back of an old letter placed on his hat, I told Mr. Waterton that this reminded me of a party of University men who were disputing as to the superiority of Oxford or Cambridge, when he resumed his seat, desiring me to tell him the decision of what he called the "Varsity disputation." I did so, observing that one of the controversialists remarked that the decision could not affect him because he was educated at both Universities. "That," said an old gentleman present, "puts me in mind of a calf which I remember when I was a boy, was suckled by two cows." "Really," said the University man of duplex attainments, "and pray sir, what was the consequence?" "Why sir, he turned out the greatest *calf I ever saw in my life.*" The Squire laughed heartily and observed "the double distilled gentleman caught it with a vengeance."

Mr. Waterton was at ease and in his element when on the lake; he was thoroughly skilled in the art of rowing, scudding through the water with perfect ease to himself, and delighting his friends by his graceful handling of the oars,—ever anxious to do the work. He prided himself, and I believe with great justice, on being an adept, and indeed, on being thoroughly conversant in the scientific management of the sailing boat. He appeared to be perfectly at home in tacking, and in so changing the position of the sails as to always accomplish what he desired without difficulty.

I observed, that the Squire was continually caring not merely for the personal comfort of his freight, but that he was also endeavouring to engage their attention by pointing out objects of interest in order to rivet the eye on land rather than on water, and thus free them from the fear of a watery upset. But I believe that notwithstanding the thousands of times that he must have wielded the oars on this lake, no mishap, nor indeed any thing approaching one, ever occurred under his able and careful guidance.

CHAPTER V.

THE Squire was proverbially liberal in gifts of friendship, but singularly determined not to accept the merest trifle directly nor indirectly in return however, delicately presented, and occasionally his mode of refusal would amount even to what, in another person would have been deemed somewhat ungracious.

On one occasion, his fondness for what he termed "a bit of surgery" upset his hitherto firm determination not to be a recipient. On my arrival alone one day unexpectedly at Walton Hall, I observed a countenance evidently betraying anxiety to enter into some explanation which was painful to him, and the moment I was seated he said, "I am, my dear sir, very very solicitous that all nonsensical professional etiquette should be hurled to the bottom of the sea until you can accomplish a wish that sorely distresses me. It is that you would condescend to soil the M.D., by opening an abscess for a poor, poverty-striken but amiable patient of mine. I have carefully examined it, and I assure you that it wants digging into very much." I replied, if the case be one of absolute poverty, and the abscess is in the condition and situation you represent, there can be neither difficulty nor impropriety in your opening it. This reply was just what the Squire wanted, as his object was to get what he considered a legitimate privilege "to do a bit of surgery." In fact, he had long yearned for such an opportunity in order to practically exercise a vocation of this character. "This is one step gained" he observed, "but I have no surgical instrument proper for the purpose." I drew a Syme's knife from my pocket which I generally carry with me to supply a country surgeon, in case of urgent need. The Squire's eyes glistened with delight as he admired the form of the knife. He evidently luxuriated in anticipation of the exploit in prospect.

I thought this a happy occasion to get him to receive a trifle from his friend, and therefore presented him with the Syme's knife, on condition that he would keep it to be ready for future operations if required, not supposing that he was alive to my inward thoughts. He immediately replied with a smile, "You have tackled me on one of my many failings, I accept the knife with many thanks, it will be invaluable to me," and he then formed loops in his memorandum book, into which to introduce the knife for safe keeping, and was ever afterwards proud of "*his operating knife.*"

From infancy to death, Mr. Waterton's habits were ever scrupulously abstemious. Even to nearly the close of his life, when our age is described as one of labour and sorrow, he knew no indulgence whatever. He had no additional "hour of rest" during the day. Up to a late period in life, he would walk to Wakefield in preference to going in the carriage; occasionally, but with difficulty, he might be persuaded to get into the carriage on his return home. Neither

the arm-chair nor the sofa had any charms for the
Squire. On the contrary, he would absolutely work
when there was no occasion for labour, saying "*labor
ipse voluptas*," "even labour itself is a pleasure," and
insisted on a personally strict observance of that rigid
discipline which his Church required only from the
middle-aged and the hale adult.

Mr. Waterton, in early life being predisposed to
pulmonary disease, was encouraged, under medical
advice about the year 1800, to largely deplete by
venesection, in order to subdue a recurring tendency
to pulmonary mischief. This was at a period when
pneumonia, unless vigorously and fearlessly met by
depletion in its incipient stage, quickly cut short the
thread of life. Thoroughly satisfied by experience of
the relief instantaneously obtained, convinced of the
salvation of life from the effect of large depletion
by the lancet, and being at that time a wanderer,
or, as the Squire would have himself said, in vaga-
bondage in the wild forests in South America, for eleven
months in succession, where no medical consultation
could be had—where no operative aid could be secured—
and when and where it might be death to wait until
to-morrow, Mr. Waterton determined to be, as far as
possible, prepared for the worst, and independent of
ordinary surgical aid ; he therefore was himself taught
venesection, "*secundum artem*," "according to the rules
of art," by a professional proficient, (the late Dr. Marshall,)

which operation if at any time it should be required, he could perform upon his own arm and with his own lancet, in the desert where he "loved to roam."

" Ignotis errare locis, ignota videre
Flumina gaudebat, studio minuente laborem."

"He loved to wander over unknown spots, and to see unknown rivers, his curiosity lessening the fatigue."

I have repeatedly witnessed the Squire operate on himself with the lancet, using either the right or the left hand as dexterously as if he were a practised expert; and I believe that the wisdom of this precautionary measure as regarded depletion, was amply verified on several occasions in the forest, as well as after his return. In bleeding himself, he was seldom satisfied or obtained sufficient relief, until he had drawn from sixteen to twenty ounces of blood. He would never permit any one to render the least assistance in tying up his arm on such occasions; and would receive no help of any description whatever from any one excepting his servant, whom he designated his " cup-bearer," allowing him as a sort of favour, now and then to hold the basin into which the blood flowed; but usually he insisted on supporting it himself.

In the most delicate manipulations of any kind he notoriously excelled, having fingers as nimble, as pliable, and as sensitive as those of a well-bred lady. With one hand and his teeth he tidily bound up his own

arm preparatory to wielding the lancet, which was
not always in the best order. With either right
or left hand he opened a vein without the least difficulty when furnished with an instrument in good
condition, and was equally skilful in applying his
compress and fillet. The amount of blood taken,
entirely depended on the relief obtained in respiration
and in general feeling. He was not at all influenced
by any particular number of ounces of blood. The
Squire's rule was, not to close the vein until he could
freely expand the chest, and allow this expansion to
be made without suffering the least pain.

I may add, that on one occasion, when sent for to
see Mr. Waterton late in the evening, I found him
suffering from very acute pain, and vainly trying to bleed
himself. He repeatedly punctured the arm, but always
ineffectually as regarded getting a flow of blood.
On an examination of his lancet, I found the edge,
if it could be said to have one, was so blunt that
it shirked the vein every time he punctured the arm.
I therefore set it for him on a common slate-stone.
He then used his lancet with the utmost precision, and
succeeded at once. The Squire greatly astonished
me by never in the least degree flinching, when he
repeatedly pierced his arm with so blunt an instrument. On explaining to him the danger of such
bungling operative practice, he replied after his
humorous fashion, " Teach your grandmother to suck
eggs. How could any mortal readily open a vein
with an instrument that had been from under his

care for the three previous months, and, during that
period, had been the common corn-cutting hack for
the servant girls of the establishment? And you
may rely upon it, that it has had some tough structures to encounter by way of extraction, and probably, not been very artistically handled by our female
chiropodists."

In his special case, habit must have had something
to do with enabling Mr. Waterton to endure depletion
so frequently, and to such a liberal extent with
impunity. The marked mitigation of painful oppres-
sion obtained by venesection, was invariably so immediate and complete, and the freedom from all distress
so permanent, that it was literally next to impossible
to prevent the use of the lancet by the Squire's own
hand.

I have, over and over, again and again, entreated the
Squire to deal less extravagantly in what he termed
"tapping the claret;" and although I sometimes prevailed
upon him to restrain his hand for a short period, yet in
my absence, his resolution generally failed him, and he
reluctantly I believe, yielded to a feeling which he
really did endeavour vigorously to combat, but was
seldom able to conquer.

Even in his eightieth year, he did not hesitate
to take away from twenty to twenty-four ounces of
blood, with not merely temporary freedom from all
suffering, but with all the permanent benefit that
could be desired. It is very surprising that the largest bleeding never appeared in the least degree to

enfeeble him. If, previously to venesection, he had
been so ill, oppressed, and prostrate, as not to
be able to leave the house, he invariably after his
arm was tied up, became sprightly and in his usually
cheerful and merry mood. He would express himself
as relieved from a painfully overpowering and oppressive load—he would go out to superintend his workmen, or to trim his beautiful and lofty yew fences,
using the very arm he had recently bled without
reserve, or he would attend to any other of his ordinary occupations whether mere amusements or absolute
labours, or he would gladly receive his friends,
—and, from that moment, you would certainly not
hear a murmur as regarded indisposition. In order
to support this artificial, and occasionally, I venture
to suppose, unnecessary waste, there was no extraordinary supply in any form nor at any time; and
when I hazarded an admonition he would reply,
"*Multo plures satietas quam fames perdidit viros.*"
"Surfieit has killed many more men than hunger." To
this I answered, "As a general rule I assent to your
assertion, but that is no reason why you should volun-
tarily sacrifice your own life with your eyes open to
such a termination by adopting an opposite extreme."
"Ah, my dear Doctor Hobson, you are out at the
elbows this time at all events; even a black fast
always does me good when it is all over, and when
my stomach has regained its usual tone and mechanical
power to tear asunder portions of animal food which
my grinders hesitate to tackle."

The Squire was not in the habit of allowing himself any increased amount of sleep nor any indulgence from his rigorously religious discipline,—nor indeed, any diminution of his positively laborious occupations, which he often very unceasingly courted, even to the injury of his health, and, I thought, frequently to the destruction of all comfort. I often counselled him from the authority of Seneca, that "rest and repose should sometimes be granted to the weary," "*detur aliquando otium quiesque fessis,*" but it seldom availed much, although he would occasionally promise me that he would "pull up and be an idle and jolly fellow for a few days at least," but it was not in the nature of the man to fulfil such a promise, although I quite believe that he persuaded himself at the moment, that the action would crown the intention.

Mr. Waterton, during his long life, even from 1799, never partook of either wine, spirit, or malt liquor. In addition to simple water, a cup of excessively weak black tea was his favourite, indeed his only beverage on all occasions, into which he put a large quantity of sugar but no cream. On entreating the Squire to substitute some more nutritious diet, rather than indulge in his favourite "tea beverage" so continually, I jocosely remarked that we should some day see him transformed into Pope's Tea-pot. Without a moment's consideration he rose from his chair, and suiting the attitude to Pope's words, replied

"Here living Tea-pot stands ; one arm held out,
One bent ; the handle this, and that the spout."

The Squire always insisted upon his cup being so liberally filled with this "pale-faced" compound, that a considerable portion had to find its way into the saucer before he would taste it. He ever most rigidly cultivated the "early to rest, and early to rise" plan to the letter, having himself for many years uniformly retired to rest soon after nine o'clock in the evening, and as invariably, he arose at half-past three o'clock in the morning, when he lighted his own fire which had been the previous evening prepared for that purpose, and forthwith set to work in good earnest in some Natural-history pursuit. The Squire seldom materially exceeded the mediæval aphorism, viz., that "seven hours of sleep is enough for old or young." "*Septem horas dormisse sat est juvenique, senique.*"

By this never-failing early rising measure, an immense amount of the preliminary labour of taxidermy in arrangement and in preserving the skins of birds and of other animals, so as to represent life itself, was frequently accomplished before an eight o'clock breakfast. Morpheus had no seductive charms for the Squire. For more than thirty years he never day nor night, stretched his "wearied limbs" on a bed. Neither pliant springs nor the softest feathers, nor the eider-down pillow, were temptations to him — luxuries of such a nature had no decoying influence over the Naturalist—they comforted not the bones of one during life, who yet cared that these "wearied bones" should rest in peace at the foot of the cross after death. His only covering during the night when resting on the hard boards, was a much-worn cloak with a napless blanket if required, whilst his pillow was a slightly hollowed out beech-wood block, in which to place his cheek, but without any covering upon it. It is difficult to conceive that such rigorous measures and health could be co-existent. Milton evidently entertained an opinion contrary to the practice put in force by my late friend, when he said—

"Secret refreshings that repair his strength;"

whilst Ovid has not less beautifully described the beneficial effects of sleep in the following lines :—

"*Somne quies rerum, placidissime, somne, Deorum*
Pax animi, quem cura fugit, qui corda diurnis
Fessa ministeriis mulces, reparasque labori."

"Sleep, thou repose of all things : sleep, thou gentlest of the Deities; thou peace of the mind, from whom care flies; who dost soothe the hearts of men wearied with the toils of the day, and dost recruit them for labour."

Such were the gratifications—such the voluptuous indulgences of the man who was ever most anxiously and unceasingly devising various means to lessen the distress, the difficulties, and the miseries of others— whose private charities scarcely knew a limit, and certainly no distinction of creed—who hesitated not to relieve with a generous heart and open hand that man who had even been his avowed and open enemy. Two instances of such a character were personally known to myself.

Thrice, from serious disease, did death with all its terrors of speedy dissolution stare this good man in the face during my intimacy with him; and as often, I

am delighted to add, to the heartfelt satisfaction of an
extensive neighbouring district, and to the extreme
gratification of a host of warmly attached friends, was
the Squire mercifully spared. It was my melancholy
pleasure to attend Mr. Waterton professionally on all
these occasions; and on one of them, when for a lengthened
and intensely anxious period he lay in an utterly
helpless, hopeless, and totally unconscious condition, and
for many, many hours, appeared to be hovering between
life and death. Never shall I forget the very moment
when returning intellectual expression first beamed on that
countenance, on which an entire blank had so recently
and for so long a period existed—when even the
preceding hour had chilled, nay destroyed the last
ray of hope—and when and where the really disconsolate friends of the apparently dying man were mutter-
ing, in mournful accents, "we shall never see his like
again." "*Nulla ferent talem secula futura virum.*"
And now, time having afforded an opportunity for
reflection since that period, I can still, from my own
feelings, confirm their then sorrowfully expressed sentiments. Lucy, a warm-hearted and faithful domestic,
then deserved unlimited praise, most judiciously using
every possible exertion to preserve her master's life.

In politics, the Squire was a staunch Conservative;
although, to the deep regret of many of his sincere
friends, he condemned the union of Church and State.
His faith though, in either party or in any one of the
three if there be a third, was not extreme. Taxation of

every kind, and the National Debt, were the odious and
virulent sores with Mr. Waterton.

When taxes were accidentally alluded to, he would
support his anti-tax opinions, by stating that "there were
no poor-rates before the Reformation, when all gentlemen
kept a sparrow-hawk, and the priest a hobby, that then
the charitable doles given at religious houses and
churches in every parish—did the business."

The Squire was passionately fond of the medical
profession in both its branches, indiscriminately distributing what the neighbouring poor called "Squire
Watterton's Pills," with, he persuaded himself wonderfully
beneficial effect. He was also warmly and immutably
attached to the priesthood of his Church, and especially
so to the Jesuits, being their firm and abiding friend
on all occasions. He was ever ready to have his joke
with me, by extolling the tenets of the Romish
Church over what he termed our sectarian dogmas
observing, "You have no unity of principle, and are in
fact, acephalous monsters,"—and would waggishly pledge
the Romish *caput mundi*, against the Protestant *caput
mortuum*.

On showing him the following lines, he observed "they
are very good and true."—

> "Eternity, which puzzles all the world
> To name the inhabitants that people it ;
> Eternity, whose undiscovered country
> We fools divide before we come to see it,
> Making one part contain all happiness,
> The other misery, then unseen fight for it.
> All sects pretending to a right of choice,
> Yet none go willingly to take a part."

In a Letter to me he writes, in his merry mood,

"My dear Sir,—Father ———, of Stonyhurst, is staying with us. You, will remember that you once over-hauled and prescribed for him. He will join us to dine with you on Tuesday, He is a professed Jesuit; one of that very confraternity held up to modern gulls by Eugene Sue the French infidel, as full of machinations, malice, and mischief. But I will take care that our Father ——— has no gunpowder in his pocket on Tuesday next, and I am certain that he cannot get at any of my poisoned arrows, and I believe that his pen-knife has no point to it: so you see he will be quite unarmed. And moreover, I deem him incapable of doing harm by any kind of mesmerism or occult science or diabolical agency, as he has never frequented Doctor E——'s school in London, and he consults no wise man; nor can I perceive the least smell of sulphur about him nor is there any appearance of a cloven foot. There is therefore, nothing about him that can cause the least alarm to our bodies. As for our souls, I must frankly own to you, that he does not handle them in the way that your Dr. H—k does. Still, this is allowable in England the supposed land of liberty, where we are all allowed to go on board either St. Peter's Bark or Charon's Punt, without much molestation from the bystanders.

"Very sincerely,

"CHARLES WATERTON."

I have already remarked, that when any religious

observance was in question, the Squire, in spite of the
priest and the doctor, would now and then act
imprudently as well · as disobediently as regarded
doing that which might endanger his health. In fact,
however indiscreet or absolutely improper it might be,
under certain circumstances, to fast when health was at
stake, and when, at his time of life fasting was not
required by his own Church, yet fast he would, and most
rigorously carry out its sacred observance. I do not
doubt but this scrupulously exact adherence to fasting
absolutely enfeebled the body, and thus permanently
impaired his health. Age seemed, in the opinion of Mr.
Waterton, to exempt no one from fasting, at least if he
was by his own acts to form the example.

In reply to all written professional advice on this
subject, although it was always most courteously received,
and as gratefully acknowledged, yet, an ingeniously
equivocating reply would be invariably transmitted
by return of post. I occasionally jeered him as to his
disobedience to the priest and the doctor, observing, that
he was acting in direct violation of his faith, and
especially so at his age. No one however, had
any influence over him unless he was dangerously
ill. In such a dilemma, I must admit that he
was scrupulously obedient to every prescribed rule,
with one exception; no persuasion could induce the
patient to go to bed. Reclining on a sofa was the
utmost concession that could be obtained, and that was
yielded with by no means a good grace. When I
advised rest, he would reply, " *Corpori tantum indulgeas*

quantum bonœ valetudini satis est."   "Indulge the body only so far as is necessary for good health."

On one occasion during Lent, in reply to a Letter from me, advising him as regarded the extent of fasting, he playfully returned the following answer:—

" My dear Sir,—When I call to mind that you have three times saved me from the dreary tomb, and when I reflect on your valuable letter of advice as regards my health, I feel how utterly impossible it is for me to make an adequate return. I shall ever be in your debt were I to live the length of the days of old Louis Cornaro. Doing then all that I can do at present, which is to thank you for what your skill and your friendship have conferred upon me, I will briefly tell you how I am going on, and will explain to you what kind of ground I intend to pasture upon and stray through until Easter Sunday morning shall put me on the high road, which leads straight forward to the happy regions of roast beef and plum-pudding. St. Francis of Assissium, (your spiritual director will tell you about this glorious saint,) very aptly gave the name of *ass* to that part of our human composition which is generally known under the denomination of our earthly frame. This comes so home to myself in particular, that I often make use of the word, when I know that those to whom I address myself are above putting it down to the score of an ill-timed attempt at wit, or of an unbecoming levity. I have then, great pleasure to inform you that my ass is at present very vigorous and sleek in his appearance, and even becomes frisky when the radiant sun of March shines warm upon it; and if it were not that certain parties thwart it now and then, by trying to pull the dried thistles from its mouth as it trots along, I should say that nothing has intervened since Ash Wednesday to cause it to deviate from the path which it is pursuing. You are aware that this is a penitential time; dried thistles therefore are very appropriate food for asses, in order that they may in some degree, make satisfaction for past unruly behaviour, and also to prevent similar occurrences in future.

" Fearful of subsequent mischievous pranks, I have considered it necessary to stint my ass to this hardy kind of food; and if I may judge by internal feeling and external appearance, we may safely jog on for a few short weeks longer, without being reduced to the necessity of regaling ourselves with a quartern or two of good old oats should Peel's income tax allow us to indulge in that sumptuous fare. In the mean time, your good and valuable instructions shall be continually in view; and if I find that my ass begins to droop his ears lower and more frequently than it has been wont to do—if I see that its eye is heavy, its pace slackened, its skin hard to the touch, its mouth dry, and that it appears to loathe its food, which in my opinion, under existing circumstances, is quite good enough for it, I will not fail to meet your wish, as regards an increase of food.

" Very faithfully and sincerely,

" CHARLES WATERTON."

On personally remonstrating with Mr. Waterton, and contending in a somewhat admonishing tone, that his advanced age necessitated a more liberal diet, less physical exertion, and a diminution of mental labour, he would with the utmost apparent gravity, observe :— ".Age! Well, my dear fellow, I am scarcely yet in the prime of life, this question can be mooted many years hence." Or he would take an opposite tack, remarking that I was in error in supposing that increased years required more liberal diet; on the contrary he would say, and on more than one occasion has quoted Cicero as his authority for disputing the soundness of my advice, — " *Habeo senectuti magnam gratiam, quæ mihi sermonis aviditatem auxit, potionis et cibi sustulit.*" " I owe many thanks to old age, which has increased my eagerness for conversation, and has diminished my hunger and thirst." To this the Squire afforded a *true convert.*

The Letters I have quoted are specimens of the perfect illustration of humorous evasions frequently received in reply to my prescribing a more generous and nutritious diet. Their character is tolerably convincing, that the necessity for an increase of nutriment and diminution of labour, at least in the Squire's opinion, never arrived, and therefore I really believe that fasting was the order of the day until the close of life. Some time ago, in reply to an invitation to dine with me, he observed in his facetious humour, — " You will have learned from the pastoral lips of your D.D., that we have not quite yet arrived at mid-Lent, therefore you may be sure that the Pope's padlock is still on my grinders."

Mr. Waterton's personal apparel was of so peculiar a character,—of such a primitive style, and occasionally so much worn, and his hat generally in so dilapidated a condition, that he was, now and then addressed by strangers as a person very much below his own grade in society. He usually rejoiced in a blunder of this kind, and was greatly delighted to carry on the misconception in apparent earnestness, by cleverly personating the man of poverty.

On one occasion, when calling on a neighbouring colonel, the butler showed him into the servants' hall to the Squire's great amusement. The colonel, on its being intimated to him that a person of the name of Waterton wished to see him, shrewdly suspected the blunder that had been made, and hastened, himself to welcome his friend, and to express great regret in consequence of the supposed annoying mistake, whilst the Squire was chuckling in his sleeve at the lucky incident.

On another occasion, the Squire was loitering leisurely on the road near to the neighbouring village of Walton, when a countryman accosted him by "Good morning, my man, can you direct me the road to the Hall belonging to Squire Watterton? I want to try to buy some wood of him, but they tell me he is a queer old chap if he happens to be the wrong side out; do you happen to know aught of him?" "Yes," replied the Squire, "I know him well.

Indeed no one in the neighbourhood knows him so well, or is so much in his company as I am. He is as queer as Dick's hat-band; you will have to get up early in the morning if you mean to get to the blind side of the old Squire." "Well," rejoined the countryman, "this is a lucky hit; you are the very man for me; come into "the public" close by, and I will stand a pint of beer, and bread and cheese also if you will make it worth my while." Mr. Waterton civilly declined the proffered bribe, saying, "that he had already breakfasted," and advised the countryman to have nothing to do with "the old chap," but to go direct to the woodman "who," he observed, "was a very decent fellow." The woodman was found; the purchase was made; and on the countryman's return, along with the salesman through the park, they accidentally came in contact with the Squire. The countryman was so highly satisfied with his purchase, that he could not refrain from tipping a sly and grateful wink to Mr. Waterton, in having recommended him "to have nothing to do with the old chap," when to the countryman's horror, the woodman doffed his hat after the rustic fashion, with a profoundly obedient bow to his master. The cat was instantly out of the bag. The countryman realised the mess he had got into, and stammeringly attempted an apology, but was instantly cut short by an order from the Squire to the woodman, that the purchaser should be taken to the Hall and well regaled,—a finale which speedily set the countryman at ease; and gave him an opportunity to receive at Walton Hall, instead of having to pay at "the public."

The Squire always displayed a happy taste, for picking up any thing curious, unique, or interesting in the science of natural history ; and having a peculiarly skilful tact of preserving these specimens in all their natural form and attitude and with the striking similitude of life itself, his labours in natural history produced a result as valuable as it is marvellous. The moment you enter the mansion, you are forcibly struck with the peculiarity, variety, and rarity of objects which never fail to delight and deeply interest not merely the eye, but the reflecting and investigating mind.

Within the mansion there is one very extraordinary and most interesting freak of nature at the foot of the grand staircase, which Mr. Waterton obtained from Roberts the taxidermist at Scarbro'. This "*lusus naturæ*," is the head of a sheep, having a horn growing from one of its ears. The ear itself is normal. The horn is natural in appearance, and is as firm and hard as horns usually are. It is semi-transparent, and in fact, presents nothing in its structure, form, or length, different from ordinary horns on a similar breed of sheep. There is no appearance whatever, of any fellow horn on the other ear, nor on any part of the head. This single and dangling appendage had its origin on the outer surface of the ear, about two inches from its root, and about one inch from its tip. Its primary source therefore, is entirely free from the slightest union, or even appearance of connection with the skull; neither is it attached to the periosteal membrane immediately investing the bone.

Horns are usually given to animals as weapons of defence, but in this particular instance, this horn would be not merely useless, but detrimental for such purpose, as it would seriously interfere with the natural mode of defence and, consequently, this poor sheep if ever in a difficulty during its life, could never have verified the accuracy of Cicero's assertion : "*Hic est mucro defensionis meae.*" "This is my weapon of defence."

Inasmuch as horns naturally arise at an equal distance from the centre of the skull, there is generally no great inequality of weight to interfere with the balancing power of the head, whereas in this case, the weight of the loose horn continually hanging on one side of the head, without any counterbalancing equivalent on the opposite the muscles on the hornless side, became so elongated, that the head had actually rotated one-fourth of a circle, and of course, was so far out of its natural equilibrium. It is also well authenticated that such was the position of the head for a considerable period before the animal was slaughtered. This head is deservedly much examined by visitors, as an unusual, if not unique, deviation from nature.

I have a great desire that this volume should not be embarrassed by narrow nor by distinctive limitations. On the contrary, I have been especially anxious that it should afford in the widest acceptation, matter intimately associated with the every-day occurrences — natural-history incidents, and the unravelling of interesting discoveries, or corroborations of such—by the widely known Squire of Walton Hall, *i.e.* consistent with the current reading of the age.

With these preliminary observations, I trust, as the horn of a ruminating animal has been the subject of the last two or three paragraphs, that it will not be deemed irrelevant nor an inappropriate deviation, should I venture to inform such of my readers as are not conversant with natural history,—that all the *ruminantia* having horns, have neither canine teeth nor incisors in the upper jaw, and that they are incapable of reducing their herbage to a state sufficiently pulpy by the ordinary mode of mastication.

The substituting provision as an equivalent for this apparent deficiency is secured by an instinctively physical power capable of conveying the grossly pounded-herbage, in its imperfectly macerated condition directly forward from the mouth to the first of the four stomachs with which all ruminants are provided.

The first stomach being large and elastic is consequently capable of containing an immense amount of imperfectly masticated herbage. The second, into which this mass in due time is passed, is small and globular with powerful parietes, rendering it capable of grasping and compressing portions of its contents into separate pellets, after having been subjected to maceration and chemical action of the secretion from its lining membrane. Subsequently, these pellets are regurgitated into the mouth, in order that they may be finally and effectually blended into a homogeneous pulp by re-mastication, and then descend into the third stomach.

This pulp there becomes thoroughly amalgamated, and in that condition is admitted into the fourth stomach, eventually passing into the larger intestines.

Without due consideration, it might be supposed that the *ruminantia,* unlike the non-ruminant animals, can have no enjoyment of their food. Doubtless, the simple act of grazing and a hasty and coarse crushing of the herbage in its dry state, its juices not being imparted to the palate, are little more than mechanical operations, and therefore, so far as gustatory gratification is concerned, must be inconsiderable, but we are ignorant what amount of pleasure these instinctively preparatory acts for future re-mastication may contribute to the animal, in anticipation of chewing the cud.

That chewing the cud, the ultimate voluntary operation, as regards digestion, is a pleasurable one, none can doubt, who have attentively observed cattle in a recumbent position, with their heads to the breeze during the re-masticating function.

> " On grassy banks herds ruminating lie."

Wild animals of the antelope, deer, and buffaloe tribe, are admirably adapted by this ruminating provision for the country they inhabit, as it is a well-known fact, that these animals could never cross the almost boundless desert and barren tracts in search of food, or in their spring and autumnal migrations, if they were not furnished with four stomachs.

Many of the *ruminantia* require very little water, and being able, in consequence of the peculiar character of these accommodating receptacles of digestion, to carry so large an amount of herbage, their physical powers and life itself, are thus sustained a much longer period without a fresh supply of food than the non-ruminants are;—a proof of adaptation to the soil.

During their migratory passage in herds across the barren wastes, they are frequently so harassed by beasts of prey, that in continual fear they have little time and few opportunities to pick up any isolated, stunted, and dried plants they may accidentally meet with, thus they are wonderfully aided and reinforced by this peculiar and more than usually complicated arrangement of the digestive organs, which affords another convincing proof of the widely ordained and admirably adapted provisions in nature to meet the wants of the great variety of climate and location.

I may observe that as regards the teeth, the camel is an exception as a ruminant, being supplied with both incisors and canine teeth, but singularly enough this peculiarly formed animal is hornless.

In alluding to natural curiosities, I am ignorant whether the occurrence of the sponge, in fresh water lakes, is so great a rarity as to be deemed one ; and I am not aware whether the production of the sponge depends on the quantity of water, the peculiarity of soil over which it passes, through which it may permeate, on which it may rest, or indeed, from what it does primarily originate.

Neither do I know whether it is more frequent in some than in other localities, but at all events, I have several times found it in the lake at Walton Hall; and Mr. Waterton himself also on two or three occasions, discovered some tolerably large specimens of the sponge in this lake. The specimens which I met with, were generally attached to dead twigs of trees, or to portions of dried or decayed wood.

Until within the last few years, the water in the lake was allowed to pass away at its surface-level, consequently, all the soil and decayed vegetable matter remained in the lake; but in 1857, Mr. Waterton so arranged the waste-sluice as to permit the superfluous quantity of water to escape at the base of the lake, which important alteration necessarily lessened the amount of mud, and consequently, increased the depth of the lake. Its deepest part however, does not exceed eighteen feet. Its form is somewhat singular, resembling a comma with its extreme and curved point reversed, its caudated portion terminating by a narrow strip of water, which is literally secluded by wood on both sides; and, therefore, so thoroughly screened and retired, that it is admirably calculated to tempt every species of water-fowl to assemble here, where they find food, privacy, and protection. To this interesting portion of the lake we were often indulged by a pleasant trip in the *sailing* boat from the mansion, which agreeable excursion by expert tacking, could generally be accomplished, to and fro, without the aid of oars.

When the day is serene and there is scarcely a

perceptible breeze on the lake, it is very delightful and highly interesting to the naturalist, to linger on the still water close to its banks, and gaze on the numerous and happy water-fowl, rejoicing in their simple, exposed, and unadorned nesting retreats. They seem to be devoted in admiration of the treasures they so carefully conceal and protect, and with their wide-spread wings, and extended abdominal feathers, apparently manifest an anxiously inborn solicitude to impart a genial warmth to their eggs, as if fully aware that this extension of feathers would absolutely tend to develope the embryo contained within them. It was also now and then, extremely interesting and instructive to watch the bird which had just become a painfully anxious mother of a numerous and scattered brood, displaying her self-reliant and ingenious schemes of protection for her off-spring, which under fear, are suddenly and unpremeditatedly determined by natural and instinctive impulse, and which, it cannot be denied, closely assimilate, nay in many instances, absolutely represent reason itself. From their courage in defence of their young, and their assiduity and perseverance during incubation, the coward may learn to be brave and the rash to be patient.

> " Reasoning at every step he treads,
>   Man yet mistakes his way ;
> While meaner things, whom instinct leads,
>   Are rarely known to stray."

When this lake was dredged in 1857, a quantity of broken portions of glass—of glass bottles, and a variety of broken ordinary crockery, were found em-

bedded in the mud, which medley of revealed acci-
dents had been evidently thrown into the lake in
past ages, in order to get rid of them, probably to
get them out of sight, and possibly out of mind.
The surface of many of these frgaments, when found,
was so smoothly and firmly encrusted by a thin
film of some deposit during the time they had lain
in the mud, that it appeared to be a portion of the
glass itself, and not simply incrustation. The varied
and vivid tints of this deposition yielded a brilliancy
and lustre to the surfaces of the *debris* which were
beautiful in the extreme. Specimens of these were
recently preserved at Walton Hall, which shone as
brilliantly as when they were taken out of the water.
The mud in which these gems have rested for so many
Years when excavated and spread on the grass, has
enriched the surrounding land; and this fertility,
from its application, reminds me of the kitchen-garden
which is prolific in an unusual degree.

Mr. Waterton, thoughtful in the extreme for the cook
and the kitchen, made a point of having a profuse
variety of herbs and vegetables for sallads and soups,
as well as an abundance of fruit, filberts, walnuts, and
asparagus, indeed an abundance of everything in the
way of garden-produce in proper season, not forgetting
the leguminous products, green peas for ducks, and beans
for home-fed bacon. In addition he cultivated an extensive water-spring for cress, which he had in great plenty
and perfection.

These considerately supplied acquisitions afforded an

annexation materially influencing both the comfort and
expenses of the household establishment.   The garden
is large, and from its having a southern inclination
as regards position, ripens its produce early, and
consequently its fruit has always a richness of flavour.
Its fecundity is not surprising, when it is known that
its situation is sheltered from all the destructive
winds—that it has a most genial aspect—and that
the whole of the garden is " made ground," composed
of thousands of cart loads of the best and richest soil
that could be procured.   In it, an enbankment or
elevated portion of ground is supported and "faced"
by a substantial wall, having the form of a segment
of a circle.   Here, in this sunny aspect, numerous
bee-hives were usually placed, being sheltered on all
sides, excepting on the south.

When this wall was being built, Mr. Waterton had a
vast number of nesting-holes prepared in it for sand-
martins, in which to safely deposit their eggs and
hatch their young.   For many years, martins in
great numbers frequented these separated compartments, and brought up swarms of their offspring, but
recently, they have entirely deserted the place.   This at
the time was considered a singular and unaccountable
caprice, as the holes, which had been so judiciously
and carefully provided for them, were in every way, as
agreeable as they could be made.   They were remarkably favourable for incubation, being perfectly dry
and entirely out of the reach of all vermin.   Neither
was there any living creature within the walls of this

garden excepting a tortoise, which had its home here for many, many years. This freak of the sand-martins is a proof of a harmonious understanding being arrived at among themselves, and that they acted in complete concert.

The Squire, some years ago, was happy in antici-pating the arrival of the sand-martin, as it made its appearance the first of the swallow tribe, so long as it visited Walton Hall. After its unaccountable desertion of this immediate district, the chimney-martin following the house-swallow speedily succeeds it, the swift arriving the last, although it leaves this country the first, or about the same time that the sand-martin leaves us. The chimney-martin then takes its departure, whilst the house-swallow is the last to be seen here.

In attempting to direct attention to objects in the park, on the lake, the island, and in "the grotto" and its immediate confines, I have doubtless, omit-ted to notice many well worthy of being examined, which may strike the eye of an enquiring stranger,— nay my very familiarity with them may, possibly plead my best apology for such omission.

> " What place is here !
> What scenes appear !
>   Where'er I turn my eyes:
> All around,
> Enchanted ground,
>   And soft elysiums rise."

CHAPTER VI.

I NEVER met with any one at Mr. Waterton's age with so retentive a memory. If during conversation a similitude or corroboration of a statement was needed to elucidate or amuse, he was seldom found wanting, and if he had recently read, or heard, an anecdote in Latin or English, he could generally reproduce it word for word.

I well remember that there was a disagreeable stench near the Grotto, where a pic-nic party of the working class had assembled to dine a few days previously, and seeing a parcel resembling an envelope on the ground, I observed, rely upon it that letter contains some dead animal matter, (which turned out to be a stale herring), when the Squire after a moments consideration, and with great gravity of countenance said, "Well, Jones complained of a bad smell about the Post-office, and asked Brown what it could be. Brown didn't know, but suggested that it might arise from the dead letters. I immediately remarked you do astonish me, to find how indeliby everything is written down in your brain." "No," he observed, "the ink is not so permanent now as it used to be. At one time I could have bottled up any thing I heard, and have drawn the cork years afterwards, and have reproduced its contents at pleasure in as sparkling a condition as Madame Clicot's champagne, a mischevous product which I never allow to be brought into my house.

About that time a lady wrote to me relative to the destruction of the spawn of fish by swans on the lake close to their house, which letter I submitted to the Squire. After having descanted at some length on this subject in a letter to me, he seized upon the watcher as more destructive than the swan, and in his ire said, "This is the era for defamation. Many a poor bird be it gentle or ferocious, is doomed to death for imaginary crimes. If your friend would hang her game-keeper and flog her watcher once a week, for his poaching transgressions, she would always have more than enough of fish to admire, to eat, and to pickle, But the gun and poison are in perpetual use. There is no living now-a-days, said the louse to her mother, when she saw the nursery maid handling a comb to rake the children's heads."

There were two reasons always prevailing in the Squire's vivid memory to account for his unwarrantably severe condemnation of understrappers in general, and for his half declared acquittal of the swan.

The former had its origin in his innate attachment, long continued, unbroken, and unalienable familiarity with the feathered race—the latter arose from ingratitude experienced several years previously from a watcher, who whilst he was being benevolently supported by his master was secretly a traitor to his interests.

If I have but sparsely gathered from the really numerous good deeds of the "South American Wanderer," I have at all events, the satisfaction to believe that sufficient have been rescued from oblivion, to afford ample conviction as to the truly estimable and engaging character of Mr. Waterton. If an excuse were needed for such a preservation, I should say with Tacitus,—that "I hold it to be the special office of history that virtuous actions be not buried in oblivion, and that men feel a dread of being deemed infamous by posterity for their evil words and actions." "*Præcipuum munus annalium reor, ne virtutes sileantur, utque pravis dictis factisque, ex posteritate et infamia metus sit.*"

In attempting to rescue some of the noble deeds of the Squire from oblivion, I am not labouring under the dubious feelings which Pope modestly admitted, when he said, in the office of collecting his previous writings, that he was altogether uncertain, whether he looked upon himself as a man building a monument, or burying the dead. My object has ever been that the memory of the dead should not be buried. Let us permanently bury the actions of those whose deeds are these of darkness, but let us disseminate, cherish, and render enduring the memory and deeds of the virtuous.

The chief part of the Natural-history specimens within the mansion at Walton Hall, when they were in what may be termed an elementary state, were subjected to a thoroughly immersed maceration for a considerable period, in a saturated solution of oxymuriate of mercury, after which careful preparation of the skin of either bird or animal, neither moth nor any insect whatever will ever attempt to destroy it or deposit its eggs in any portion of the skin or feathers so prepared and "mounted." But it must be strictly observed that simple momentary

immersion was never relied upon by the Squire, nor
had recourse to, excepting in the most favourable specimens. The subject intended for preservation, particularly
if not in a fresh condition, might require to be thoroughly
covered in the solution for a day, or in some instances
a greater length of time.

Taxidermists say that "corrosive sublimate is expensive,
and then there is the trouble attendant upon wetting and
drying the feathers. Now, the additional cost is in reality
trifling, it is the additional trouble they don't like, which,
after all, is a mere flea-bite ; and in compensation they
would have the satisfaction of knowing, that their
mounted specimens would be permanently safe from
hat penetrating and destructive foe the moth."

Some birds at Walton Hall, thus preserved by Mr.
Waterton, have been purposely exposed, having been
experimentally located in their present position without
shade or any protection whatever for upwards of fifty-
five years, and are now as fresh in appearance, and as
perfectly free from any trace of the moth, or of any of
its pernicious and despoiling influences as they were
the day they were "set up."

Notwithstanding Mr. Waterton's repeatedly publishing
his mode of preservation in detail in his works, and also
now and then in ordinary newspapers for the benefit of
all,—yet you continually hear of parties, professing a
knowledge of natural history and taxidermy, even yet
enquiring the best mode of preservation from the moth.

All the birds and animals, as well as all other speci-

mens of natural history preserved by the Squire, are
indebted for maintaining their correctly anatomical form,
natural life-like attitude, and their permanently well-
sustained position, entirely to modelling by internal
manipulation.   This admirable method is unquestionably far superior to any other yet adopted.   Its
advantages are numerous and really important, and they
are certainly very convincing to all taxidermists who
will, with nice accuracy, follow out the method recommended and invariably adopted by the Squire.

This mode of manipulation within the skin gives
great scope and wonderful facilities to the taxidermist,
in enabling him to produce and bring out at pleasure,
not merely local elevation of feathers on any particular
portion of a bird, but it gives him the power also of
raising perpendicularly, and of sustaining in a permanent position, even any individual feather that may be
required to imitate nature by standing erect.   It also
enables the taxidermist to elevate any patch apparently
inflated however small, or any extent of bristling feathers
however large; for instance, in order to represent anger,
as in the male turkey, or the assumed dignity, conspicuous pride, and self-conceit of the peacock.

Another great advantage is obtained by this ingenious
method, inasmuch as it requires neither stuffing nor
wires to sustain and preserve the attitude or position
once given.   In fact, the skin of either bird or animal
by being soaked in the saturated solution of oxymuriate
of mercury and daily manipulated by modelling *within,*
until the required form and attitude are ultimately

gained, and until the absorption of all moisture is completed, becomes thoroughly and effectually tanned and durably unalterable in its form and position, needing no artificial support of any description whatever. If by accident, any bird so prepared should be crushed into an unseemly or unnatural form, the skin, from its inherently elastic property of recovering its former figure, will revert to its original form the moment that detrimental pressure is removed and the skin and feathers are simply adjusted. A weasel and indeed other larger animals, were so ingeniously mounted by the Squire, that you could instantaneously detach the head or the limbs, or even one half of the body from the other half, and replace them as quickly;—and without the slightest appearance of any defect, the different parts could be again united in a moment so as to produce a perfect animal, to the astonishment of any accidental spectator. Indeed the head and legs could be thus detatched and placed within the body of the animal so preserved.

Such splendid specimens as the male turkey and peacock in the extension-staircase at Walton-Hall, (both being magnificent in plumage,) would each cost the Squire a considerable amount of labour daily, for several weeks before completion; but it must be remembered, that half a dozen specimens might be in hand at the same time. In some stages of this mode of preservation, one single bird might probably require an hour's labour, whilst another in a more forward stage of being preserved, might not need more than five or ten minutes. It is however, always abso-

lutely necessary that more or less *internal* modelling
should be *daily* had recourse to, so as not merely to
obtain, but to preserve the form and attitude which have
been secured the previous day.

Simple pieces of hard wood of arbitrary lengths to
suit the modeller, and from three quarters of an inch
to an inch in circumference, with smooth and rounded
heads of various sizes, were the only mechanical materials
Mr. Waterton used for all his modelling purposes.

The objection urged by taxidermists generally against
this method, is the difficulty of execution and the length
of time it is supposed to occupy. If however, three or
four or half a dozen birds are in process of being mounted
at the same time, this objection ceases. Nothing, it is
evident, but an unheard-of perseverance and labour,
coupled with lengthened experience, could have accomplished what the Squire has actually perfected in taxidermic execution; but he who has determined to be
incomparable, must encounter and submit to an infinite
amount of both physical and intellectual exertion, that is,
"he who would eat the kernel must crack the shell."
"*Qui e nuce nucleum esse vult, frangat nucem.*"

Mr. Waterton was so ardently attached to every thing
pertaining to natural history, that any labour connected
with this department of science, which would weary
most men, never appeared to have any fatiguing influence over him; and more especially, if his
subject was either beautiful, rare, or one somewhat
unique or difficult of execution.

The Squire was always singularly liberal in his desire to communicate information, in what he jocularly termed the "bird-stuffing line," to any one who was really anxious to be taught; but if the *should-be learning pupil* ever so far forgot himself as to suppose, that as an expert in taxidermy, he was closely treading on the Squire's heels, this professing pupil would pretty soon be in disgrace, and in an inglorious position.

On the other hand, if any one wanted a hint, and in a proper spirit manifestly realised his own inferiority in the art of "setting up" birds, the Squire would speedily recognise his anxiety for improvement, and forthwith display an evident and unmistakeable pleasure in supplying his intellectual wants,—and always in an agreeably instructive manner.

In however humble a position of life a man might be, yet if he was in mental distress, in consequence of a lack of taxidermic skill, the Squire would feelingly say, "Poor fellow! I pity him."

"Quemcunque miserum videris, hominem scias."

"Whenever you behold a fellow creature in distress, remember that he is a man."

This kind feeling and generous conduct on the part of Mr. Waterton, had, doubtless, its origin in a similarity of taste as regarded natural history. The old proverb says, "Birds of a feather flock together," and I presume, from the somewhat strange associations we sometimes see, they do so regardless of plumage. Ovid happily elucidated and confirmed these sentiments, when he wrote the following lines :—

> " *Scilicet ingeniis aliqua est concordia junctis,*
> *Et servat studii fœdera quisque sui.*"

"In truth, there is a certain alliance between kindred minds, and each one cherishes the ties of his own pursuit."

If a man either had, thought he had, or was supposed to have, any knowledge whatever in the science of natural history, the door at Walton Hall was always open to him by asking permission at the fountain head!

As a general rule, no unknown party was admitted beyond the threshold of the lodge doors, unless he could give some apparently satisfatory reason for his entrance within the park walls; but now and then, the feminine janitor was outwitted by some contrivance or other, so specious as to secure a stranger's entrance;—under such circumstances, the Squire's patience was occasionally severely tested. On the whole however, the arrangement of exclusion at the lodge to all strangers was gently and reasonably made, and so effectually carried out, as to preserve entire privacy in the whole of this extensive domain, so that there could be no disagreeable nor unexpected intrusion at any time.

If a stranger did get access to the house, the questions that Mr. Waterton put to himself, on one occasion at least, in a half-whispering tone, in my presence, before the final determination, " to be, or not to be," were these " Has the man come here in quest of gape-seed? Has he come with a profession of a knowledge of which he is really ignorant ? Has he come to teach the old Squire how to stuff birds ? Or, has he come, in all humility, to gather a few crumbs of information ? If he have come for any of the first three reasons, he may wend his way home again as soon as he likes ; if for the last reason, I will admit the poor fellow."

In reality, it was of very little moment what the man might have come for, as the Squire's kind heart could rarely refuse admission to any one ; hence hundreds of these "poor fellows" still breathe the spirit of the following quotation :—

" *Vita enim mortuorum in memoriâ vivorum est posita.*"

" The life of the dead is retained in the memory of the living."

Although Walton Hall is, in many respects, a very convenient house, yet it has in my opinion, one great disadvantage ; for instance, as a matter of necessity, every thing weighty or unwieldly has to be received into the house on a tier below the ordinary front ground floor, and in order to gain such admission, all these things have to be conveyed across a portion of the lake, on the south-west side of the mansion, by a large flat-bottomed boat to a place, I admit, well adapted for their being easily and safely landed.

The Squire from long continued habit and usage, I presume, considered this little or no inconvenience, although by this transit was conveyed all the fuel consumed in the

SOUTH-WEST VIEW OF WALTON HALL, AND OF THE SAILING BOAT ON THE LAKE.

house in the form of coal and wood; also, all stone and bricks and mortar for reparation or alteration as regarded building purposes, hogsheads, furnitnre, &c., &c. A considerable quantity of fuel must have been always required, as Mr. Waterton could never get on satisfactorily or with any comfort, without large fires.

If the Squire came to my house unexpectedly during my absence, even in July or August, when a fire was generally, not merely unnecessary but disagreeable to most people, he would, immediately on his arrival, rush into the kitchen until a fire could be made for him in its proper place; and on my return, he would say, "How I have enjoyed myself at a roaring fire in your kitchen."

I apprehend that this morbid sensibility as to cold arose from excessive fasting, a too frequent repetition of "tapping the claret," and a prejudicial habit of abstracting an inordinate amount of blood at one time, or probably from both causes; and, I feel confident, that these combined acts, which I always unreservedly disapproved and endeavoured to disuade him from resorting to, materially cut short his life.

It gives me great pleasure to record any act or occurence connected with the late subject of this memoir which tends to establish a correct conception of the natural disposition and true character of the man; and it affords me special gratification when any such contribution is obtained from a source at once conveying a convincing impression that such event has been actually witnessed by an intimate friend of the Squire.

Now to my knowledge there existed for several years not only a very agreeable natural history correspondence, but a confiding friendship between the old Squire and Sir James Stuart Menteth, Bart., and therefore any incident authorised by Sir James is doubly welcome, and more especially as I have a generous permission to insert it in my future editions.

" My Dear Doctor Hobson,

" Having read ' Charles Waterton, his home, habits, and handiwork,' perhaps it may gratify you to hear how much pleased I am with it, and also to know I consider it very truthful in all you describe of the pursuits and character of our dear old friend the Squire of Walton Hall.

" For nearly forty years I enjoyed his society, and occasionally partaking of his hospitality I had ample opportunity of being well acquainted with his sound and excellent views of natural history, and of witnessing in his park the various and ingenious contrivances he adopted to make it a home and paradise for the feathered creation.

" As I have always, from being a boy, taken the liveliest interest in natural history, you may easily conceive how much I used to enjoy my visits to Walton Hall.

" After one of these visits I committed to paper a slight sketch of what I saw in the park and in the house.

" This paper appeared in Loudon's Magazine of Natural History, vol. viii, page 28, in January, 1835.

" If you will read it you will find that I agree with you in the delightful portrait you have drawn of the dear old

Squire, and of the different ways he devised to make his park a safe retreat and paradise for every bird that entered its precincts.

"I never knew a man of kinder or more amiable disposition.

"After the death of Mr. Loudon, editor of various useful works on gardening, &c., he left his widow not over well provided for. Mr. Waterton having been acquainted with Mr. Loudon, invited his widow to Walton Hall, and during this visit of a month, composed his third volume of 'Essays on Natural History,' which he presented to Mrs. Loudon to make what she could of it.

"Few country gentlemen were more versant in the classics than Mr. Waterton. He had Virgil, Horace, and Ovid at his finger ends, and readily composed verse in English and Latin.

"From Ovid's Metamorphosis he took many hints to adorn his three volumes of 'Essays on Natural History.'

"These beautifully written Essays will long survive the amiable author and instil in many a youthful mind a love of natural history, and also teach a good lesson of showing kindness to every dumb animal; and I wish I could add, infuse in the minds of our rural aristocracy a love of preservation of life of many of our birds and animals which the gamekeeper has now orders to destroy, and hang on his gibbet. I hope that Mr. Waterton's good example may be followed by many of the English Squires by making their parks the home and asylum of the much-persecuted birds, so useful to man in clearing his woods and fields of insect vermin.

" Books like Boswell's life of Doctor Johnson are always interesting to the reader.   Imparting the conversations of a distinguished man acquaints us with his mind and thoughts.   In your ' Waterton's home, habits, and handiwork,' you have given us these in a lively and interesting manner.   By doing so your book will be valuable and interesting to every lover of natural history ; and it will diffuse far and wide a knowledge of a man who has done more for the cultivation of natural history than any one of his day.   There was not a British bird nor animal, whose habits and character he had not studied by watching them out of doors at every season of the year.

"Hoping you will be amply rewarded for all the trouble you have taken in recording the doings in natural history of such an interesting and good man as Charles Waterton, of Walton Hall.

"I am, my dear Doctor Hobson,

"Yours sincerely,

"JAMES STUART MENTETH.

"Mansfield House,

"Near Cumnock, Ayrshire.

"25th October, 1866."

To describe the interior of the mansion at Walton Hall, and do justice to it, would require a varied extent of knowledge which few men possess, and would be a labour of so Herculean a character that few men would care to undertake the task, whilst a still less number would be able to creditably accomplish the laborious and difficult undertaking.

MR. WATERTON MOUNTED ON THE CAYMAN, WHEN LIVING.

Rare, exquisitely beautiful, and truly gorgeous birds from all countries, uninterruptedly and with unbounded satisfaction, meet your eye at every step in the magnificent grand staircase and its extension. You can scarcely conceive it possible that even *living* nature could surpass, nay could equal the simple dead representations here displayed, to such a state of perfection has art attained. But the "great object of art is to conceal art." "*Ars est celare artem.*" In taxidermy, you have here unrivalled execution. In attitude, you have life itself in all its varied phases. In plumage, you have lustrous beauty unsurpassed even in life. In anatomy, you have every local prominence, local depression, curve, nay, even the slightest elevation or depression of each separate feather, to accurately represent nature in all her imposing grandeur and apparent animation. You are delighted with each bird, animal, reptile, and insect. You are charmed with each group, whilst you are literally fascinated and amazed with the "*tout ensemble.*"

On the top of the staircase is the veritable cayman, mentioned in "Waterton's Wanderings," and on which the Squire was mounted in Essequebo, after being caught by a shoulder of mutton bait, and when under the control of the natives and his own servant. Here you see the actual line and hook which captured and safely secured this alligator in the river, and by which he was dragged on to "*terra firma,*" evidently much against his own inclination, now that he was favoured with a barbed hook in his stomach, by which his man-eating propensities were doubtless thoroughly subdued. You also see, in this enchanting staircase, the huge snake with which the Squire contended in single conflict, and which, by his never-failing courage, presence of mind, and power, he bravely conquered, even when it had coiled its vast and powerful length around his body, with so tight and oppressive a grasp, as to nearly suffocate him.

It is utterly impossible, either by any written or verbal description to convey even a faint idea of the reality in this extraordinary collection. Surprising as it may appear, yet the preservation of every bird, animal, insect, and their name is legion,) in the whole of this unparalleled assemblage abounding in rarity, beauty and eccentricity, is the work solely of the Squire's own hands. We may well exclaim in admiration, "When shall we find his like again?" "*Quando ullum invenicmus parem?*"

Although I dare not attempt to describe, even generally, the numberless objects of curiosity within the house, yet I will venture to draw attention to two or three, because of their extreme peculiarity, and the marked attention bestowed upon them by strangers.

In the first place, allusion may be made to an enormous crab, really a monster in size, beautiful in colour, natural in attitude, and splendidly preserved and "set up."

Mr. Waterton, when in one of his merry moods, and such jocular humours were by no means either unfrequent or unwelcome, waggishly represented this crab, which he called his "crustacious favourite," in Latin verse, as one of the twelve signs of the summer solstice, thus playing on the word Cancer, and placed the verses within the case containing the crab. "He anticipated," he was accustomed to say, "a bit of criticism from the *cognoscenti*, a hearty laugh from those who had as mattering of the dead tongue, but not learned enough to understand it, and great gravity from those who had never thumbed a Latin grammar, and he was not disapppointed," he observed, "in the long run."

" Cancer.

Solstitium Æstivum.

Jussu fatorum, non audet, limina cancri,
Unquam curriculo, Sol superare suo
Juxta autem portam, cursum repressit equorum,
Unde dies longa, et nox brevis esse solet.

CAROLUS WATERTON."

The Latin verse may be thus translated :—

The Summer Solistice.

Sol dare not drive—such the decree of fate--
Past Cancer's bounds, but when he nears the gate,
Pulls up his coursers in their fiery-flight,
Hence, come the longest day and shortest night.

When Mr. Waterton saw any one who modestly and unaffectedly acknowledged his ignorance of the Latin language, he politely and very kindly afforded every possible explanation relative to his verses, and to the habits of the crab; but when his quick eye caught any one professing that of which he was evidently ignorant, the Squire invariably "passed by on the other side." The

Scholar had an utter detestation of pretended assumption of a knowledge by any party not possessing it; and he never failed by his manner alone, to convey an unmistakeable and unenviable impression to the erring individual The crab which incited Mr. Waterton to represent it in Latin verse as the fourth constellation in the Zodiac, is really a magnificent one in nature as a crab, and the Squire's skilful manipulation in "mounting" it, has rendered it, as a specimen of art, an object of equal admiration.

I have already described "John Bull and the National Debt," in the representation of the filbert-tree and mill-stone in a state of nature; but Mr. Waterton, from his extreme horror of all taxation, was induced to illustrate this subject of nature by a very singular work of *art*, placed within the extension staircase.

These two subjects of nature and art are synonymous in appellation, "John Bull and the National Debt" being used by the Squire as applicable to both; in appearance however, they are very dissimilar, yet their dissimilarity to the eye will not allow us to draw any other conclusion than that the ultimate result will be the same in both cases. The Squire always stoutly maintained, that although the death of the filbert-tree might be of a somewhat distant and lingering character, yet that its fatal termination would not be the less sure, simply from the effect of strangulation; whilst in the case of art, although John may boast of his coat of mail with which he is clothed as a protecting armour; and of his peculiarity of construction, as indicating strength and endurance,—yet it is evident, that the immense weight he has to sustain must ultimately bring him to the ground.

This most singular and ludicrous subject of art represents John Bull as standing on four legs, to denote power and capability to support a heavy weight. His back is formed from that of the tortoise, whilst a sturdy-looking visage peeps out from under the over hanging shell of the anterior extremity of this artificial roof. His legs are short and representing double the number allotted to man as I have already stated, in order to indicate power and stability, whilst a well-filled sack is slung across his back; on one side of which is written transversely in legible characters, "John Bull and the National Debt," and on the other, "Eight hundred million pounds sterling." This is a most extraordinary, and indeed, what may be termed a most unearthly looking object; one that excites intense curiosity as to its composition, and invariably tickles the risible faculties of strangers.

Mr. Waterton had considerable inventive genius, especially in the actual formation of supposed extinct animals, and generally of the most horrid form and appearance, by a skilful union of separate portions of reptiles. By the way, his inventive powers, though exercised more than forty years ago, had nearly carried his experimental ingenuity to a fatal issue. He had for a considerable period, conceived some crude and ill digested idea, that the act of flying was within his grasp, and that in a short time, he would become a second Pegasus in execution.

Under this surprisingly delusive impression, he invented
and manufactured duplicates of a peculiar character of
mechanism as substitutes for natural wings, to be fixed
on each arm, and to be united by their surrounding
the thoracic and dorsal portion of the trunk.

How the Squire proposed to dispose of his lower
extremities he did not explain to me, but I remember
he stated that a man's legs however symmetrically formed,
were inconveniently long and heavy for an "atmospheric
trip," unless they could have something more sustaining
than air on which to rest, or to sustain the lever they
represent, and consequently, were too unwieldy and
unmanageable to be of any service to the aeronaut in
navigating the atmosphere ; adding, that the only time,
during his life, he had found his legs in the way, was
when he attempted to fly.

At all events, Mr. Waterton not only manufactured
fictitious wings, but actually attached them to his arms
and trunk, and also formed and fixed the remaining
mechanism which he conceived was necessary to be
attached to the other parts of the body, so as to complete,
and as he imagined, perfect this really chimerical project;
and in order to carry his scheme into practical execution,
he arranged to make his first essay from the eves of
the roof of a building in the farm yard being an elevation of several yards, from whence his flight, it is true,
would be of limited extent in a forward direction, and
where an abundance of litter would break the severity
of a possibly uncontrollable and rapid descent.

Fortunately, however, when the Squire was "clipped

and heeled" for his first attempt to take an *aeriform* cruise, "an intimate friend," "*Alicui toto pectore deditus*," accidentally walked into the farm yard, and happily had sufficient influence over the would-be aeronaut to persuade him to take his incipient trip from a less elevated position.

Of course, it is needless to minutely detail the many perils and dangers he actually encountered in attempting to carry out this delusive conception, as the Squire afterwards unhesitatingly admitted to me, that unlike Pegasus, he could neither fly to the " top of Mount Helicon," nor further imitate him "by then flying up to heaven." Also, that his affinity for the earth, to his great surprise, woefully out balanced his attraction to the clouds, and that on coming in contact with "mother earth," he received, as he was wont to say, when jocosely using the Walton dialect, such a "foul shak," as to be satisfactorily convinced that soaring in the atmosphere was not his *forte*, having in his unwilling, unintentional, and disagreeably hasty descent, like Phaëton (who lost command of his horses) thoroughly lost all command of *his* wings, and thus narrowly escaped a broken neck, by pitching lightly and softly upon his head in spite of the faith he had entertained in his all-supporting wings.

"Since that egregious and unpardonable blunder of mine," observed Mr. Waterton, "I have realised the rebuke given by Apelles, 'Let not the cobbler go beyond his last'—'*Ne Sutor ultra crepidam.*' My legs, which are all that mortal man can desire, so long as they are used as nature intended, have never failed to come to my rescue

when in difficulty, so long as I trusted to them, whilst my
wings have never been put to the test but once, and
then ingloriously left me in the lurch.

"The publicity of my rash attempt to confide in
wings, together with my failure, which at the time was
comparatively in a nut-shell, where I had hoped it would
remain, soon, contrary to my wishes, spread abroad, and
the rumour in its route gathered nothing that was
enviable on my behalf, but just the reverse. This
was somewhat annoying, but I must admit that the
chaffing I fell heir to was ultimately beneficial to me,
inasmuch as it convinced me that I had no earthly chance
to lay claim to the motto of the Earl of Thanet,—"He
flies with his own wings," "*Alis volat propriis*;" an
accomplishment which I had fully intended to have
acquired. I was however satisfied, that in popular language, I had been "out of my element," had laid
myself open to the sneers of professing friends, and that
I had in future, much better tenaciously adhere to my
favourite natural-history labours, in which I encountered
neither danger nor derision. And yet, no man cares
less for these two bugbears than I do ; in fact, the former,
the public say, has now and then been somewhat courted
by me, whilst the latter is insidiously patronised by the
professor of friendship whom I despise."

"Forty years ago I had a hard struggle to keep my
head above water against a host of self-constituted censorious scoundrels, but the unprejudiced public took
my wandering bantling by the hand, affording it even-

handed protection until it arrived at maturity. When armed *cap-a-pie* and floating in smooth water, it bravely hoisted the colours of self-defence, and confidently threw down the gauntlet, anxious to be overhauled by honourable and impartial reviewers."

It frequently happens that, in reviewing the character or writings of a man, those self-appointed censors are the least qualified to form a reliable judgment,—are the most prejudiced and perversely obstinate in promulgating their opinions, and the least inclined to put a favourable construction on any doubtful point.

It is, indeed, an admitted fact, that many disputed the varacity of "The Wanderings," published in 1825; but the subsequently repeated and astounding feats of the Squire at length convinced all worthy of notice, that in every natural-history instance recorded by Mr. Waterton, his word was truth.

This ungenerous scepticism did to a certain extent, as I have previously observed, rankle in the heart of the good old man, or he would never, at so remote a period, have dwelt on these invective animadversions as he did to his old friend, Mr. Harrison of Lancaster, who for the last twenty years was accustomed to frequently see the Squire at his own residence and at Lupset Hall, near Wakefield, the seat of Mr. Daniel Gaskell, a very old and valued friend of Mr. Waterton.

To Mr. Harrison, the Squire observed, "that after his removal of a host of rattle-snakes from one compartment of a case to another," an old fellow who had witnessed, what he termed this dangerous and courageous transfer, cried out, "Well! after this fact I'll believe 'The Wanderings.'"

Now what can be more convincing of the worthlessness or rather of the undeservedly damaging influence of an opinion founded on a limited knowledge of the subject entertained by such ignorant or inconsiderate parties, than the one here recorded?

Had disparagement or even disbelief, been limited to parties moving in a sphere of life similiar to the instance to which I have now alluded, such impediments would have been trifling, but the moment the naturalist had hatched his offspring, and before the deliberately judging portion of the public had an opportunity to form their own opinion by perusal as to the veracity of its contents, war to the knife was waged against "The Wanderings," consequently before being fledged it had to suffer the deteriorating pressure of unjust accusations.

Some of the regularly constituted reviewers at once emphatically stated that the contents were untrue, and on that false assumption these censorious critics, proceeded to pour out their ill nature.

Notwithstanding, however, the degrading position in which some of the detractors had most unjustly placed "The Wanderings" it gradually emancipated itself from so undeserved a condemnation. Some of the imputations were so spiteful that the cloven foot peeped out, whilst the bitterest reviewers betrayed so malignant a feeling that many of the more charitable public, from utter commiseration for the Author ventured to judge for themselves, and immediately "the tables were turned" to such an extent as to induce the thinking and

unprejudiced portion of the people to read and believe,
Gradually, as the Squire's powers became more known.
"The Wanderings" in a relative ratio crept into summer plumage, working out a reputation and eminent
distinction for the Author, which thousands would be
delighted to inherit, and which have shed a lustre on the
name of Charles Waterton that succeeding ages will be
loth to efface.

As a further and definitely individual confirmation of
what I have stated relative to the loose and incongruous
opinions of many reviewers of "The Wanderings;" on
which they formed their judgment and promulgated
their harsh and undeserved ridicule, I may select the
Squire's "riding the cayman," as the chief stumbling-
block on which they seized as "an uqualified untruth."

Now, Mr. Waterton admitted to me that when he
mounted the cayman, " I had no fear, because I knew
it was impossible that the hook, from its peculiarity of
construction, could be returned through the mouth, and
having made it myself, I had carefully ascertained that
there was no flaw in it, and had also tested the strength
of the rope.   You may rely upon it that I made all
secure for the sake of number one, as I had a pre-
determined intention to mount the saurian if he should
give me a chance.

"My enemies, if I have any, have played the fool in
disputing my having accomplished a feat, which any
old lady, minus her crinoline, might have easily done."

Somewhat similarly· was the first edition of this volume
recently received by the Editor of the Zoologist. Not-

withstanding its restrictive title and the Author's disavowal
in the preface, as well as in the body of the work, that he
had the slightest pretension of being the *biographer* of
Waterton, and notwithstanding his distinctly stating
that "it would be little less than an insane act on his part
to attempt to write the life of a man of whose antecedents
he was totally ignorant, and of the former half of whose
life he knew nothing," yet the reviewer beyond all
courteous precedent chose to designate him the *"biographer"* of Waterton, and on this unjustifiable assumption
of his own creation, founded an acrimonious and depre-
ciatory review, which malevolent poison he disseminates,
but withholds the Englishman's right, by an undignified
and delusive reply, refusing to insert the author's remonstrance against his distortion of facts.

I have already pretty broadly hinted that Mr. Waterton did not shine in the management of land, that his
knowledge of agriculture was limited, having neither
taste nor relish for practical farming. He unfortunately
never gave land the credit of being grateful, nor of its
being a reimbursing recipient, whilst on the other hand,
the really good farmer chiefly depends on a spirited and
judicious outlay. Mr. Waterton was not, what in the
present high farming age, would be termed an agricul-
turist. For instance, even the trifling drainage which
was accomplished by the Squire on the land at Walton
Hall, was absolutely coaxed out of him by a favourite
agricultural friend and neighbour, and this atom was
not granted without a protest of disapprobation, and

I might add, under a firm conviction that his pasture would suffer considerable depreciation by this "new-fangled and expensive mode of farming," which he contended, would ruin the crops by laying the land far too dry, especially if the drains should be insanely cut upwards of three feet in depth.

Mr. Waterton had peculiar and erroneous notions as regarded the improving or detoriating land by drainage, he insisted that drains, however judiciously made, would not influence the land to yield a better and more nutritious quality of grass, and that the land which was left a little swampy would produce a greater abundance of equally good pasturage and more milk and butter for the dairy.

He contended that animals, horned cattle especially, required quantity, so that they could speedily fill their stomachs, lie down, chew the cud, and take rest. He would point out as an instance of what sort of grass he approved within a short distance of the mansion,—viz. :—the swampy ground where the herons were accustomed to feed and pass many of their leisure hours.

Now it had evidently never entered into the Squire's calculations, that the reason why the grass was so long in this spongy ground, was because of its being of so hungry and coarse a nature from want of drainage that the cattle would not eat it.

I suspect, that inasmuch as this spongy ground afforded an agreeable lounge and fertile feeding resort for his special favourites the herons, the Squire could not divest himself of a similar feeling, and that he

was in reality, enamoured of the swamp because the
herons were enraptured with it. His excessive love
of ornithology led him astray on this all-important
question to the farmer.

Independent of Mr. Waterton's naturally humane
feelings influencing him to prevent the destruction of
the mole and the owl, he warmly contended that they
undoubtedly were two of the farmer's best friends.

"I have myself accurately ascertained" said the
Squire, "that an owl which had a brood in the old
ruin to nurture, brought to its nest, on an average,
not less than four or five mice an hour, for several
hours in succession. Indeed the large amount of food
devoured by a brood of voracious young owls is, to
any one inexperienced in these matters, inconceivable."

It would be difficult to find a dissentient voice, as
regards the owl, but there may be some conflicting
testimony as to the farmers deriving benefit sufficient
to counteract the damage sustained by the burrowing
propensities of the mole. The Squire believed, and
strenuously urged his opinion, that the "runs" made by
the burrowing of the mole near the surface, were more
beneficial as drains to the farmer than those made
by man. So far as the mole's labours go in this
direction, few farmers would be found to coincide or
approve. But when the naturalist stated that moles,
in their under-ground burrows destroyed an immense
number of slugs, &c., &c., his opinion and arguments
gained him many disciples among agriculturists, and

some good and experienced farmers, although they condemn the mole because of the unsightly mounds of earth which it raises on the surface, and the ravages it sometimes commits by devastating the tender roots of young wheat, yet hesitate to positively determine for or against it as regards its beneficial or detrimental services to the farmer. They occasionally leave it an open question, and for the following reason. Mr. Waterton is not without supporters on his side of the argument.

A respectable authority relates an interesting experiment which proves the service rendered to agriculturists by moles, and the impolicy of destroying these little quadrupeds.

In a commune of the Canton of Zurich, the municipal council were lately about to proceed to the election of a mole catcher, when M. Weber, a distinguished naturalist, laid before the board the following facts.

M. Weber observed that—" he had carefully examined the stomachs of fifteen moles caught in different localities, but failed to discover therein the slightest vestige of plants or of roots; on the contrary, they were filled by the remains of ascarides or earth worms." M. Weber not satisfied by this fact, shut up several moles in a box containing sods of earth, on which fresh grass was growing, and also a smaller case of grubs and earthworms. In nine days two moles devoured three hundred and forty of the white worms, one hundred and ninety-three earth-worms, twenty-five caterpillars and a mouse, skin and bones, which had been enclosed while alive, in the box. M. Weber next gave them raw meat cut up in small pieces, mixed with vegetables. The moles eat the meat and left the plants. He next gave them nothing but vegetables. In twenty-four hours two moles died of starvation."

It has been long known that moles live a very short time, unless they are frequently supplied with food.

Another naturalist of eminence calculated that two moles would destroy twenty thousand white worms in a single year.

Having alluded to the peculiar kind of food essential to the sustenence of a lower grade of animal, the mole, I am reminded of its liberal distribution by Mr. Waterton for the susport of the neighbouring poor, of every political shade, and every religious creed, as a marked trait in the character of this good and kind-hearted man. If a suffering creature was too poor to employ the surgeon in the district, Mr. Waterton was always anxious that I should see him; and if the patient was unable to pay the chemist, the Squire himself, not only furnished the needful for that purpose, but took special care to supply the particular kind of food required in each case. If the patient was able to walk to the mansion and dine in the servants' hall, there was the opportunity afforded to enjoy a good dinner; — if not, a liberally supplied plate was directed to be sent for from the hall. Bread, meat, milk, and eggs, were freely distributed to the sick and broken meat, &c., &c., to the needy. New shoes to the naked feet were seldom refused, and were occasionally given in a very peculiar way.

Mr. Waterton, at one time, had for a considerable period, an understanding with a shoemaker in Wakefield, that if any poor fellow should call upon him and present him with his knife, which the cobbler knew, he should retain the knife, and furnish the mendicant with a pair of serviceable shoes, calling on Mr. Waterton for payment.

On naming the circumstance to the Squire, and asking if it was a correct version, he replied, " Yes, you have got the right sow by the ear. It is as true as that Pope Pius the IX. is a holy man; and I will tell you the reason why I made the arrangement to which you have alluded, with the man of leather and wax at Wakefield.

" Many years ago, a miserable, half-starved looking wretch, and apparently terribly foot-sore, met me near the village of Walton, and entreated charity in such a piteous tone, and in such apparently genuine humility, that my flinty (scientifically termed silicious,) heart was softened;—and having nothing less than half-a-crown in my pocket, I was speedily minus that amount. In the latter part of the day, on passing through Sandal, on my way to Wakefield, I accidentally came in contact with this scoundrel who had done me out of half-a-crown in the morning. Although very drunk, he recognised me by a very familiar ' How do you do, old boy? I owe you one; come into the public - house, and I will treat you with a pint of heavy wet out of your own half-crown, as I have fifteen pence in button-park yet.'

"This drunken exhibition so annoyed and so thoroughly disgusted me, that I set my wits to work to discover a better method of affording relief to the poor than by giving them money. It has so far, answered well, consequently, my old and well-known knife has gone the same errand so frequently, that I think it would find its own way now to the cobbler's shop at Wakefield.

"But even this plan would not have made me perfectly secure in one case, if Jack Ogden my keeper, had not come to my aid. We were repairing a tree, outside the park walls, which had been severely handled by a violent hurricane, when an apparent object of distress in the form of man, accosted me in a mournful and tremulous strain and, at the same time, directing my attention to his bare feet. His case seemed to be one so deserving of relief, that I quickly had my trusty knife in my hand, ready to send on its mission of charity to the Wakefield cobbler when Jack Ogden came up, and knowing my Wakefield dodge, and seeing me knife in hand, whispered to me that he had seen this vagabond take off his shoes and hide them in a thick fence, before entering the field where we then stood,—that he had taken them from their hiding-place, and then actually had them in his shooting-jacket pocket.

"I immediately said aloud, 'Jack, do you think my shoes would fit this poor fellow, who is barefoot?' 'No, sir,' he replied, 'yours wont fit him, but I have a pair in my pocket that seem to be about his size; try them on to these poor feet of yours,' said the keeper, in an apparently sympathising tone of voice. The culprit at a single glance, recognised his own property, his countenance fell to below zero, and he at once pleaded guilty. Jack pulled his dog-whip from this universal pocket of his, and was anxious to inflict summary punishment; however, having nothing 'silicious' as the scientific now say, in my composition, I begged the scoundrel off, substituting a threat to imprison him, if he should ever appear in the district of Walton again."

The misletoe, which is commonly suspended in houses to announce Christmas, was a favourite plant with Mr. Waterton; not because it was used as I have stated, nor in consequence of the formerly Druidical custom to usher in the New Year by youths presenting it to their elders, but because, in many country places, it had acquired, and still maintained in this district a widely reputed celebrity as a cure for epilepsy.

The Squire endeavoured, by grafting the misletoe into various trees, more especially into the apple tree and the thorn, to cultivate it at Walton Hall, in order that he might gratify the poor who had great faith in its exhibition; but it, somehow, never succeeded to any extent. It did live, it is true, but it never really flourished, and a severe winter generally almost destroyed it.

When I told Mr. Waterton, that inasmuch as epilepsy arose from such a variety of causes even if curable, no one agent therefore, would be a remedy for all cases,—the Squire replied, "Very probably, but it may furnish hope to the sufferer, and 'hope deferred, maketh the heart sick.'"

The Squire had the universally acknowledged capability of vividly representing animated nature in hideous and gastly aspect, as well as the faculty to portray and adorn her in the most fascinating and attractive elegance of formation, nay " to snatch a grace beyond the rules of art," and he was also gifted with the singularly rare, inventive, and imaginative endowment, of constructing and organising animal representation of supposed extra-mundane characters, even on the spur of the moment.

Indeed, from the vast variety of his artificially prepared demonstrations, widely and conclusively substantiated, he might have had a sly peep into a retrospective age, even beyond that of a knowledge of the palæontologists of the present day, and yet still apparently harmonising with the *fauna* of the animal kingdom of this generation, the modified deviations from known extinct animals assuming a gradual metamorphosis from antiquity.

CHAPTER VII.

MR. WATERTON was a wonderfully keen and very staunch supporter of the "infallible Church," consequently, now and then, was greatly delighted by a vehement and caustic attack on what he always designated "our Reformed Church as by law established," as he was wont, in sportive criticism, to thus speak of it. In order to carry out his own individual notions more efficiently, and to more thoroughly humiliate us Protestants in what he termed a "savoury mode," he jocosely and practically represented many individuals, who took an active part in the Church Reformation upwards of three hundred years ago, by means of an actual and substantial illustration composed of the most disgusting creatures that his flight of fancy could conceive, from the animal, nay from the loathsome reptile creation.

Still more signally to mark the horror he entertained of the ground-work of Protestantism, and to enrich in contumely, the distasteful and nauseous spectacle so ludicrously got up, the Squire assembled in solemn conclave the most prominent Reformers of the age as special objects of his sarcasm and antipathy by name, attaching such appellation to each reptile as he conceived most suitable for the character he intended to lampoon, assigning the most absurd and disagreeable position and attitude to each representative of this professed "*senatus-consultum*," "decree of the senate." He also associated with our most prominent and distinguished characters of Church Reformation a sprinkling of his fancifully suggested or supposed inhabitants of the infernal regions, not of course forgetting to introduce in apparent gravity, the "Old Gentleman" under the cognomen of "Old Nick."

This representation is so cleverly "got up" in taxidermic execution, so ludicrously and artistically ridiculous and absurd in appearance, character, and singularity of attitude, and evidently, in the Squire's opinion, so precisely *appropos* to those most distinguished in the age of Church Reformation, as regarded the individual appellations which he conceived and selected for criticism, that I have strong reasons for believing Mr. Waterton deemed this practical illustration his *chef d'œuvre* in the art of taxidermy.

I have also a well-grounded suspicion, but no absolute certainty, that this Reformation display was gravely intended as a sarcastic and contumelious retort on the Socinian boast of having brought disasters on the Romish Church.

> "*Tota jacet Babylon ; destruxit tecta Lutherus,*
> *Calvinus muros, sed fundamenta Socinus.*"

> "All Babylon lies prostrate ; Luther destroyed the roof,
> Calvin the walls, but Socinus the foundation."

It must be observed, whenever allusion has been made in the preceeding pages, to either words or acts on the part of Mr. Waterton apparently trenching on profanity, or on what might be considered as expressive of a want of due respect or veneration for the Supreme Being, that I have invariably and truly represented him as jocose.

Watts however, says, "If the subject be sacred, all ludicrous terms, and jocose or comical airs should be excluded, lest young minds learn to trifle with the awful solemnities of religion."

The Squire's inherent eccentricity of character, so universally known, from personal intercourse and from his various publications, coupled with the admittedly extreme views held by him in regard to his own Church, invariably allowed him, by sufferance, permission, or a sort of sanction, to say and do many things which the ordinary usages of society would not tolerate in others.

Mr. Waterton had an inordinate, and I am sorry to acknowledge, in my opinion, an injudicious amount of credulity in his composition,—a feature, by the way admitted to be prominently marked and extensively indulged in the Romish Church. In the Squire's case however, many who were strict adherents to the discipline of their own Church, lamented and were greatly surprised with this excess of credulity in so highly educated a man, and in one who had seen so much of the world and its obliquities.

Unsuspiciousness, a trait abstractedly considered, is worthy of the highest approbation, and is most frequently associated with youth, but as years roll on, this admirable quality is occasionally found to have been the germ of future self-delusion, and is apt to gradually slide into a credulity which is satisfied without requisite evidence.

" *Tam sæpe nostrum decipi Fabullum quid*
Miraris, Aule ? Semper bonus homo tiro est."

" Why wonder Aulus, that our friend Fabullus is so often
deceived ? The virtuous man is always a novice."

To show the playful levity of my octogenarian friend
I may mention a circumstance which occurred without
a moment's warning of a very unexpected nature.

In the north-east corner of the front entrance hall
of the mansion stood a table on which to place the hats,
great coats, gloves, &c., of arriving visitors, which was
covered by a large cloth, hanging down to the floor. On
seeing me drive up to the bridge in front of the house,
the Squire has, more than once, secretly crept on all fours
like a dog under the table, waiting my arrival in the
hall, in order that I might place my great coat &c., &c.
upon this table; and whilst I was thus unsuspectingly
engaged, he has in his private retreat commenced to growl
like a savage dog behind the cloth, and has siezed my
legs in such a practically canine manner, that I really
had no idea at the time, but that some fierce dog was
attacking my lower extremities.

Mr. Waterton's kindness and generosity were unbounded.
Almost invariably, on my leaving the hall, when about
to return home in the evening, I was sure to find my great
coat pockets well stuffed with apples, pears, filberts,
or some other fruit which might be then in season, whilst
my carriage box was as repeatedly most liberally stored
with cherries, eggs, or other edibles.

In order to manifest his warmth of heart and a welcome reception to his friend, the Squire would, on my

arrival, even in the most boisterous weather or in the
depth of winter, nay in a snow storm, come out to meet me
at the bridge, without hat or any other covering on the
head, although his hair was always cropped as short
as the most dexterous expert in the hair-dressing line
was able to cut it. He would frequently come out to '
welcome me, even in his slippers, and prove his pleasure
to receive me by actually dancing down the whole length
of the broad flagged walk, occasionally throwing one of his
loose slippers from his foot high up in the air above his
head, and expertly catching it in his hand in its descent.
The wetness of the flags underfoot, or a shower overhead,
never constituted any impediment to an exploit of this
character with Mr. Waterton, when he was even approaching his eightieth year.

Although the Squire rigidly abstained from all stimuli
in the form of fluids, yet he was incautious, and by no
means even ordinarily discreet, as regards the consumption
of solids. He had naturally a good appetite, and as he sometimes heedlessly indulged it, the consequence was, that
when the Pope, as he facetiously observed, " removed the
padlock from his grinders," instead of his eating sparingly
for two or three meals as he ought to have done, he would
at once, unwisely gratify his palate, (until very late in life,)
with a hearty relish of rich soup and also solids in the way
of animal food. The result was as others anticipated, the
stomach, which had occasionally been subjected to absolute starvation by severe fasting, was for a long time,
totally unequal to perform its healthy and normal functions,

when suddenly loaded, or rather, over-loaded with that of which it had been so long deprived. Hence succeeded a train of painful feelings, and, *for the moment*, a conviction that Dr. Kitchener was not grievously in error when he stated that "the stomach was every man's master."

At these times, I can bear testimony, as an eye witness, to the acute agonies of the Squire; and, as a convincing proof that he did then suffer severely, he would silently retire and even condescend to betake himself to the sofa, which was a very unusual concession for the rigid Roman Catholic to submit to, and, of course, he was then by his own admission, thoroughly determined to be more wise for the future, but

"*Ægrotat dœmon, monachus tunc esse volebat;*
Dœmon convaluit, dœmon ut ante fuit."

"The Devil was sick, the Devil a monk would be;
The Devil got well, the Devil a monk was he."

When the Squire was well and mentally undisturbed by trifling mishaps or unanticipated annoyances, which are difficult to always prevent under any circumstances, even in smaller establishments than the one at Walton Hall, he enjoyed an exuberant flow of spirits, and was never niggardly in their distribution, if appreciated by those around him, so as to convince him that his hilarity contributed pleasure. On the contrary, however, if he experienced an ungracious or repulsive silence, a frigidity of manner, a gratuitous or intentional hauteur, he could and would be contemptuously taciturn to the precise extent to convince that he had (to use a mercantile phrase) taken stock of their deportment, and that he intended to meet out measure for measure.

His mode of communicating such determination to characters so discourteous was singularly significant and effective. Indeed so thoroughly did the silent system of punishment on the part of the Squire sting to the quick, that you might occasionally see the arrogant reduced to a position of absolute humility, and the torpidly indifferent to one of apparent cordiality.

Mr. Waterton's patience was now and then severely taxed by parties gaining admission from the introduction of friends to see the staircase, many of whom were not only totally ignorant of ornithology, but ten to one equally unacquainted with every other ology. In this unenviable position the Squire had to resort to various expedients rather than give offence by a palpable want of attention.

A countryman once gravely asked Mr. Waterton if he thought he could turn him out "a complete curer of birds in two months, and if he could, what he would charge per month, and board and lodge him into the bargain." The Squire replied that he never worked for money, hoping thus to cut short this *ignoramus* without further trouble, when the countryman, not understanding figurative expressions, but thoroughly comprehending realities, observed that he was very much obliged, and would enter on these terms on Monday next. This free and easy acceptation of terms that had never been offered, set the Squire's bristles up, when he coolly remarked

"He was surprised that his mother had allowed him to come alone," and forthwith took French leave of what he called "the unlicked cub."

Mr. Waterton's chief and never-failing delight appeared to be in beautifying his park and enriching the scenery immediately surrounding the mansion, as well as in rendering Walton Hall distinguished, unexampled, and unique in its peculiarities.

The Squire, by his refinement of conception, his purity of taste, his singularity, and wonderful and unparalleled execution in handiwork, has created a lasting memorial of himself, which can in no way be more faithfully delineated than by the inscription on the monument of the late Sir Christopher Wren, in St. Paul's Cathedral :——

" Si monumentum requiris, circumspice."

" If you seek my monument, look around."

A specially favourite amusement with Mr. Waterton was, the trimming his beautiful fences with a light hedging bill. On one occasion, whilst thus engaged, he accidentally cut his foot very severely with this sharp hook. On the arrival of his surgeon from Wakefield, he ventured to gravely admonish the Squire as to the inexpediency and danger of his recent occupation, and strictly enjoined absolute rest, with an elevated and horizontal position of the limb, as well as the continued application of folds of linen dipped in cold water on the wound.

On the surgeon's re-appearance the following day, the

Squire had slily and unobserved, escaped from his thraldom, of course without leaving any message to that effect. A "hue and cry" was raised, and when discovered, the culprit was found working in the grounds as usual with his favourite hedging bill, and to the astonishment and great annoyance of the surgeon, was standing in a ditch ankle deep in water. On a respectful and really serious remonstrance being made, Mr. Waterton gravely insisted that he was strictly and perseveringly carrying out the surgeon's injunctions, by having slit open the upper leather of his shoe to allow a free admission of water to the wound on his foot; consequently, it had been continually immersed in cold water for the preceding two hours, and as he was not walking, he contended that the limb was at rest.

On Mr. Waterton's recovery from the accident to which I have alluded, he wrote me the following Letter :—

"WALTON HALL.

"My Dear Sir,—A letter from Park House always acts on me as balm on the way-worn traveller's wounds. The less we say about wounds the better, recollecting recent occurrences. We want no inviting to your table. We are forcibly urged into Leeds as the loadstone drags iron to itself. I have been vagabondising. The old proverb says, "*Qui multum peregrinantur raró sanctificantur.*" *

"I wanted a vampire, and have succeeded. This morning I am off to our dear Jesuits at Stonyhurst. There will

* "He who travels much is rarely sanctified."

be no need for me to enter into any kind of plot with these good fathers for the destruction of our government. Lord John Mummery has done the needful. Considering the very great interest you always show to our family, when things go bodily wrong, I should deem myself an ungrateful sinner, were I not to drop you a line by this day's post.

"Yesterday, I eat my breakfast unfeelingly, having spent the previous night coughing. Finding that the pulse was feeble and below the standard mark, I thought it high time to put things peremptorily to rights, so produced the lancet, *longo post tempore visum.* * Father ——— stood looking on. John Warrener our servant was my cup-bearer, and in a pet I called him a noodles, when he said, ' he might well be one, as he had not never seen nobody bled before.' I let out above five-and-twenty ounces of blood. The pulse returned to its normal beat. The cough no longer pained me. I could make my elbows meet behind me, which I can always do when in good fettle.

> *' Dixero quid si forte jocosius, hoc mihi juris*
> *Cum veniâ dabis.'* †

"A week ago I had well nigh put myself into a state which would have enabled my dexterous friend Sam Smith to pay his assessed taxes with increased facility. Whilst I was cutting off the dead branch of an elm tree, the ladder on which I stood slipped sideways, and down I came

---

* " Not seen for a long time.

† " If perchance I shall speak a little jocosly, you will kindly allow me that privilege."

in full twelve feet of descent soss upon the earth. I had just presence of mind in the act of falling, to forcibly restrain my breath, and from fasting, being meagerly supplied within, when I reached the ground, I may say with truth, that I literally bounced upon my feet in an instant, and then continued my occupation. My transit from high to low merely produced a stiffness in my neck and right leg the following day. Had my ass been full of beef at the time, I might not have gone further, but assuredly should have fared worse.

"By the way, feeling how much store we rustic inhabitants of Walton Hall set by you, and at the same time knowing how fervently you always obey the ecclesiastical edicts of Queen Victoria, we wish to know how you have managed to bear the discipline in submitting to the humiliation of the tremendous national fast on Wednesday last. We ourselves have not materially suffered, as we are not in the habit of paying attention to any spiritual authority that comes not from the sacred inclosure of the eternal city; so that Wednesday passed off with us as usual.

" Very sincerely,

" CHARLES WATERTON."

In the Squire's letter just quoted, he alludes to making his elbows meet behind him, which apparently juvenile volatility seems so simple and easy of accomplishment that I had never dreamt of its difficulty. Its practical solution however, is an embarrassing puzzle to most men.

Mr. Waterton was formed by nature to scatter to the

winds dilemmas of this character. He could in truth
"make a long arm" and consequently, as the upper
portion of the trunk of the body was spare and somewhat
narrow, he possessed unusually overbalancing advantages
in his favour for the achievement of this manœuvre,
because, whilst the abnormal length of arm afforded the
advantage of a more lengthened extension than ordinary
the diminished capacity of the chest lessened its necessity,
hence the Squire's facility in consummating a feat which
seems to be such plain sailing in theory, but which in
practice proves so perplexing to most men.

Mr. Waterton and I have very frequently together
narrowly and perseveringly watched the exciting season
of ornithological incubation, and by the various resources
and appliances which we frequently had in our power,
have now and then, settled many knotty points as to
habits and distinguishing peculiarities, which could be
decided only by our absolutely witnessing them. The
"little island" in the centre of the lake at Walton Hall,
was our favourite ground of observation in the spring
months by means of the telescope, being admirably
situated and adapted for that purpose, when this lake-
girt locality yearly contributed much that was valuable,
interesting, and instructive to the ornithologist, and much
that was amusing to the merely ordinary observer, during
the period of the incubation of, at least, three species of
water-fowl, viz., the Canada goose, wild duck, and bald
coot.

These birds nested freely on the "little island," the

THE DISTANT MANSION; THE RUIN; THE LITTLE ISLAND; AND THE LOMBARDY POPLAR.

elder trees, bramble bushes, and long and coarse grass which here abounded, always affording a safe, shaded, retired, and concealed retreat, as well as perfect quietude to numbers of the females whilst silently and instinctively discharging a solitary yet pleasing duty imposed on them by nature, being necessarily a whole month virtually separated from the male bird.

It is really quite delightful to see how papa and mamma play into each other's hands, if I may be allowed the allegorical expression. For instance, if the *mallard* should not be in the way when the duck leaves her nest for the purpose of feeding, and for the pleasure of refreshing herself by a wholesome wash in the lake, she invariably, before her departure, so arranges her little temporary abode that the eggs should be entirely concealed from the eye of any intruder, by a covering of down and feathers, previously and instinctively plucked from her own abdomen and breast by her bill, whilst this simple but efficient covering, being a bad conductor of caloric, materially prevents the escape of heat from the eggs, so that only a trifling or unappreciable decrease of temperature takes place until her return.

This instinctive arrangement for the protection of her eggs having been accomplished, she rapidly glides into the lake for her brief holiday with apparently great delight, repeatedly and forcibly flapping her outstretched wings on its surface, a sportive exertion of power of all waterfowl when in a merry mood. The noise thus produced is peculiar, and generally soon heard by the male bird who, having caught a glimpse of his partner, speedily and rejoicingly approaches her by the same flapping progression which the female had previously resorted to on leaving her nest.

These birds having exchanged cordial congratulatory inclinations and declinations of the head, and achieved sundry other evidently pleasurable as well as playfully physical gesticulations on the lake, the mallard without further ceremony, directs his impetuous course from the lake to the island, hurriedly waddling along to the nest so recently occupied by his spouse, round which he repeatedly walks, continually and gracefully bowing his head over it. He then, with his bill, gently removes the feathers covering the eggs in the centre of the nest, to its circumferential portions. He afterwards, by the same means, disposes the eggs in such positions as to render his entrance to the nest safely and. easily accessible, and in situations the least likely to cause damage to the treasures of his faithful consort, which had for the time, been taken under his charge, a duty which he gravely settles down to, in the necessary absence of his better half.

Occasionally, the kind-hearted mallard would stealthily approach the immediate neighbourhood of the nest, whilst the duck was still performing the dreary office of incubation, when by his fidgetty and restless movements here and there in immediate proximity to the duck, and by the repeatedly graceful declinations of his head towards his spouse, it was evident that he was coaxing and tenderly inviting her to leave her nest in order to feed and have a refreshing dip in the lake. Usually

she was neither unwilling nor tardy in yielding to his
evidently anxious solicitations to leave her eggs for a
short period, but it was invariably observed, when she
did so at the mallard's request and in his presence, that
she never, on her departure on these special occasions,
attempted to cover them, manifestly well aware that the
mallard would take careful charge of her treasures until
she returned to attend to her duty.

Now and then, these birds would boldly venture to
nest on the very brink of the "little island," and even
closely approximating the margin of the water, being
then conspicuously exposed to the anxiously scrutinising
surveillance of the inmates of the drawing-room by
means of the telescope, the powers of which agreeably
and instructively revealed every habit, however trifling,
of the particular species of water-fowl under examination, during the anxious period of incubation.

With every-day opportunities of such a character for
Mr. Waterton to gain an unparalleled amount of information which could be entirely depended upon, it would
have been strange indeed, if so observing, zealous, and
vigorous a mind, could have remained ignorant of a
thorough knowledge of that very subject which he had
ever, during his whole life, had most at heart. And, it
must be acknowledged that "the testimony of nature
is of greater weight than the arguments of learning."
"*Validius est naturæ testimonium quam doctrinæ argu-
mentum.*"

The Canada geese have occasionally nested on the

island on which the house stands, and on more occasions
than one within ten yards of the dining-room windows,
but the very close proximity to man and his daily and
hourly movements and accompaniments, necessarily placed
the birds in a position subjected to a disagreeable amount
of observation and restraint, and doubtless, in many
instances, prevented them from invariably resorting to their
natural and undisguised habits ; hence, information gained
from birds nesting close to the house was never to be so
fully relied upon as knowledge gleaned from the "little
island," although at a much greater distance, but which
was obtained at a time, and from a situation when and
where the birds had no idea that they were under the
inspection of any human eye.

The most interesting points to attract the attention of
the naturalist, as regards the habits of these birds during
the period of sitting on their eggs for the purpose of
hatching their young are, on the part of the *female*, viz.,
her plucking down and feathers from her own breast and
abdomen, in order to use them for a special purpose,—
also, her covering and thus concealing her eggs when
she leaves her nest, by distributing those feathers which
she has secured, over the eggs, in accomplishing which
another important end is gained.

For instance, inasmuch as feathers are imperfect con-
ductors of heat, the duck with instinctive design, uses the
material, of all others best calculated to prevent the escape of
that caloric with which she has previously supplied her eggs.
Another interesting point is, her leaving her nest at the
special request of her husband, in order to feed, wash,

preen, and refresh herself. A third point almost amounting to reason, is her apparent knowledge of there being no neccessity to cover her eggs when the mallard is about to take upon himself the office of discharging her special duties, until she is desirous and prepared to conveniently attend to them herself.

The acts worthy of notice as regards the *mallard*, are in the first place, his anxiously hastening to occupy the nest so soon as he is aware that the *duck* has left it, and that it is then unprotected by either of its owners; in the second place, the *mallard's* tender care for his better half, by his affectionately requesting her to feed and refresh herself, should be recorded; and thirdly, his anxious readiness to supply her wants until she returns,—also his carefully removing the covering of down and feathers from the eggs by his bill, to the circumferential portions of the nest, before he ventures to put his foot into his lady's abode.

These natural and ordinary habits of both sexes to which I have now drawn attention, having been for many years repeatedly witnessed through the medium of the telescope, by Mr. Waterton and myself at Walton Hall, may be received as established facts in natural history.

The "little island" could never boast of entertaining more than the three species of water-fowl to which I have alluded. It seemed singular, but the herons never condescended to visit it, although daily crossing it in their flights and hovering around its precincts. They would assemble on the banks of the lake immediately opposite it to plume themselves—in the swamp, to dabble in the

Q

shallow water where they seemed to be actively engaged in quest of frogs—to roost in the heronry, and remain in it for the purpose of incubation, and visit the head of the lake and its tributaries in order to fish during the day, but never in the night, as they then hunted the neighbouring streamlets or the various estuaries at ebb tides within distance.

I may here state, that formerly there was a generally, but absurdly prevailing opinion that herons, during incubation, rested on their nest with a leg hanging out on each side, in consequence of the limbs being so long that they could not be conveniently accommodated within the nest. I suspect that such idea has not yet, even in this knowing age, entirely vanished, although a moment's reflection ought at once to dispel such an absurd and illogical impression, when it is explained that the heron's nest is from ten to twelve inches in width, whilst the heron itself is not more than one-half this width, and, I may add, that the Squire and I have several times had very favourable opportunities of watching herons on their nests during incubation, through the medium of the telescope, by which means, we could clearly ascertain that their legs like those of other birds, were within the nest, and that such a position did not appear to interfere with the comfort of the heron in the slightest degree. On the other hand, if the heron, occupying a width of not more than five inches transversely as regards the breast and thighs conjointly when in the act of incubation, should attempt to bestride a space of ten or twelve inches diameter, by suspending its legs over the edges of its nest, it would find it an utter impossibility to accomplish such a feat, even supposing its anxious determination to submit to such an inconvenient position.

When alluding to Mr. Waterton's want of relish for agricultural pursuits, I ought to have stated his very equivocal skilfulness as regarded horses; for although in his younger days he always lived in the country, and was continually surrounded by a certain class of the equine race, yet it must be admitted, that they were generally not of that stamp calculated to fascinate a high-mettled and plucky youth, such as the Squire then really was; consequently at that period of life, when a know-ledge of the horse ought to be gained, if ever such skill is to be thoroughly acquired, and which most desirable acquisition all country gentlemen should assuredly possess, Mr. Waterton had no probable chance to become a proficient in that science.

His father however, thinking that when grown up to man's estate, he would be materially benefited by mixing with his equals "in the field," spiritedly and liberally procured for him a couple of accomplished hunters; and as there was always, even in infancy, an immense amount of naturally inherent courage in the Squire's composition, he did what few men under similar circumstances would have dared to do, that is, "he rode to the hounds," and never shirked a five-barred gate when it came in his way, which feat, trifling as it is represented by the closet sportsman, is always more agreeably, and now and then more easily discussed over a bottle of Port than accomplished "in the field."

Two or three, who were deemed "fast" young men at that date, and who were regularly to be seen at the cover side, and invariably gave extravagant prices for their horses had, from other reasons totally unconnected with hunting or any of its accompaniments, been obliged to succumb to their creditors, "which unfortunate occurrences," the Squire observed, "so scared my father that he said, ' Charles, I fear this hunting may ultimately lead you into similarly disgraceful difficulties, now that I frequently hear of your jumping five barred-gates, and being so highly complimented by sportsmen like Lord Darlington for your bold riding.

'Praise from an old and acknowleged thoroughly good sportsman, and more especially from one of the "right sort," and with a sprig of nobility attached to his name glibly glides into the brains of young men, and now and then turns them upside down, and it would greatly distress me if you should slip the cable and come to grief. You obliged me by commencing to hunt—will you still futher oblige me by giving it up?'

"I instantaneously replied, 'Yes father, I will do whatever you desire me to do, but I am satisfied that hunting has had nothing whatever to do with the failure of the parties to whom you have alluded. On the contrary, I believe that hunting has been of material service to them, in warding off the evil day for a certain period.

"'The hunting field substantially invigorated the physical energies of these men, and whilst in it, they were neither guzzling Champagne, throwing the dice, nor transgressing the bounds of morality, all of which habits extracted infinitely more guineas from their breeches pockets than ever the most extravagant-priced hunters did ; and, as to moral comparison, we will let that pass, but from this day agreeably to your wishes, I shall never again appear in crimson, nor risk my neck over a five-barred gate.   So far I have kept my promise. and a pledge to my father was recognised by him in as sacred a light as if it had been made to the Pope himself.'"

Whilst this check in the Squire's hunting career, in a great measure accounts for his being below par in the knowledge of that noble animal the horse, it furnishes additional information of his surprising innate courage and ready aptitude to succeed in almost any thing he chose to attempt.   It also displays a singularly fine and exemplary character as a son, in so promptly acquiescing in the wishes of his parent, as the Squire had become unequivocally attached to this popular, glorious, and invigorating diversion, and felt thoroughly convinced that his father's conclusions were derived from false premises.

If a horse stood upon a short leg, and had short and nearly upright pasterns, and carried a good head and tail, he was, in the eye of the Squire, perfection.

Mr. Waterton had no idea that there was a happy medium as regarded the length and obliquity of this portion of the limb which constituted in the hack, the lady's pad, the hunter, and the race horse, the most desirable formation for each distinction of duty or of service.

His opinion was, that his favourite combination to which I have alluded, constituted a sure foundation for the greatest amount of speed, endurance of labour, lasting properties to the leg, and ease and comfort to the rider in all cases and for every purpose.

You could never convince Mr. Waterton that a lady's pad should stand on a somewhat longer and less upright pastern than a hack destined to carry a gentleman's weight, or that a more lengthened and oblique pastern contributed greater elasticity and resiliency of spring than the short and upright pastern did.

It was therefore evident that the Squire had based his original learning on opinions established in his youth from the hairy leg and a lack of quality so much in request in that day among country gentlemen.

Mr. Waterton had quite as great a partiality for the application of the lancet in the stable department as he had in the mansion, bleeding to the amount of half a pail being generally followed by a drachm each of calomel and tartarised antimony, whether the horse was suffering from a plethoric condition, or might be as hungry as a hawk from sheer starvation, in fact the Squire was a second Doctor Sangrado.

Whilst he was liberal of oats beyond measure to my horses, he was in the same ratio, parsimonious to his own, contending in unaffected sincerity, that a great many horses were ruined by conceited and empty-headed grooms who believed that all diseases arose from a want of oats, and that all diseases were prevented and cured by their inordinate exhibition.

That Mr. Waterton was, to a limited extent, on the

right track, I will not dispute, but being naturally so
sanguine a character, he was apt to hunt his game too
closely, and therefore now and then to unwittingly over-
shoot his mark.

When no vaunting superiority of endowment or of surpassing talent was vaingloriously professed, Mr. Waterton
invariably refrained from any thing bordering on sarcasm,
but if undeserved pretensions were indulged and ostentatiously displayed, and especially if officiously claimed as
meritorious, his ridicule or even satire was expressed with
a caustic contempt and a silent but an evidently marked
disapprobation which made the boasting party wince
under his chastening and castigating reproach, causing the
magniloquent pretender to repent and bitterly regret
having incautiously ventured out of his depth. And
he would probably turn towards me and say in a half
whisper,

> " It's hardly in a body's power,
> To keep, at times, frae being sour."

A self-opinionated and conceited young coxcomb, who
was visiting the staircase at Walton Hall, and whose
dress, exquisite, and extreme in the fashion of the day,
had, from this very circumstance, already unfavourably
attracted the keenly observant eye of Mr. Waterton.
This aspiring youth, having separated himself from his
accompanying party, coolly called the Squire's attention
to "two or three little errors in the attitude of the peacock" in the extension staircase, terminating his criticism
by saying, " On the whole Mr. Waterton, the execution

of this bird does you considerable credit, but I have a strong suspicion that it is not an honest bird, or in other words, that it is decked with a few borrowed plumes in its tail which is unusually long."

The concluding uncalled-for as well as undeserved and insolent remarks, roused the Squire's ire to the extreme of endurance, and in recounting the fracas to me, he observed, " I looked this man-milliner so profusely got up full in the face, and enunciated what I had to say with an emphasis which would not fail to leave an indelible recollection, that 'the mark of the hatchet was against the wall,' and that I had taken an accurately-estimated measure of his natural history attainments," when I immediately observed in reply, " Sir, I should degrade myself by holding any cavilling argument with so mere a stripling in natural history as you, and the more especially, as it is palpably evident, from your remarks, that your ignorance far outshines any ordinary qualifications which you may possess in the bewitching science of ornithology. Go home Sir I beseech you, and carefully pore over some elementary A. B. C. work relative to the anatomy of the peacock, and endeavour to ascertain *where* the tail of a peacock is situated, as at present, your ignorance may constitute *self-bliss*, but it must give much pain to your friends if they happen to possess any knowledge whatever of natural history.

" After the lapse of several years my friend made his second appearance on the stage, when he was dressed like a Christain, and on this occasion, conducted himself like a gentleman." In fact, he not only did not assume any

ornithological knowledge, but earnestly entreated the
Squire to pardon his former absurdly ostentatious display
of science, the very rudiments of which he was totally
ignorant, admitting that he had richly merited the severe
castigation which was then meted out to him, and was
grateful in the extreme, that his punishment had not
been carried out to absolute ostracism, appending in all
humility an ample apology, by saying, "Mr. Waterton I
admit that I then thought myself a Solomon, and am
ashamed to add, that I even considered myself competent
to instruct you, but now, by close application in consequence of your invective cat-o-nine-tails, I am beginning
to discover my incapacity, and to clearly see how little
I really do know, and at the foot of Gamaliel I shall now
be thankful for the falling crumbs."

Mr. Waterton was much pleased, saying "there was an
evident sincerity in this spontaneously expressed atone-
ment which no gentleman could slight," and when he
named this circumstance to me, he observed, "I was
myself half inclined to apologise for my original warmth,
but, on further consideration, I merely remarked, that I was
much pleased to see the once barren and unprofitable tree
bringing forth fruit, and that a learned Bishop of the
Orthodox Church as by law established, had said, 'I had
rather confess my ignorance than *falsely* profess knowledge, as it is no shame not to know all things, but it is a
just shame to over-reach in anything.'"

My friend sometimes rushed into extreme views, and
thus necessarily into exhorbitant measures, and then

unfortunately found himself on unsubstantial and indeed untenable ground.

The witholding an amount of oats sufficient to afford his horses power and energetic spirit adequate to accomplish the labour required, was a failing which the Squire never could conquer; but I believe this arose chiefly from ignorance of the management and the essential requisites necessary for the preservation of genuine health in the animal, and not from any stingy motive.

In order to convince him that his horses would not only do more work, but accomplish it more easily and more speedily, I have reminded him of what Burns said to "Auld Maggie."

> "When thou was corn't, an I was mellow,
> We took the road, ay like a swallow ;
> At Brooses thou had ne'er a fellow,
>   For pith an speed ;
> But ev'ry tail thou pay't them hollow,
>   Whare'er thou gaed."

> "When frosts lay lang, an snaws were deep,
> An threatened labour back to keep,
> I gied thy cog a wee-bit heap,
>   Aboon the timmer ;
> I ken'd my Maggie wad na sleep,
>   For that, or Simmer."

Inasmuch as Burns was sometimes quoted by the Squire as "a knowing farmer," I took advantage of the Poet's expressed opinion in his " New-year morning salutation to his auld mare Maggie," in which he advocates a liberal supply of oats, he having evidently been convinced that in order to secure and maintain "the pith and speed" of the swallow she must be well " corn't," and when " frosts and snaws" retarded agricultural operations beyond their usual time, she was prepared to meet the anticipated difficulties by her "-cog," (measure) having been slightly heaped above the "timmer" in addition to her usual fare.

Mr. Waterton replied "however correct Burns might be in feeding auld Maggie, it was no reason why he should become 'mellow,' and thus make a beast of himself."

A young gentleman, a thoroughly clever "cross-country" man, accompanied me a few years ago to Walton Hall, and in the course of some animated conversation, or what is usually termed chaff, the Squire was relating a hunting anecdote connected with the late well and widely known Martin Hawk, who hunted with Lord Darlington for many years.

Each recounted his own hunting exploits until a little rivalry began to manifest itself, when they arranged to jump a bar for some trifling wager, more from love than money, Mr. Waterton contending that with the exception of bridles, the horses should come to the scratch, and perform their feats "*in puris naturalibus*," and, with this proviso, dared at seventy-four years of age, our friend to the mark, who having a private signal from me, to my great satisfaction, prudently declined the dangerous contest.

Had they carried out this absurd rivalry, on the bare backs of their steeds, in all probability, one or both might have realised the perilous descent of Icarus, as a man, accustomed from his cradle, to ride upon a saddle, would cut a sorry figure on the bare back.

I merely allude to this contempt of danger, to show the Quixotic character of the veteran at seventy-four.

About the year 1847 or 1848, a clever and ingenious fellow living in Leeds of the name of Green, very adroitly duped some *would-be* scientific proficients, who, it was then said, modestly estimated their own natural-history attainments at no inferior rate, but the sequel will better inform us on this delicate point. Green cleverly managed to accomplish his mechanical labour, and to gain his ends for a time among those self-esteemed cognoscenti with considerable ability and decided success in the following manner. He destroyed a toad without in any way disfiguring it, and having procured a large block of coal, he split it into two parts; he then neatly excavated a portion in the lower half, the form and size of this indentation being precisely adapted to correspond with that of the toad, into which cavity he placed the reptile already prepared for its berth, leaving its back slightly projecting. In the upper half of the block of coal a trifling excavation was made, just sufficient to admit the trifling but necessary projection of the back, which I have already named.

When these two halves were placed in close apposition the toad exactly fitted the excavations, and the two halves of the block precisely fitted each other, so as to convey the impression that the toad had been thus accidentally imbedded in its present position in by-gone ages, when it might be supposed that the surrounding matter was in so fluid and yielding a condition as to form a mould for this batrachian reptile.

Green plausibly asserted, that this block of coal was from a colliery at or near Osmondthorpe, and professed to know the precise number of fathoms below the surface whence it was obtained. With great apparent simplicity he detailed the various circumstances of his becoming possessed of this monstrosity by saying, that when walking up Wade Lane in Leeds behind a coal cart, a large block of coal accidentally fell from the load, and by its concussion on the pavement, split into two parts,—that he was thunderstruck to see a living toad in the lower half, — and that he immediately seized both halves, and took them home as a valuably booty. On exposure to the air however, he observed, "the toad died, without a struggle."

This fellow, whose powers of assumption were largely developed, not only succeeded I have understood, in persuading three different parties to credit his absurd and false statement, but actually gulled them into being purchasers of what he very truly, but very unintentionally, called unnatural productions.

It is somewhat singular that these three artificial products should have fallen into the hands of three *reputed* naturalists. By the way, Green did not display his wisdom nor his usual tact, in disposing of so many specimens of his handicraft at no greater distance from each other than York, Leeds, and Holbeck, as of course, the discovery of one deception would be very likely to expose and lead to the revelation of the other two, and so it turned out.

This gross imposition, however strange it may appear

remained undiscovered for so long a period, and the sums received for these fictitious specimens were so richly remunerative, that Green was emboldened to fly at higher game, and actually hazarded a call at Walton Hall, ambitiously hoping to dispose of his hitherto highly approved, although misrepresented wares, to the universally recognised giant in natural history. The foundation on which Green rested for success was errone-ous as he made his essay in a quarter highly gifted with the powers of acutely distinctive discrimination. He dwelt too much upon his previously experienced ability to deceive, without carefully weighing the ordeal of the keen, intelligent, searching, scientific, and antagonistic eye he had on this occasion to encounter. This indiscreet step was a woeful mistake, on the part of the hitherto skilful and experienced impostor. The Squire, fortunately was at home, put in appearance, and received the stranger without the slightest pre-vious knowledge of the man, and without a suspicion that the kidnapping toils were to be so skilfully spread for him, or that dust would be thrown in his eyes by so cleverly manufactured a falsehood.

I will endevour to state what passed during this inter-view, as nearly as possible in Mr. Waterton's own words, having repeatedly heard him narrate the conversation with apparently great pleasure, and especially as regarded his immediate discovery of what he always termed the "clumsy fraud."

Whenever the subject was broached, the Squire usually commenced by saying, "On the occasion of Green's visit

to my house, I happened to have a gentleman in the room
with me, learned in many things, but not in natural history. When this fellow Green, exposed his counterfeit
and fabricated monstrosity for a professed inspection, but
in reality for nefarious sale, I without any difficulty,
instantly discovered the deception, and anxious to let
my learned friend into the secret, without letting Green
know what my private opinion was, I said to my visitor,
'*Annosa vulpes haud capitur laqueo,*' but did not anglicise
by adding, ' An old fox is not to be caught with a springe.'
As however, I smiled when addressing my learned friend,
who was still in the room and manifestly enjoying the
prospective finale, Green evidently concluding that my
scrap of Latin although unintelligible to him, was laudatory of his exhibition, and therefore appeared more and
more satisfied with his apparently exalted and self-
established but really unenviable position. At length,
gathering still more assurance, he coolly looked me
in the face, and with a grinning smile of self-appro-
bation observed, ' Did you, Mr. Waterton, ever witness
so great a curiosity in your life ? and you must have
seen many curious things in your travels in foreign
countries I suppose.' My reply was expressed with an
intentionally stern countenance. Sir, in all my travels,
at home or in ' foreign countries,' I never met with so
great and so unpardonable an impostor as you. Get
out of my house instantly you scoundrel, and if I
ever hear of your offering this gross imposition for
sale again, rest assured that I shall expose you right
and left.

"When this vagabond had fairly taken his departure and finally turned his back of the house, my friend, who vastly enjoyed the concluding stormy scene, and more especially what he jocosely designated my terminating benediction, expressed his great surprise that the flimsy fiction should have escaped a detection which I so instantly discovered, particularly, he observed, as this unparalleled imposition had been previously examined by so many experienced naturalists, when, really without any intention of lacerating the thickened cuticle of these self-styled natural history celebrities, I could not refrain from replying, 'Very true, sir, and I assure you that I am and ought to be grateful. '*Beati monoculi in regione cæcorum.*' 'Happy are the one-eyed in the country of the blind.'"

CHAPTER VIII.

I HAVE already alluded to the hollowed-out beechwood block for Mr. Waterton's pillow during the night, but the providing an unyielding "*sleeper*" for the cheek to rest upon was not limited to the Squire's bedroom. This very singular caprice was invariably resorted to on board ship, as, when the weather would permit, and even when of a very dubious character, he delighted to sleep the whole night on deck, and always to gratify and indulge in this peculiar fancy by resting his cheek on what he called his velvet cushion,—viz., the outward soles of his strong shoes, which were furnished with a profusion of stout nails.

When the Squire was in a light-hearted mood, and detailing to me *his* mode of curing an ulcerated leg, which of course involved the exhibition of a host of "Squire Watterton's Pills," I asked him if he gratified his sides alternately, when softly luxuriating all night on the hard boards. His decisive reply was, "No, it cost me too much to prepare one for its endurance to induce me to make a second experiment on the same subject."

Some years ago (my memory does not furnish me with the date), I had a portrait presented to me, in consequence of my fortunately bearing the same surname as the subject of the painting to which I shall now allude. It was the portrait of the late Mr. Tobias Hobson on horse-back, who so generously and munificently contributed to the town of Cambridge, by the erection of public edifices. On its arrival at my house Mr. Waterton happened to be dining with me, and was wonderfully delighted with the newly imported production, probably more so in consequence of Mr. Hobson having been a universally recognised and avowedly good man, coupled with a considerable amount of eccentricity of disposition. This gentleman, representing an individuality or an acknowledged peculiarity of character, I suspect had a material influence with the Squire. Some verses having been published, in 1734, by that celebrated Latinist Vincent Bourne relative to the subject of this painting, I, in a casual way, and really without being in earnest, asked the Squire to turn poet and Anglicise them, in order to attach them to the painting we were then admiring. The following day, to my great surprise, he returned me a copy which I now transcribe, from Bourne's original, and which Mr. Waterton told me "he had turned into his doggrel verse whilst in the railway carriage on his return to Walton Hall."

" HOBSONI LEX.

" *Complures (ita, Granta refers) Hobsonus alebat*
 In stabulo longo, quos locitaret, equos.
Hac lege, ut foribus stai et qui proximus, ille
 Susciperet primas, solus et ille, vices.
Aut hunc, aut nullum—sua pars sit cuique laboris;
 Aut hunc, aut nullum—sit sua cuique quies.
Conditio obtinuit, nulli violanda togato;
 Proximus hic foribus, proximus esto viæ.
Optio tam prudens cur non huc usque retenta est ?
 Tam bona cur unquam lex abolenda fuit ?
Hobsoni veterem normam revocare memento;
 Tuque iterum Hobsoni, Granta, videbis equos.
     " VINCENTIO BOURNE."

"HOBSON'S LAW

" In his long stable, Cambridge, you are told
  Hobson kept steeds for hire in days of old ;
  On this condition only--that the horse
  Nearest the door, should start the first on course
  Then next to him or none, so that each beast
  Might have its turn of labour and of rest.
  This granted, no one yet, in college dress,
  Was ever known this compact to transgress.
  Next to the door --next to the work--say why
  Should such a law, so just be doomed to die ?
  Remember, then, this compact to restore,
  And let it govern as it did before.
  This done--O happy Cambridge, you will see
  Your Hobson's stud just as it ought to be.

" CHARLES WATERTON."

Addison, who was born about forty years subsequent to Vincent Bourne, thus describes the subject in a paper in the Spectator.

" I shall conclude this discourse with the explanation of a proverb, which, by vulgar error, is taken and used when a man is reduced to an extremity, whereas the propriety of the maxim is, to use it when you would say there is plenty, but you must make such a choice as not to hurt another who is to come after you.

" Mr. Tobias Hobson, from whom we have the expression, was a very honourable man, for I shall ever call the man so, who gets an estate honestly. Mr. Tobias Hobson was a carrier, and being a man of great abilities and invention, and one that saw when there might good profit arise, though the duller men overlooked it. This ingenious man was the first in this island who let out hackney horses. He lived in Cambridge, and observing

that the scholars rode hard, his manner was to keep a
large stable of horses, with boots, bridles, and whips, to
furnish the gentlemen at once, without going from college to college to borrow as they have done since the
death of this worthy man.   I say, Mr. Hobson kept a
stable of forty good cattle, always ready and fit for travelling ; but when a man came for a horse, he was led into
the stable, where there was great choice, but was *obliged*
to take the first horse which stood next to the stable door :
so that every customer was alike well served according
to his chance, and every horse ridden with the same
justice : from whence it became a proverb, when what
ought to be *your* election was forced upon you, to say,
'Hobson's choice.' This memorable man stands drawn
in fresco, at an inn, (which he used) in Bishopgate-Street,
London, with an hundred pound bag under his arm,
with this inscription upon the said bag :—

'The fruitful mother of a hundred more.'

"Whatever tradesman will try the experiment, and
begin the day after you publish this my discourse, to
treat his customers all alike, and all reasonably and
honestly, I will ensure him the same success.

"I am, Sir, your loving friend,

"HEZEKIAH THRIFT."

I may add, that an artist was desired by the authorities of the town of Cambridge to furnish a large painting
of Mr. Hobson mounted on a powerful horse, and, anxious
to prove, and to publicly establish, their deep sense of

gratitude by a lasting memorial, and one specially worthy
the occasion, they stipulated with the " coming" artist,
that he should previously produce a smaller one for
approbation. The artist, on his first essay, succeeded so
satisfactorily in pleasing the authorities by the proba-
tionary one, that he had not the slightest difficulty in
immediately obtaining an order for a very large portrait
for the town. · By an agreeable and fortunate accident,
the lesser and really original painting has fallen into
my hands. The horses tail in this painting flows to the
ground. The bridle is a snaffle, having a pink rosette
below the ear. The saddle cloth is large, appearing both
before and behind the saddle, and is party-coloured. Mr.
Hobson himself, to my astonishment, wears a wide-awake
hat, and a short cloak tied with ornamental tassels in
front. He rides in top-boots and spurs, the former being
so short as to allow a considerable portion of stockings
to be displayed. The costume of both man and horse
is materially different from that which is in use in this
fanciful age, excepting as regards the present day's similarly Vandalic and unbecoming wide-awake hat, which it
seems was then in use.

In speaking of the dress of Mr. Hobson, I am reminded
of that of the late Mr. Waterton, which did not precisely
accord with the fashionable habiliments now worn. The
Squire pertinaciously adhered, until very recently, to the
blue coat and metal buttons, that is, on extraordinary
occasions. His usual dress when at home, and when
attending to what he conceived his ordinary and necessary

duties, was a brown jacket without skirts—very wide trousers—worsted stockings—and shoes that were always worn so loose on the foot, that he could, by giving his leg a sudden jerk, throw them a considerable distance in any direction he might desire, and which singular exploit he delighted to perform when in happy harmony with all around him.

You would never err far in telling Mr. Waterton that he had "a shocking bad hat;" when he would immediately, with the utmost gravity, reply that a half detached crown or a few air holes were really desirable, as he was ever anxious to keep his head cool, excepting when ornithologising on the highest terrace in the grotto, when and where he delighted to bask in the sun's hottest rays without his hat. His shoes were also often in the same dilapidated condition. I must admit, that the Squire had rather a pride in not only dressing peculiarly, but shabbily, which crotchet, his best and real friends neither admired nor approved.

The supposed and ever-to-be-lamented imaginary proof of independence, by his usually sporting a somewhat eccentric and threadbare attire, pleased and captivated the vulgar, and by this "*aura popularis,*" "breeze of popularity," he was himself unfortunately caught, and permissively wafted on the wings of the multitude, at all events, for the moment. Notwithstanding that I sometimes professedly jeered him, as to the character of his apparently "cast off" ordinary attire, whilst, at the same time I was, to his knowledge, unambiguously and intentionally in good earnest, yet he would jocosely quote Cicero, whose

advice, he said, he always followed, "*Adhibenda est mun-
ditia, non odiosa, neque exquisita nimis, tantum, quæ fugiat
agrestem, ac inhumanam negligentiam.*" "We should
exhibit a certain degree of neatness, not too exquisite nor
affected, and equally remote from rustic and unbecoming
carelessness."

The Squire's kindness of heart was, in reality, the origin
and the primary motive power in first seducing and in
latterly influencing him to somewhat indiscreetly yield to
popular approbation. For many years, as the decline of
life slowly but surely advanced, he could never muster
sufficient resolution to refuse the applications for mob
pic-nic parties of *unlimited* numbers, and occasionally,
even of *dubious* cast, who, being beyond all measure
gratified and exalted by his condescension, vociferously
and fulsomely flattered his open-hearted generosity, consequently, that which was, in earlier life, positively
irksome, became by degrees, and unfortunately, long
before the close of life, a too unlimited pleasure to him.

Whilst disapproving, and occasionally, unnecessarily
harsh censurers, were ready to say, "*Plausu petis clarescere
vulgi,*" "You seek celebrity through the plaudits of the
mob," this single-minded man would, in earlier life, have
supplied his reply very probably from Byron,—

> " I seek not glory from the senseless crowd ;
> Of fancied laurels I shall ne'er be proud :
> Their warmest plaudits I would scarcely prize,
> Their sneers or censures I alike despise."

Mr. Waterton, I am quite sure, persuaded himself that
he was entirely free from any influence exercised by the

multitude; but the precept, "Know thyself," which was
inscribed in letters of gold over the portico of the temple
at Delphi, is extremely difficult of accomplishment, the
more especially, when adulation is the insidious means
used to gain an end :—

> "O popular applause! what heart of man
> Is proof against thy sweet seducing charms?
> The wisest and the best feel urgent need
> Of all their caution in thy gentlest gales."

Mr. Waterton, notwithstanding all his temerity and
absolutely indiscreet recklessness in exposing himself to
personal danger with poisonous snakes, in descending by
means of ropes dangerously precipitous cliffs in quest of
birds' eggs, and by repeatedly and very unnecessarily
jeopardising life in various ways, was after all, specially
watchful in preserving the health of himself and his
household generally. For instance, he was a determined
advocate for throwing open doors and windows to secure
free ventilation, whilst he was at the same time equally
anxious to keep up large fires throughout the house. As
to supplying fuel, sweeping up the fire-side, and having
it always in tidy order, no housemaid could accomplish
these little labours more speedily, nor more artistically,
nor with more pleasure than Mr. Waterton, who really
prided himself on performing a feat of this sort in better
style than it was ever done by the footman.

In 1857, the late Mr. Ainley, Surgeon, of Bingley,
informed me that there was a very singular hatch of the
domestic duck in his neighbourhood, every one of which

had some generated or inbred malformation. I desired my friend to procure the whole hatch for me, in order that I might have them "mounted" as specimens of "sports of nature." Mr. Ainley intrinsically shrewd, and well skilled in ornithology, and whose heart was immersed in natural-history pursuits, returned home immediately, anxiously hoping to lay hold of the whole hatch, but, to his great disappointment and regret, only just in time to secure a solitary male bird, the remaining number having been destroyed, from a vulgar and superstitious idea being entertained in the neighbourhood, that if any thing assuming an unnatural or a monster-like form should be allowed to live, some bad luck would attach to the owner.

On becoming possessed of this bird, which fortunately arrived at my house when the Squire was spending the day with me, it was forthwith carefully examined by Mr. Waterton and myself, and found to be devoid of a particle of web between its toes. My old friend, who had a keen eye for the discovery of any peculiarity, was in an ecstacy of delight, and instantly on this discovery, proposed that it should go on to the lake at Walton Hall, until matured and dressed in its most captivating plumage, when he would then show me a specimen of his handiwork in taxidermy, if we could only harden our hearts to return a verdict of execution by chloroform.

Mr. Waterton became much attached to this bird, which was, on its arrival at Walton Hall, named by him, and consequently by all in the establishment, "Doctor Hobson," a name which it continued to retain

so long as it floated as a living mallard on the lake,
and indeed, singularly enough, for a short period after
its death.

In 1860, a somewhat ludicrous circumstance, connected
with this water-fowl, occurred. A farm servant, hat in
hand and with elongated visage, approached the Squire,
saying, "If you ple-ase Squire, Doctor Hobson is de-ad."
My good old friend, who was always much more careful
of my life than of his own, instantaneously pictured *my*
death and not that of the bird. He urgently interrogated
the hind as to the source of his information, and to the
trustworthiness of his authority for the assertion he had
made ; when the reply was, " I seed him mysen liggin
de-ad, all on a lump at dam he-ad." The mystery, hitherto
inexplicable to my well-wisher, at once vanished, and Mr.
Waterton combining the grave with the gay, immediately
wrote an exceedingly clever and most entertaining letter
of condolence and congratulation to me, in which, in
melancholy strain he regretted the death of this favourite
bird, but rejoiced that his friend was not "liggin all on a
lump at dam he-ad," and added, "I shall, in due time,
'set-up' your namesake, so that no taxidermist in existence shall have just cause to display a fault-finding
physiognomy, and that is saying a good-deal, as we
bird-stuffers are admitted to be a snarling and pugnacious
tribe."

In July, 1860, the Squire, on presenting me with this
beautifully preserved mallard, declared that he felt as
much delighted on the occasion as if he were treading on
enchanted ground. Its attitude is perfect, whilst the

various elevations and depressions of feathers give the appearance of actual life. Within the case is written, by Mr. Waterton's own hand, the following memorandum :—

"THE COMMON DUCK.

In the year 1857, My friend, Doctor Hobson, brought this bird to Walton Hall, where it lived over two years, and then died. It was hatched without any appearance whatever of web in its feet.

"CHARLES WATERTON.

"*Walton Hall, July* 8, 1860."

I may add, that one duck in this extraordinary brood was hatched with its head reversed, having its bill as regards its horizontal position, appearing and indeed actually situated immediately above its tail, so that when food was placed on the ground, behind its tail, this duck always had to seize it by turning a somersault.

This bird inherited doubly interesting peculiarities,—one specially arising from its being individually abnormal as regarded its deficiency of the ordinarily decussating webs between the toes, universally assumed to furnish a mechanism to materially aid propelling power in the act of swimming, and yet, in this instance no appreciable difference in apparent power nor in rapidity of motion from its companions was discernible when gliding at an ordinary rate along the lake, nor even when breasting and buffeting the waves on a tempestuous day. The other peculiarity is its being one of a hatch of seven or eight, all of which unmistakeably betrayed some singular physical malformation.

A collection so numerous of defective formation from even various sources would constitute an interesting one, but such an assemblage from one hatch only would have engaged the deep interest of all naturalists, and I regret beyond measure my inability to have obtained a phenomenon so rare and yet so nearly within my reach.

The Squire, very much to the regret of his most intimate friends, at all times positively delighted in wearing " a shocking bad hat," and also in never allowing it to be brushed. On one occasion, when dining with me, my servant had previously had private orders to carefully sponge the Squire's hat with very weak vinegar and water whilst he was at dinner, and to then thoroughly brush it until its outward aspect had undergone an entire change, in my opinion for the better. When about to return home, Mr. Waterton took up his hat in the entrance-passage many times and as often put it down again, in evident doubt, distrust, and apparent distress,— at last observing, under a countenance of some irritation, and in a tone of indubitable displeasure, " Now this is really too bad; some one has taken away my hat, leaving in its place a Miss Nancy looking concern, which none but some fashionable Tom Fool would put on his head." I saw that the Squire was becoming annoyed, " that the shoe pinched," and therefore, told him that the hat was really his own, but that I had desired it to be brushed up a little, and to convince him, pointed out the letters, C. W., written by himself in the interior of the hat. He immediately remarked, " Doctor Hobson, if any other person had taken such a liberty with my hat I should never have forgiven him, and I hope you will never do so again, as you have completely ruined my long-worn and favourite beaver."

From this very moment he calmed down again, his countenance changed from the grave to the gay, and, in genuine amnesty, he ever afterwards allowed me to joke him on the once tender and susceptible subject though never forgetting to wind up with an half in earnest, and half in jest rebuke, adding, "Well but after all, you really did ruin my head-gear for all useful purposes, as I never could wear it with either pleasure or satisfaction afterwards, until it had lapsed, in some measure into its former unaspiring condition, by getting rid of that sleek-looking surface which gave me such a priggish appearance."

I have more than once alluded to Mr. Waterton's natural kindness of heart, and this amiable trait of character, I may add, was daily manifested by having his capacious pockets constantly well filled with scraps of bread, for distribution to all living creatures that would eat this material during his daily perigrinations from morning to night, in the neighbourhood of the mansion and the farm buildings. His admirers and followers, therefore in this numerous class of recipients, for such he never failed to secure, were familiarly friendly with him, pecking "the staff of life" from his hand without fear, and without any apparent suspicion of its being a deceitful decoy, which friendly confidence, manifested by the feathered tribe, always delighted him.

The Squire had a numerous appointment of cats about the farm buildings, which were diligently and daily attended to. When fish was in requisition, he would carefully collect, in an old newspaper, after dinner, all scraps of fish and their bones, and take them himself to the saddle-room, and would bruise the hard relics gathered from the table with a tolerably heavy hammer, by which operation the bones were so softened as to be masticated without difficulty, swallowed without danger, and devoured evidently with an insatiable relish, by the whole feline retinue, which he could at any time assemble at the saddle-room, by calling out somewhat loudly, " My Pretty." In the evening, Mr Waterton generally regaled his favourites with new milk direct from the cow, so that the cats were well cared for, and, being thus liberally fed at home, there was less temptation for them to sneak into the grounds in quest of a leveret or of a young pheasant or partridge.

On asking the Squire if the cats would not hunt better if he would provide less luxuriously for them ? he replied " you are not the first person who has fallen into that error. Remember that it is the cats special nature to hunt vermin altogether independently of satisfying hunger. Such a notion as you have suggested is applicable to the animal which kills and immediately devours, whilst the cat is impregnated with an instinct which prompts her to hunt for pleasure. Observe her pounce upon a rat or a mouse with all her energy, exerting herself to the utmost of her physical power as if implacable in order to secure her prey, but the moment it is within her gripe, you will see her countenance relax from the previously apparent animosity with which she clutched her victim. Nay, she seems to simply preserve and tenderly retain her hold until in a little while she alternately liberates and retakes it for her future amusement."

I thanked Mr. Waterton for his information, and with a mischievous intention to puzzle him observed with a grave countenance, how is it that the cat, which is not a ruminant, and has also canine teeth and incisors, yet seems to take so little pains to grind her food by mastication? when he replied, "how can she *grind* when she has no lateral motion in the lower jaw? adding, you have not caught a weasel asleep, although I am pretty sure that you had set that down as an achievement."

His pointers, numbering three or four, very much to my surprise, were left entirely to the care of the keeper, as, during the protracted period of my friendship with Mr. Waterton, I never knew him pay the least attention to them, nor manifest any special care about them, having laid aside the gun a long time before his death.

If he had not had entire confidence in the humane attentions of his keeper in the kennel department, he would have, I doubt not, supervised their apartments and have, if necessary, personally administered to their comfort.

Many years previously to Mr. Waterton's death, when on one occasion, we were sitting alone in the grotto, admiring his favourites flitting around us from spray to spray, and calmly discussing their habits, or musing on their varied character of life, the Squire was apparently in the genuine enjoyment of his nature. In the midst however of our pleasures, and without a single preliminary remark as a harbinger of his hitherto hidden woes, his countenance suddenly changed its aspect, from apparent cheerfulness to one of unusual gravity, gradually increasing to an intensity of despair. Recovering quickly again from this smothered mental distress, he could no longer refrain from open-hearted admissions.

He then introduced and freely indulged in cool and calculating speculations as to the ultimate fate of his vast and varied handiwork. In general terms, he observed, that the diversified assemblage of all his labours might be moonshine—a flash in the pan—a Will-o'-the-wisp—a merely ephemeral gathering together of the productions of nature, the result of his unceasing and unwearied labours.

In thus giving vent to his grief, when tears rolled down his furrowed cheeks, and when truly "wearing the willow," he suddenly roused from his depressed condition, and with a smile, expressed a hope that the work of his hands might yet be a spark from which, at some future period, a flood of light, by numerously radiating powers, might illuminate another generation of the scientific of their day, adding I do believe, even if I were aware that the whole of my collection, which has taken me a lifetime to procure and put in order, should be consumed by fire to-morrow, I should still set to work again in good earnest, perseveringly and resolutely continuing to pursue that aristocratic (?) craft, which has always appeared to me to be my natural vocation; not I admit, with the same pleasurable feeling, unless I could be satis‐fied and thoroughly convinced that my labours had a fair chance to benefit and instruct a future generation."

I wish to be understood from what I have stated as now speaking of the time *to come*, when *it* will be spoken of as the time gone by, just as the modern architect does when he admits the cementing superiority of the ancient thin mortar grout, compared with that of the present age—as the modern painter is wont to do, who candidly acknowledges the superiority of certain com‐binations of colours prepared by the ancients, as com‐pared with those used by artists of the existing age, acknowledging and deeply lamenting the loss which all their ingenuity and all their scientific attainments can neither reproduce nor so efficiently replace.

Although during our long familiar intercourse and cordial friendship, we now and then had occasion to intro‐duce private and not always agreeable affairs, necessarily connected with an appeal to the finer feelings, affections, and passions generally, sufficient to tempt the lachrymal gland to shed its briny and crystal drops, yet on no pre‐vious occasion, did I ever see the Squire shed a tear.

When we were about to leave the grotto, and return to the house, I quietly remarked, " Where the treasure is, there will the heart be also." The Squire immediately rejoined, "You never quoted a more true proverb, nor, probably one more *apropos;* I do delight in natural history, and especially in a bit of bird-stuffing."

With a heart acutely sensitive—by nature delicately

s

susceptible of the tenderest and most refined feelings
and impressions, and ever brimful of sympathy and
unbounded affection for his friends, or even for the
stranger in difficulty or distress—how singular that I
should never see Mr. Waterton give vent to his feelings
by a single tear, until the occurrence I have just named.

It seemed to me, that in order to reduce the Squire
to a positively lachrymose condition, there was a something wanting beyond simple grief—that he must be
roused by some secretly cherished suspicion betraying
a want of confidence in the future, or by some mortifica-
tion mixed up and amalgamated with his favourite natural-
history labours.

Mr. Waterton's great anxiety manifested on all occasions, appeared to me not only that he should lead a
spotless and untarnished life among his fellow men in
all sublunary matters, but that he should be distinguished for his high attainments, in those pursuits to
which he had been so ardently and faithfully attached
from infancy, and that his memory in after ages should
be signally distinguished by posterity with a feeling that
he had at least done something worthy of a grateful
recollection from the man of science and the philosopher
of a future generation.

For many years Mr. Waterton entertained an unconquerable horror of being the subject of an artist, consequently,
it was only by a carefully preconcerted manœuvre arranged
between the artist and myself, of which the Squire was
entirely ignorant, that we succeeded in obtaining even

MR. WATERTON AND THE AUTHOR PHOTOGRAPHED BENEATH THE
LOMBARDY POPLAR.

the present unsatisfactory apology for the man. In accomplishing this I had to feign fatigue, and proposed to refresh myself by resting a while on the grass, and managing, by a little persuasion, to coax Mr. Waterton to adopt a similar course, so that he might be in such a position that it was impossible for him to see the artist or the *camera*. If he had caught the slightest glimpse of either one or the other, he would have bolted instantaneously,—hence the view of the back only. Those however, who were intimately acquainted with the Squire, during the last few years of his life, will have no difficulty whatever in immediately recognising the man, even from the present imperfect illustration, although the face is not visible.

Of course, I gladly sacrificed my own photograph, from its being necessary that I should continually talk to my companion, in order to divert his attention from the artist, and endeavour to keep him from any movement if possible to do so, which was very difficult with a man having naturally so active a mind. In this photographic view of our chief subject, without any previous intention the lens fortunately caught a portion of the well-known Lombardy poplar, which had been twice so dreadfully mutilated by lightning.

> .   .   .   "As when heaven's fire
> Hath scathed the forest oaks."

On telling the Squire that I believed we had been the chosen objects for the *camera*, he instantly assumed an erect attitude, and smilingly observed, "They might succeed in securing your face, but it was utterly impossible they could catch mine, as I had my back to them, and to that they are welcome," after which remark he made no further allusion to the subject, of which I was very glad, as I was a little fearful that the march we had stolen upon him, we hoped without suspicion, might have been a source of annoyance and have ruffled his temper.

In fact we were fairly foiled in our intentions. My idea was to have had Mr. Waterton standing alone at the base of a trée looking up and into it as if bird-nesting, the province and position of a naturalist, and an attitude in which I had frequently seen him, but the unyielding and inexorable fates were against us.

It was always very difficult to get to the blind side of the Squire, and I apprehend that he entertained an opinion that we were contemplating some mischief of this nature, as he would never remain a moment in one place until he was reclining on the ground and had his back to the region of the artists.

I then named a wish to photograph "John Bull and the National Debt" which was in the extension-stair-case, as I observed that in my opinion, it would be an interesting object in the forthcoming little volume. He appeared delighted with the proposition, and said, he thought the "nondescript" and the "Church Reformation case" also would photograph well, and in high glee brought them down stairs for that purpose himself. I suspected that his expression of countenance, which was generally com-municative of future events to the bystander, indicated amicable hostilities, betraying an inward intention to have a sly fillip against the Protestant Church, and so it was. The "Reformation case," he observed in great hilarity, and with an intentionally caustic smile on his countenance, "would be specially gratifying, and absolutely a *bonne-bouche* to those professing religious sentiments as 'by law established.'" These subjects were attempted to be photographed, but that indispensible essentiality daylight had vanished, or at least, so far deserted us that the "Reformation case" was a complete failure, whilst the "nondescript" was really excellent.

By many, it will be recollected that the "nondescript" was the frontispiece in an early work of Mr. Waterton's, a publication which, at that time, 1825, was read with great avidity, not merely from its being the production of so original and singularly amusing a writer, but because it contained a vast fund of charmingly interesting matter as well as an abundance of useful and hitherto absolutely unknown information, whilst it also contributed so materially and vitally to practical natural-history.

It was generally supposed, indeed by some freely and very positively asserted, that the "nondescript" which is assuredly an extraordinary looking object, was modelled with a view of representing by similarity of face, a certain eminent nobleman, possessing at that period the highest honour of the long robe, but who was not in very special favour with the South "American wanderer."

On my putting the question, as to whether there was any truth in this almost general belief, adding, with a view to squeeze a little information out of my old friend (but who was wide awake) that I thought there certainly was a likeness that many would recognise, but that so far as I recollected of the nobleman's face and of that of the " nondescript," they were not as had been stated regarding the similarity of Cæsar and Pompey, " whose faces were said to be remarkably similar, particularly Pompey's ; "— the Squire's only appearance of a reply for a little time was simply a smile, but having gathered his thoughts together, he gravely observed, " ' *Si poema loquens pictura est, pictura tacitum poema debet esse* ' * being muzzled, on this special question, you must patiently bear with my taciturnity, and let those who think the cap fits put it on."

For upwards of fifty years Mr. Waterton entertained a firm conviction that hydrophobia was under the remedial influence of the careful and judicious agency of the Woorali poison. He was several times sent for to distant cases, and two or three times actually proceeded to the residence of the patient for the purpose of using the Woorali, but in every instance the cases had succumbed, to this fearful malady before his arrival. On one occasion on reaching Nottingham, fully prepared to test the efficacy of the Woorali his patient had just expired, it was therefore arranged by the " old Squire " and the medical staff at the General Hospital to experiment upon a donkey. The well-known eminent surgeon Mr. Higginbottom, was one of the hospital surgeons and so delighted Mr. Waterton that they became cordial friends, of whom indeed I have frequently heard the Squire speak with great respect.

Mr. Higginbottom informed me that they then poisoned a donkey with the Woorali, producing apparent death, but

* " If a poem be a speaking picture, a picture ought to be a silent poem."

on making an incision into the windpike, and causing artificial respiration, the donkey got upon its legs and the Squire mounted and rode it round the room.

This donkey was henceforth named Woorali and lived for many years on the large grass-plot attached to the General Hospital.

Mr. Higginbottom, it is well-known has been for very many years remarkable for leading and persevering in an abstemious life, and being now I believe in his seventy ninth year, we may reasonably conclude that he has derived benefit from the plan which he has adopted. About nine years ago however, this gentleman was completely check-mated by the Squire as regarded the adoption of abstinence.

These gentlemen accidentally met in town when the temperate and abstaining surgeon asked Mr. Waterton where he had dined? Dined? Responded the Squire, no where. I take a bun and a glass of cold water when I am hungry.

In a letter to his friend at Nottingham, in 1863, Mr. Waterton says, " I am now four score and one year and three months old, and I can stand upon the upper branches of a tree, or upon the top of a high wall without fear of falling. I rise every morning winter and summer at half-past three o'clock. I do not even know the taste of wine, nor of any spirituous liquor, and sixty-seven years have now passed over my head since I drank a glass of beer, and I have passed twenty years off and on in the pestilential swamps of the tropics. During this period I have largely and repeatedly depleted by venesection."

A gentleman recently says "an amusing anecdote is reported as follows of our chief natural-historian, some friends of mine were at a German watering-place and when discoursing together, a tall and interesting looking person came up to them and said, ' I do not wish to pick a quarrel nor to pick your pockets, but I should like to be allowed to join your conversation.' 'Certainly,' replied these gentlemen, 'we were talking of natural history.' 'Oh,' rejoined the stranger, 'natural history is a favourite subject of mine. Indeed, I suppose I am the only person who has ridden an alligator.' 'No sir,' replied my friends, 'Mr. Waterton has done the same thing.' 'Mr. Waterton !' said the stranger, 'you surely do not believe what that old humbug says.' 'I should believe every thing Mr. Waterton says,' was the universal rejoinder. 'Notwithstanding what you say,' persisted the stranger 'I still believe that I am the only person who has ridden an alligator.' 'Then sir, we presume,' observed my friends, 'you are Mr. Waterton.' They were right, and a most agreeable companion they found in the Squire of Walton Hall."

When that deservedly popular and, taking into consideration the age in which the book was written, I may add scientific work the "South American Wanderings," first made its public appearance in 1825, various were the murmuring surmises as to Mr. Waterton's wanton and inhuman cruelty, in having been regardless either of torturing animal or of sacrificing human life in order to gain his own ends in natural history attainments.

In addition to what was useful and instructive, the

"THE NONDESCRIPT," IN THE EXTENSION STAIRCASE AT WALTON HALL.

"Wanderings" furnished, in consequence of the introduction of the "nondescript," a sensational subject of so novel and exciting a character that it afforded an unbounded amount of gossip of that peculiar type which was freely indulged in by a certain class in the surrounding district,—a genus of that special kind of humanity by the way, which it may be safely admitted, is being continually diminished in its numbers in each succeeding age and generation. These parties declared themselves to be so forbearing and benevolently intentioned, as to generously take charge of the supposed misdeeds of their neighbours, although such high-minded disinterestedness might occasionally sacrifice the opportunity of attending to and correcting their own. Into such merciful hands, on the issue of that publication, was the Squire of Walton Hall tenderly committed.

Suspicions of the gravest and most diabolical character were currently circulated, accompanied by dubious expressions, dismally long faces, and awfully tremulous shaking of the head, evidently foreboding a supposition of something sad in the sequel.

These vile insinuations and widely disseminated undercurrents rapidly gained ground, and lost nothing by their iterated repetition, verifying and thoroughly confirming the predication of the greatest of the Roman poets :—

> " *Fama, malum quo non aliud velocius ullum,*
> *Mobilitate viget, viresque acquirit eundo.*"

"Rumour, than which no pest is more swift, increases by motion, and gains strength as she goes.

It was whispered that the Squire had, when in the
'back woods" in South America, shot a native human
being, and actually "mounted" his head and a portion
of his bust after the fashion of his "setting up" ordinary
natural history specimens, and placed him in the grand
staircase at Walton Hall, having bribed the custom-house
officers to secure his safe transition through the grasping clutches of these vigilant guardians of the revenue.

Many were the severe and absolutely uncompromising
remarks and not a few nauseating aspersions, pointed at Mr.
Waterton, in which certain parties indulged who professed to be in the secret, and who sapiently hinted
that an inquest ought to be held on the "mounted
bust," actually exposed in the Walton Hall Museum, in
order that the Squire might be brought to condign
punishment "and no mistake."

Malicious gnashing of the teeth, from *professing* friends,
was currently indulged on the one hand, whilst wringing
of the hands and affectionate lamentations were gravely
deplored on the other, in the most heart-felt regret, for
"the poor Squire's unfortunate and pitiable position" in
which it was reported he had so indiscreetly placed
himself, and so recklessly played the part of the "dare-
devil," — at least, a liberal amount of the surrounding
residents for many miles had made up their minds to
such an absurd belief, and continued to resolutely maintain
that opinion for a certain period.

Time however, without any very lengthened interval,
convinced these deluded and would-be wise instigators of
intended mischief, that this bust was simply modelled

from the skin of the head and bust of a monkey, and that
Mr. Waterton had not criminally dyed his hands in the
blood of a human being.   And it is my firm impression,
that the Squire never entertained the slightest intention
that this unique work of art should represent by physi-
ognomical similarity, any particular individual whatever.
Indeed, Mr. Waterton had too much natural amiability of
disposition—too much cultivated gentlemanly feeling, and
was in possession of too great an amount of worldly policy,
to be guilty of so flagrant and uncalled-for a voluntary
and unprovoked sarcasm, or to commit himself to the
possibility of a glaringly deserved rebuke from the lynx-
eyed public.   The Squire had been at Corinth,—he was far
too wide awake to be caught napping in connection with
a subject so fertile in the possibility of mischief.   In the
execution of this singularly conceived work of art there was
fine scope for a display of the talent in which the Squire
so signally excelled.

In addition to his innate partiality for the substitution
of the pleasing and cheering resemblance of life for the
grim visage of death, he had in time gone by, carefully
studied the muscular anatomy of the face as an agreeable
recreation, which was afterwards indefatigably followed
up by bestowing considerable attention to the works of
Lavater.

There was an union of a variety of knowledge which
enabled Mr. Waterton to produce a prodigy in apparent
nature and when I observed, "How could you dream of
such an idea as to turn the monkey into man?"   He replied
"I fear you do not indulge in the scientific and progressive

works of the day.   Are you not aware that it is the present
fashionable theory that monkeys are shortly to step into
our shoes ?   I have merely foreshadowed future ages or
signalised the coming event, by giving to the brute a
human formation of face, and to this face an expression of
intellectuality, for which I dare say there are in the
medley of humanity a few here and there who would
consider that a fair exchange would be no robbery."

In consequence of some misrepresentation for admission to the Park at Walton Hall, the Squire wrote the
following letter to me :—

"My dear Sir,
"I saw the last swallow on the 16th October.   By the
way, 'if you admit Irishisms,' it was a house-martin.   The
last ring-dove cooed on the 17th.   Two gulls have been
here all day.   Can we have a stronger proof of an early
winter ?
"Now, as I am aware that application may be made
to you to see my lions, it being known that we are such
intimate friends, I will here chalk out a line which will
save you future trouble.
"When you wish your friends (supposing them to be
personally unknown to us) to see the staircase, you may
be quite certain that they may have their fling here from
nine in the morning until noon, and from two in the
afternoon until the light fails, Saturdays always excepted,
as on that day, the whole house is under the housemaid's
scrubbing brush.

"If any party of your friends want a pic-nic, the building at the grotto will be at their disposal the entire day, and they will have crockery, kettles, &c., from the Hall. They need not send their horses to the village, as I have such a superabundant store of hay, the little they eat will never be missed. The woman at the lodges, for the trifling gratuity of a shilling will prepare their tea, and clean all up the following morning.

"How delighted I am to hear that you have enjoyed your trip into the Arctic regions. I have fancied I was getting too fat, therefore have come down to a breakfast cup of very very weak tea without milk, and a bit of dry bread twice a day. "This diet has made me so elastic, that I am out all day pruning trees.

"Nothing new, excepting that the ladies' maid, having jilted her first lover, was herself jilted by a second, and has again succeeded in pacifying the first, who was very spooney, and now, they are seen billing and cooing at every hedge-corner when opportunity serves them. Doubtless the parson will soon be needed.

"M——— is also dead. Poor good priests. They are now enjoying their reward in glory. They are gone to where sin is never seen, and where sorrow is unknown. They have nobly done their duty, and they cared not for life on earth when that duty was to be performed. Would that my own departure from this "valley of tears" could be as happy as theirs has been.

"Are there no rosebuds among your feminine friends who would like to see the staircase and enjoy a chop of Wakefield mutton? I do long to pay you a visit to lessen the contents of your larder, but in Ember week, we have three whole days of orthodox black fast, and next week comes *Corpus Christi*, a festival of the Church of England, kept on the first Thursday after Trinity Sunday, in honour of the Eucharist, one of the greatest festivals in Christendom.

"It was reported you were dead. I always had a positive aversion to wear mourning, but if you should die before me, I swear by the Hades of Satan and Hippocrates that if you do deprive us of your services, we are so infatuated with you, that I will put on a black suit, aye, and wear it a whole year and a day, and be in sackcloth and ashes during that period.

"Should you have a leisure day to spare, be it known that the Pope, (God bless him in his sorrows) will allow us to offer you a chop on Sundays, Tuesdays, and Thursdays.

"When I went to Aix-la-Chapelle I found it choke-full of visitors from all the surrounding district. They had assembled at that ancient town for the Septennial exhibition of the relics so nearly connected with man's redemption. I have just seen an interesting letter from Rome, giving an account of the miraculous and instantaneous cure of Lord ———'s son in that city, by the prayers of the martyr-nun of Minx.

"I observe what you say about the chaffinch. You will hear its last warble on the 15th of July, and it will not sing again until the second week in February.

"Very sincerely,

"CHARLES WATERTON."

CHAPTER IX.

On one occasion, immediately before Mr. Waterton's return from Aix-la-Chapelle, which place he usually visited yearly, and where he had been staying for a considerable period, he addressed the following Letter to me :—

"My dear Sir,
'*Cernite sim qualis; qui modo qualis eram.*' *

"I may now say to myself—

"*Lusisti satis, edisti satis, atque bibisti,
Tempus abire tibi est.*"†

Eating, drinking, and lounging, are so much in vogue here that there is no spare time for ornithology. The swifts left us a few days ago, and have probably reached their southern destination. You see they pretty nearly keep time with those in England, — Buzzards, owls, magpies, carrion-crows, and ravens are not wantonly destroyed here, as in England, by our rascally game-keepers. I can therefore, always have a peep at my favourites by going a couple of miles out of the town.

"Our Queen passed through here a few days since, but I did not get a look at her sacred Majesty.

* "Behold what I am, and what I was but a little while ago."

†"Thou hast trifled enough, has eaten and drunk enough,
It is time for thee to depart."

" Your last kind Letter (without date by the way, never mind, it's all one in the long run,) gave us great amusement, pleasure, and satisfaction. I had written to you once previously, since we became vagabonds, but as you made no mention of it, I concluded that my Letter got strangled on its way to Leeds. Bearing in mind the old saying, ' *Qui amat periculum, peribit in illo,*'* we have given up the idea of visiting places where there is '*plurima mortis imago,*'† and shall quietly bend our returning steps to the well-known land of pride, heresy, and smoke.

" I here see fat and wealthy old sinners, a short time ago apparently bursting with beef and pudding, walking about now without assistance. They arrived with crutches, then hobbled in the course of a few weeks with two sticks, then with one stick, then with none at all.

" We shall return by Grenoble. In the vicinity of that ancient town is the famous Salette, for ever memorable on account of the miraculous apparition of the blessed Virgin to the two shepherd children. We shall see all the wonders there,—and, on our return, you shall have a report of the result from my own mouth.

" The Doctors here seem to be a compound of homœopathists and non-bleeders. I think I shall write an essay on blood-bleeding, what say you ?—please let

---

* " He who loves danger will perish in it."

† " Death in full many a form."

me have your opinion; and if you would do penance,
by giving me a few hours of your personal assistance,
you would do a charitable deed, and if you were not
one of the new faith, I would pray for your soul in
purgatory, in case you go first, for depend upon it, our
souls will have vast difficulty in going to heaven in a
straight line. '*Hæe scripsi non otii abundantia, sed
amoris erga te.*'*

" Sincerely,

" CHARLES WATERTON."

On Mr. Waterton's return from Aix-la-Chapelle he
always discoursed freely on the healing virtues of its
"wonderful springs," and also as to its superiority of
regulations in police jurisdictions as compared with
those in England. We must not however, forget that
his habit of travelling and of roaming in the new
world in early life, where he had abundance of opportunities of gratifying his natural-history tastes, and of
procuring in distant regions many things which he
could not obtain in England, materially biassed and
probably unduly warped his immediate impressions and
future sentiments in every point of view.

It is not indeed surprising that a man, entertaining
somewhat extravagant views on subjects appertaining to
religion, should occasionally very much enjoy a holyday
residence in a city, whose Roman Catholic inhabitants
numbered nine-tenths of the whole population, and a

* "I have written this, not from having an abundance of leisure, but of
love for you."

city also rich in historical associations, and especially of a character fascinating to the inclinations of the Squire.

Mr. Waterton delighted to describe the beautiful shrubberies and tastefully laid out walks in the ruins of the outer ramparts, the splendid Cathedral and its sacristy, sanctified and more sacred by its containing some of the relics and remains of Charlemagne, also its monasteries, and vast and valuable library, in a city where it is said all languages are spoken.

The Squire was always anxious to be at Aix-la-Chapelle during the Septennial exhibition of the relics of Charlemagne, which period of solemn display occupied a fortnight in July, when an immense concourse of strangers are invariably drawn to the city. In praising much connected with this demonstration and the inhabitants themselves, he never forgot to signally condemn the widespread practice of gambling, nor to deeply lament its being sanctioned by government.

" Waterton's Wanderings," having antecedently been extensively read abroad, procured for him personally, a distinguished position in natural-history attainments, which induced strangers to look upon him as being so entirely out of the ordinary class of men, that eulogistic expressions and acts indicating regard and admiration, were continually afloat in society of the highest grade.

Under so animating a host of approbationary evidence on all sides, a man must be almost more than mortal who could turn a deaf ear to such charms ; hence the Squire's love for another country over his own is neither surprising nor unpardonable. The heaviest accusation of this character could but charge him with the commission of a venial error, even if it be one. Mr. Waterton delighted to return by Grenoble, the first town of importance that opened its gates to Napoleon on his leaving Elba, because there was a museum containing some good specimens of natural-history, and very probably Salette being in the immediate neighbourhood might be another alluring reason, as well as the very splendid library in this town.

Aix-la-Chapelle was a wonderfully favourite resort of the Squire's. I believe that the opportunity of seeing a variety of birds of prey, on which he could gaze with extreme pleasure, constituted one of the principal inducements why Mr. Waterton annually turned his head in that direction.

On the subject of the "*famous Salette*," he of course, on his return, largely expatiated, and insisted on my chiming in with him to the full extent of his own self-conviction. He was amazed how I could be so obtuse and bigoted as not to be, at once proselytised, expressing the greatest surprise that I was so perverse and hoodwinked as not to go along with him even in his "tolerant belief."

After earnestly expostulating with me, " I have," he observed, " often heard it said, that none are so deaf as those who won't hear, but I can bear testimony that none are so blind as those who won't see." Although we were both emphatic in our disputation, yet our controversy was invariably maintained with such a thorough conviction of the sincerity of a sacred veneration for the cause we espoused, that a word in anger never escaped the lips of either of us. I entertain not a shadow of a doubt but that the Squire indulged to the fullest extent, in the firm belief of the appearance of the apparition of the blessed Virgin to the two shepherd children; and, that no argument, however sound or lucidly expressed and convincing to Protestants, nor any amount of persuasive powers, however bewitchingly used, could have created an atom of doubt or disbelief in his mind.

The Squire's pretensions "to write an essay on bloodletting," could not, of course under any circumstances, be seriously entertained for a single moment, but the difficulty I had to conquer was to convince him that such was the fact. When Mr. Waterton had once conceived an idea, which he unfortunately now and then did without due consideration, and being naturally somewhat impatient under expressions of non-coincidence, it was not an easy matter nor a pleasant one either, to put an agreeable as well as an efficient break on the rapid current of his hastily arranged intentions or predetermination, without the infliction of momentary displeasure, or even an occasional approximation to offence.

In this instance however, by a wholesome distribution of oil on the troubled waters, and by a gentle and persuasive hint that an essay on such a subject was neither his business nor his *forte*, and that professional etiquette, which was generally very unyielding, would taboo my treating any question of such a nature in unison with a

non-professional man, I escaped without a scratch of disapprobation or of censure. The only observation he ever
made on the subject being, "So you decline being joint
author, although I doubt not that by such a union we
might save many valuable lives. Your reasons," he further
observed, "are probably good, at all events they are
decisive, and I knock under."

The Squire certainly had, in *propria persona*, practically experienced the effect of venesection in a wholesale
degree, but never by dribblets, and had undoubtedly, to
my knowledge, frequently derived very great advantage
from it; but Mr. Waterton was naturally of so sanguine
a temperament, that the benefit he gained on many
occasions when suffering acute pain, led him to believe
that bleeding was a remedy in *all* cases, and thus he
deprived his judgment of maintaining an unbiassed value,
which it would have assuredly secured in a less confident
and a more coolly discriminating man.

Indeed, it cannot be denied that to a certain extent
—occasionally to a very unreasonable, and not unfrequently to a prejudicial one,—this failing, partaking so
largely of pure empiricism, is and has been in all ages,
too apt to prevail, even in the legitimately constituted
healing art.

For instance, when any agent may have, in a thera-
peutic sense, beneficially exercised its curative influence,
so as to afford the medical man an unusual and gratifying
amount of satisfaction, and now and then have actually
surpassed his most hopeful and confident expectations,
an impression and an unconquerable tendency are engend-

ered, and generally so thoroughly established in its favour, as to render it exceedingly difficult to control his resorting to it too promiscuously—immoderately, or beyond rational bounds—hence the failure of many valuable and powerful agents, simply from their misapplication, and hence the sinking into unmerited neglect of what would be inestimable remedies if judiciously administered.

Mr. Waterton was willing to acknowledge that he himself was not entirely free from some ingenerate characteristics, although probably not without their utility which certain parties thought fit to designate specialities, and even in his presence to stigmatise as eccentricities. This was too much for the Squire to patiently accept and endure; and therefore, after calmly contending that what they were pleased to call eccentricities were few and trifling, he somewhat pungently observed that "a moiety of the offences at which they were carping, would not be noticed by any who had cut their wise teeth. The present age," he remarked, "was fertile in precocious and inexperienced popinjays, who officiously interfered by attempting to teach others, but who certainly ought to be in the learning and not in the teaching class." This was a knock-down blow for the intruding fault-finders, who had that moment indiscreetly indulged in quizzing what they called the Squire's eccentricity, and unfortunately in the hearing of his coachman, simply because he had fixed a notice in the saddle-room to prevent smoking there, but what was mortifying to Mr. Waterton and ungentlemanly on the part of the strangers, was the indulging in personal remarks in the presence of his coachman. As the Squire frequently fed his cats there, he found the

smoke disagreeable to him, and he also invariably deprecated the use of ignited tobacco in the immediate
contiguity of all combustible matter.

The nut which Mr. Waterton had furnished to be cracked
by the parties to whom I have just alluded was not a
sweet one, and the gentlemen in due time acknowledged
their error by a singular mode of apology. They sent the
Squire a bird " in the flesh," rare in the district, along
with the following somewhat anomalous note :—

" Messrs. B—— and N—— send for Mr. Waterton's
acceptance, a bird, they believe, never previously killed in
Yorkshire, in exchange for their insolent remarks in the
saddle-room at Walton Hall on the ——inst., which they
wish to retract, and sincerely apologise for an indiscretion
which they are thankful to have had efficiently corrected."

I can well conceive that the Squire's manner, and expression of countenance, which on such occasions, were
any thing but agreeable, would be even more caustic than
his sentiments declared on the occasion of those gentlemen's uncalled-for and officious interference, because,
smoking was an accomplishment of all others, for which
he had no sympathy. Passing strange, however, as it
may and certainly did appear to all at the time, the
Squire one cold winter's night, on my leaving the house
for a thirteen miles drive, actually stood at the door with
a burning spell in his hand, to light a cigar for me, in
order as he observed, "to keep out the cold," which kind
offer had no similar antecedent at Walton Hall, but notwithstanding this, I had the moral courage to gratefully
decline the well intentioned overture on the part of my
friend who himself so disapproved the practice.

Although the Squire's great abhorrence of the habit of smoking might be mixed up with a considerable amount of prejudice in opposition to what he delighted in calling "that disgusting habit," yet his reasons I am induced to believe, were in some measure judiciously grounded on the universally admitted danger of its possibly setting fire to valuable property, frequently involving the loss of life from accident or carelessness, or from its being so constantly used by the free drinker, whose wits, when "wine is in," are sure to be "out."

I readily and cheerfully admit that smoking and drinking are not invariably, nor yet uniformly twin sisters, and further acknowledge, that they are but seldom, if ever so closely associated in the upper classes whilst it cannot be denied, that in the lower ranks of life, this double - relation - tendency or reciprocate affinity, is so unequivocally marked with apparently kindred feelings, that each habit seems to be a counterpart of the other·

In Mr. Waterton's early life and education, smoking was not known, much less recognised in good society ; indeed· the perniciously soothing weed, in any form for that purpose, was not tolerated in his age excepting among the humble grades. Any man who would have dared to infringe on the then usual and ordinary rules of good breeding, by venturing to smoke in the street, which was deemed an unpardonable amount of assurance, would have been instantaneously sent to Coventry. Such were the then ordinary usages in all stations above mediocrity.

Impressions imbibed in early years, by naturally self-opinionative temperaments, have hitherto been invariably, and I believe, correctly acknowledged to increase in ascendancy as life advances, until at length, they amount to an undeviating conviction that their accuracy is infallible, and undoubtedly, the old Squire was some years before his death, an unflinching instance of the character now described.

There is however, in the present age, one very marked feature, and a fearfully growing one in the use of tobacco, in a banefully depraved direction, which was frequently dwelt upon and bitterly lamented by my old friend. This demoralising habit was even more repugnant to his feelings than any to which I have hitherto made reference. I allude especially to the abominable practice of smoking, now almost universally had recourse to by mere children. No sooner has some stripling been divested of his feminine garb, than he is seen deliberately smoking his short pipe in the public streets. Wrapped up in the vain-glorious supposition and affectation of manliness, he does not attempt to conceal his disgusting transgression, nay on the contrary, he openly and exultingly displays his mal-practice, assuming and personating in miniature the man of importance.

If an immoderate use of tobacco has a prejudicial influence over the adult, whose matured organs have a greater antagonistic resistance and corrective power as antidotes, than what are possessed by immature organs,— we need not a Solomon to reveal to us the sure and fatal consequences which will be ultimately entailed on the present as well as on a future generation.

This publicly and vauntingly displayed curse is on all

sides acknowledged as a reality; and a universal censure
should be indiscriminately and indignantly lavished on
parents for their neglecting to restrain so pernicious a
habit. A moment's reflection however, furnishes a reply
difficult of contradiction. How can a parent, with a pipe
in his own mouth, admonish his child who is diligently
walking in the footsteps of his father?

If Satan should be deputed to correct sin, the reproof
would be administered with a bad grace, and with little
reasonable hope of its efficacy.

At Scarbro', in the Winter of 1854, Mr. Waterton
wrote to me, in his ordinarily enlivening and humorous
vein, the following Letter :——

"My dear Sir,—We received your last communication
with great pleasure, and read it with contented smiles.
Having now taken our last dip in Neptune's briny wash-
tub, nothing remains but to square accounts betwixt ourselves and good Mrs. Peacock, of Cliff No. 1., which we
always arrange satisfactorily to both sides.

"To-morrow morning we shall leave Scarbro' with a
sigh, and journey on to those gloomy regions, where
volumes of Stygian smoke poison a once wholesome
atmosphere; and where filthy drainage from hells upon
earth is allowed by law, for the sacred rights of modern
trade, to pollute the waters in every river far and near.

"To-morrow being our great detonating festival, I shall
have a leisure hour to ruminate on the dreadful consequence of old Guy's atrocity, had he succeeded in blowing

to atoms a few dozens of miscreants who ought all to have been hanged for their crimes against heaven and earth.

"The Vicar of this place is expected to be ferociously eloquent in the pulpit, in denouncing the horrors of Popery to a holy congregation of terrified old women."

In a previous Letter he writes,—

"Not having had a single line from us, you will naturally conclude that we have either forgotten you (impossible), or that we have all gone to the bottom of the sea in a fishing-boat. We are all alive, and not far from our great festival, about to commemorate how Guy Fawkes and his holy squad did dabble in charcoal and saltpetre, to the utter consternation of all good Protestants. No doubt the Pontifex Maximus was at the bottom of all the intended mischief.

"The parson here will ascend his pulpit, and preach a sermon to warn his congregation against having any thing to do with the Devil, the Pope, and the Pretender.

"You will be shocked to hear that Archdeacon ———, after having cruised for years among the shoals and sand-banks of heretical England, is on his way to the sea of eternal bliss—having gone bump ashore on St. Peter's rock. There he is, high and dry, and it is the universal opinion that, were all the steam-tugs of the country put into requisition, their united force would not be able to get him into deep water again.

"Ever sincerely yours,

"CHARLES WATERTON."

Mr. Waterton was for a long period, much attached to Scarbro' in consequence of its purity and supposed salubrity of atmosphere, as well as from the absence of pernicious influences, arising from filthy trade accumulations, and also from its site being peculiarly adapted for efficient drainage.

He always delighted in expressing his horror of the pollution of air and water by noxious gases and poisonous emanations from various chemical works and dye-houses, &c., &c., the more especially, as he had experienced, to his sorrow, abundant proof, that although he had been able at his own residence to guard against the latter, yet that he was to some extent under the deleterious and inextricable influence of the former, as he was well aware, that the artificial and detrimental usurpations so destructive to animal life and vegetation, were not limited to proximity in their immediate neighbourhood, but that they were conveyed through the medium of the atmosphere to long distances from the original source of their formation, and still retaining their power to prove, that where they existed or were deposited, there was sure to be "death in the pot."

The Squire never objected, when in good feather, nay he delighted to briefly indulge in a light and friendly argument, and particularly when supporting his own creed, which he always did with great earnestness, and I am thoroughly satisfied, with genuine sincerity, as well as with considerable force and ingenuity, he stoutly maintained that it was an extremely rare, if not an absolutely unknown occurrence, for a Protestant of a third generation in unbroken succession, to survive and retain a beneficial interest in property confiscated rom a Romanist; and that this punishment inflicted as a Divine judgment, was sure, at all events at no remote period, to detrimentally reach every such instance, whether lay or church-patrimony or possessions.

In order to indulge, to corroborate, and to still more confirm his convinced imagination, as well as to generously favour us Protestants with an additional and enlightening rap on the knuckles, the Squire would calmly, but very determinedly wind up his argument by saying, which he once did to a gentleman in my presence, "You now know my settled opinion, which has never been hidden under a bushel, but you shall have the benefit of another accredited assurance, infinitely surpassing any influence that my *ipse dixit* might contribute,—'*De male quæsitis vix gaudet tertius hæres.*' 'A third heir seldom enjoys property dishonestly got.'"

At the moment, without in the slightest degree desiring or attempting to raise any argument, but on merely questioning the accuracy or truth of this quotation, as regarded its known accomplishment in times gone by, Mr. Waterton, who unquestionably, had a wonderfully retentive and correct memory in all genealogical matters, was I admit, able to enumerate a series of family ancestry, in Yorkshire alone, to such an extent as to surprise, nay to stagger his opponent in argument, and to apparently substantiate the quotation he had used, if not his own assertion, as to an unqualified and uninterrupted sequence

by extinction beyond the third generation, to which he
still most tenaciously adhered.

Probably, if the Squire's theory had been fairly and
impartially tested by a searching and scrutinising examination of families generally, who had never enjoyed confiscated property at all, the result, by comparison, might
have been similar in both cases, and if so, Mr. Waterton's
idolised idea, of its being a limitedly providential judgment would fall to the ground.   Under such circumstances,
it might then perhaps, be fairly conceded, that a partial
and undue leaning to the Roman Catholic side of the
question had doubtless been, in a great measure, the
basis for his entertaining the opinion he so staunchly
maintained and promulgated.

This notion, so zealously and even religiously cherished
by Mr. Waterton, was a specially favourite crotchet with
him, and was frequently introduced, during the whole
period of our intimacy, whenever a familiar chit-chat
accidentally took such a turn as to allude to the con-
fiscation of property in former years, or to the adjudging,
by forfeiture, of penalties to the public exchequer;
and with a man of so sanguine a temperament, and
so naturally inclined to yield to the credulous, it did
not surprise me to see him ride his hobby with
doubtful discretion and somewhat unmercifully; a
mode of argumentation, by the way, ill-calculated to gain
converts.   I am well aware that the Squire was not the
first to broach the idea of the influence of a Divine
judgment in the cases to which allusion has been made,

and I merely name it to record *his* definite opinion on this subject, which, even in the present age, is contended by many to yet hang in equilibrium.

Having, in my immediately previous observations, introduced and directed attention to ancestry generally, I am forcibly, aud indeed, agreeably reminded of Mr. Waterton's own paternity, and more particularly, as the natural animus of the man habitually displayed, by a variety of accidentally occurring circumstances, so much genuinely expressed filial feeling. In three words, Virgil may have been acknowledged to have truthfully predicted and faithfully delineated the subject of our Memoir,—" *Patriæ pietatis imago."* " The image of filial affection."

His never-failing, enduring, and affectionate veneration, uniformly manifested for the memory of his late parents, was singularly gratifying to all around him ; whilst this devoted and reverential esteem for their memory was more especially evidenced and convincing when emphatically recording any anecdotes or dubiously chronicled legends, relative to his father, which might have occurred forty or fifty years retrospectively.

The simple relation of these traditionary reflections of the mind, many of them strongly marked by the rust of antiquity, always appeared to give the Squire extreme pleasure. The respect and deference shown, on all occasions, to the judgment of his late father, on any and every subject, were remarkable, as, although Mr. Waterton was not unfrequently somewhat obstinate in not yielding to the very evidently correct opinion that might happen to be advocated by any ordinary friend, yet if it suddenly or accidentally occurred to him that his deceased parent had held the opinion which his friend then entertained and was maintaining, but in opposition to which impression he himself was in direct antagonism and was vigorously, nay determinedly then resisting, he would at once alter his course, and openly and even somewhat exultingly, accord with his friends conviction, which he had up to this period, so diametrically opposed, and even occasionally, ventured to turn into ridicule or derision.

The Squire, after a perceptibly internal struggle, and a grave self-condemnation as to the interpretation he had adopted regarding the question in dispute, would then say to his rival in argument,—"I must frankly own that I see, and am fully sensible of the false impression under which I have laboured, and unreservedly acknowledge my error. I well remember, and with extreme pleasure, that the sentiments which you are now so ingeniously advocating were the very convictions entertained by my father; and as his judgment and conclusive decisions, on all subjects, were so immeasurably superior to my own, I must draw in my horns, and cry peccavi;" "I have sinned." This must be admitted as a noble recantation in a man who had been so invariably accustomed to be "the lead horse in the team," or "to play the first fiddle"—in one who had seldom met with contradiction—who was naturally somewhat self-opinionated, and who was bordering on eighty years of age, a time of life when opinions are usually supposed to be irrevocably fixed or closely approximating immutability,— at least so says the world generally. We must admit, that when the opinion of the world is all but universal, it would savour very strongly of an unwarrantable or a discourteous dogmatism to assert that it was in error, or to deny that where there is smoke there is sure to be some fire. "*Flamma fumo est proxima.*" Flame is near akin to smoke."

If this can be in honest truth, indubitably and correctly considered as an age of legitimate and veritable progress, as it is generally and even vauntingly stated to be, we should at all events, *expect* to be frequently gratified by meeting with similar instances of an unpretending and modest deference of the wayward son respectfully yielding to the sober and experienced judgment of the parent.

Is it so? Has the advanced and widely expanded scheme of scholastic and moral education so universally adopted, and by some, affording such enthusiastic and wholesale commendation, together with such a signally boasted improvement in the training discipline of youth, substantiated the expectations of the sanguine supporters of the present vaingloriously approved system? Has the recently indulgent system, the overweening estimation on the part of the parent, in confiding to early, nay to premature and inexperienced years been judicious, or has it been a misplaced trust? U

A negligence even of proper respect is in close proximity to an undue assumption in the presence of superiors, and I cannot refrain from alluding to a severe reproof by a late Bishop of Bristol, then Vice-Chancellor of the University of Cambridge, administered to two under-graduates who neglected to pay the accustomed compliment of "capping," which has prevailed in the University from time immemorial. The Bishop to their astonishment arrested their steps and inquired the reason of their neglect. The two men then trembling, begged his lordship's pardon, observing they were "*freshmen*," and did not know him. "How long have you been in Cambridge?" asked his lordship. "Only eight days," was the reply. "Very good," said the Bishop, "puppies never see until they are nine days old."

Do we, "now-a-days," see sons generally manifesting a respectful, a compliant, and a confiding deference to parents? I wish I could reply in the affirmative. On the contrary, are we not frequently grieved by witnessing in youth not only an unwarrantably self-conceited and offensively arrogant estimation of their own abilities and acquirements, not merely contending for an indiscreet, a hap-hazard, or a go-a-head progress, but also openly and lavishly expressing disapprobation and contemptuous opinions of the judgment of "our old governor?"

Nay we now and then, I regret being obliged to admit, see ignorance and self-sufficiency so closely interwoven and amalgamated in youth, that the son, although acknowledged by all to be immeasurably inferior in every respect to "the old governor," and comparatively in total darkness—yet, we find him, instead of paying a youthful and deferential respect to age and to his parent, actually with an insufferable assurance, disapproving and openly censuring the superior discrimination of the more enlightened and proficient parent.

> " He spake, and to her hand proferr'd the bowl,
> A secret pleasure touched Athena's soul,
> To see the preference to sacred age,
> Regarded by the just and sage."

If, in our inferential deductions, we are to be guided by the premature, contemptuously inattentive, and off-hand manners of the present age, apparently the result of the recent "go with the stream" system of discipline, it would appear as if there had been an encouragement adopted, tending to the production of an undue and unbecoming precocity of intellect, the result of which short-sightedness is sure to ultimately defeat its own purpose, and eventually, generate what a powerful author designates "the fools of that paradise," who do not understand that which they profess to teach, and are too vain of their own imaginary attainments to learn knowledge from others.

The indorsing countenance, the absolutely laudatory encouragement, and the woefully mistaken zeal so invariably bestowed by parents upon their children, in order to promote and to advance precocity of intellect, is thoroughly destructive of healthy cerebral function, as also ultimately of general physical development.

The moment the mind in early life, takes an undue lead of the body, the normal condition of both is banefully interfered with.

If we have, too lavishly bestowed artificial measures, tending to produce a premature ripening of the brain, in all human probability we shall ultimately have to witness premature death, or what is infinitely more deplorable, we may eventually calculate upon painful and permanent evidence of a lamentable and distressing imbecility of mental power in various degrees, but to what extent, no human foresight can divine.

" *Modestè tamen et circumspecto judicio de tantis viris pronunciandum est, ne, quod plerisque accidit, damnent quæ non intelligunt.*" "We should however, pronounce our opinions with reserve and cautious judgment, concerning such eminent men, lest, as is the case with many, we condemn what we do not understand."

Mr. Waterton was, during his whole life, anxiously punctual and extremely exact in all his pecuniary transactions, ever having the greatest horror of being in debt. Indeed, the position of his being indebted to any one, however trifling the amount might be, or without consideration as to its having been recently incurred, was little less than an agonising condition for the Squire to realise. He also disapproved and excessively disliked all paper pecuniary payments, much preferring what he was pleased to call "solid tin" to a cheque, although it might bear the signature of an intimate friend, or even that of an acknowledged *millionaire.*

His management, or in rigid truth, I ought to say mismanagement of money in any and every form, was unexceptionally anomalous; and, I trust, without incurring severe or even merited censure, I may add, that it was somewhat savouring of the last rather than of the present century. For instance, many years ago, he determined to encircle his park by a very high and substantial stone and mortar wall; but as he himself observed, " I had then no loose cash in my drawer with which to meet so indefinite, and in all human probability, so large an expenditure, and although never reputed to be needle-witted in the acquirement of pounds, shillings, and pence, yet I trust that I had sufficient mother wit and inborn honesty in my composition to prevent my ever ordering anything for the payment of which I should have had to borrow the amount; and catch me directing or authorising any thing to be done that I can't pay for. In that respect at all events, I am a chip of the old block. Although this was in truth my real position, I firmly resolved at all hazards, to gain my ends, and zealously set to work, by joyfully amassing reiterated instalments, in order to accumulate a substantial hoard, by frequent deposits of spare cash into my idolised safe although of the vegetable kingdom only, until it should contain five hundred sovereigns, the predetermined sum requisite for the commencement of my intended ' castle in the air.'

" This being accomplished, in my humble opinion, by a laudable and thrifty economy, yet without descending to the cheese-paring system, which I ever did and ever shall abominate, I at once engaged masons to build the then contemplated, but now existing and circumjacent wall, which I had so long and anxiously set my heart upon; but it was commenced with a most distinctly mutual understanding that when the last sovereign was drawn

from its hiding-place, the masons should instantly cease
their labours, although this state of poverty (that is, when
the drawer should have yielded its last sovereign), might
accidentally occur on a Friday night, and not on Saturday,
the usual wage night. It was fortunate, for the sake of
preventing any misunderstanding, that such a prophetic
provision had been previously arranged, as it did so occur;
—that is, my hitherto fund-supplying treasury pleaded
'*nulla bona*,' 'no effects;' there was, consequently, a
'suspension of payment,' and I therefore, strictly according
to our pre-arrangement, discharged 'every man jack' on
the Friday night until further orders.

"My favourite deal-drawer was at once a receiving, a
protecting, and a subsidising depository, over which I kept
an argus-eyed guard, as the lock having been manufactured
in an age of greater honesty and less roguery than the
one to which I allude, was of ancient and simple construction. This affianced custodian of my pecuniary
capital was subsequently again and again replenished by
frequent spare cash reserves, until it had gratefully
admitted and ultimately as liberallly yielded the last
sovereign needful to complete the noble barrier which
now stands as an invaluable and permanent rock of
defence between the poacher and myself, and within
which I can with pleasure, and at all events, figuratively
echo the following lines :—

'I am monarch of all I survey,
  My right there is none to dispute ;
From the centre all round to the sea,
  I am lord of the fowl and the brute.'

"On suspending all building operations by discontinuing the masons as I have already stated, agreeably to the contract antecedently and mutually indorsed on the commencement of their labours, until my sovereigns should increase in number, a professing friend, about whom I always had my own well-balanced opinion and that a suspicious one, officiously and impertinently censured this act of mine by remarks unworthy of a gentleman, and of much too coarse a nature to be gratifying, or even palatable to me, but I speedily settled his unneccessary and discourteous interference, by simply asking him if I had performed my portion of the original contract. He replied, 'abstractedly, you have.' I then observed, Sir, when my father disapproved of any thing I was saying, or was evidently about to say in the presence of a third party, he would very audibly whisper, '*tace* is the Latin for a candle,' which was tantamount to saying, hold your tongue, and don't make such a fool of yourself. This, Sir, is the observation I should have thought it my duty to have made to you, if a third party had been present, which, unfortunately is not the case."

I admit the extreme severity of the rebuke, yet probably an overwhelming majority of my just, equitable, and high-principled readers may be induced to concede even its necessary propriety, as the Squire observed, "it required a giant's blow, or something tantamount to steam power, to level this gentleman with the ordinary usages of society."

When I expostulated with the *sovereign* hoarder and store-keeper in the most gentle way imaginable, as to the possibility or even probability, of robbery in his own house and the very evident insecurity and inexpediency of treasuring up so large a sum in an ordinary deal drawer, and also in a financial point of view, as regarded the loss of interest whilst the sovereigns were accumulating, he remarked, in apparently intense gravity, that, "according to the political aspect of the times in which we live and are so unmercifully taxed, the money is quite as safe in my favourite drawer as it would be in the Bank of England, and I shall have infinitely more pleasure in paying the masons in solid gold than in flimsy paper, which a drunken mason might accidently use in order to light his pipe, and thus, by this simple inadvertence or sottish stupidity, deprive his family of sustenance for the next month. I will have nothing to do with the shadow when I can lay hold of the substance. And I think you will agree with me, when I tell you that a nobleman's footman in Hampshire (at least, so says Hone), to whom two years' wages were due, demanded the sum from his master, and gave notice that he would quit his place. The master inquired the reason of the man's precipitancy, who told his Lordship, that he and a fellow-servant were about to set up a country bank, and that they wanted the wages for a capital.

"I am well aware," continued the Squire, "that your Leeds merchants, who are keen, crafty, and wide awake in 'their generation,' would have designated me a flat, or, according to the fashionable slang of the present day, 'a muff,' and would have regarded me as having taken leave of my senses, by robbing my sovereigns of daylight for so long a period, and myself of interest for the cash in reserve, or as they would have commercially contended, in a useless heap; but this is a question which I shall not contest, as I strongly suspect that ninety-nine out of a hundred would vote against me in this new-fangled age, which means, make money honestly if you can, but if not honestly, yet make it, as my old favourite Horace whispered to me in my Stonyhurst days, and which sentiment, some parties who are prepared to sail as near the wind as possible, now cordially indorse, although I never did, and most assuredly never shall so steer my craft, although I should live to number the days of Old Parr."

Notwithstanding Mr. Waterton's inaptitude and generally undisciplined mode as regarded the management of money, and its yielding or unyielding business-like returns, yet in detailed expenditure and receipts no one could be more acutely sensitive or accurate. I well recollect that when our conversation with a mutual friend took the turn to which I have now alluded, the Squire remarked, " I have long entertained a wholesome fear of ' being done,' as the vulgar say, whilst, at the same time, I have an equally anxious desire to prevent the possibility of any one in truth, saying that I have not paid him the uttermost farthing that he is rigidly entitled to.

"In early life, like many other young, inexperienced, and unenlightened swells, (if I ever deserved that odious appellation,) I was twice victimised to my heart's content. In making this admission, I may add, that the first swindle never opened my eyes, but the second time the pigeon was plucked, the sting dipped through the feathers, and so inconvenienced me that I coolly and firmly resolved never to be caught in a similar trap again.

Although I did not relish either my first or my second spoliation, yet, excepting for the sake of the awful position of the plunderers, I do not now lament the calamities to which I have alluded, as they exercised so marvellous and salubrious an influence over me, that in after-life I have so far escaped all serious losses.   I do not however, mean to convey an impression that I have steered clear of minor frauds, but where poverty has been their matrix, I have endeavoured to reconcile myself to the loss, hoping that the little I have been deceitfully deprived of may have benefitted some poor creatures after all."

Here we are again reminded of the distinction Mr. Waterton invariably made between a criminality committed by men in the upper ranks of society as compared with a similar act in the lower orders.   He was accustomed to speak of the seductive vices to which poverty was almost necessarily exposed, and of the nearly insuperable difficulties she had to conquer.

He would add to his plea for mercy on behalf of the delinquent, the acknowledged depravity of the human heart, and hence its natural proneness to yield to the temptation of vice, and more especially in a body enfeebled by want, contending still further in aid of charity, that if the body was insufficiently supported, the mind would be necessarily deprived of its energies, and would consequently lean to apparently present comfort, nay possibly tempting luxuries.

As an ample confirmation of what I have stated, I may adduce an instance which bears me out to the letter.   In 1828 a gentleman, living in the neighbourhood of Wakefield, but now a resident in Nottingham, called upon the Squire one morning, when he had just received one hundred pounds from his publisher, as a portion of his profits for the "South American Wanderings," when Mr. Waterton told him that having no present use for the money, he determined to distribute it to the poor in the immediate neighbourhood. This intended liberal and disinterested, proposition, was carried into execution that very day. The first house he entered on his charitable mission was that of a Protestant who had eight children, and who came in for his fair share of the hundred pounds, although he had been accustomed to publicly abuse Mr. Waterton in consequence of his being a Roman Catholic. This noble act prompted by a generous and forgiving heart was only one of many similarly admirable ones during a long life. Such an example was truly heaping coals of fire on the heads of some pharisaical professors, who could see no virtue in any charitable act but those of their own, which, like Angel's visits, were few and far between.

Mr. Waterton's experience of a return for pecuniary or other equally valuable assistance was, he always stated, gratitude from recipients of known good principle, but frequently no acknowledgement, nor even any recognition whatever from those devoid of principle, and is not this a sufficient proof of the impropriety of indulging in promiscuous charity?

CHAPTER X.

I HAVE previously hazarded the liberty and propriety of alluding to Mr. Waterton's politics, which were of somewhat singular texture, and I think the opinion then recorded is pretty accurately corroborated by the following Letter to me :—

"My Dear Sir,—I shall not vote. You know my sentiments. If driven to extremities, I had rather be slain by the sword of a Tory at noon-day than be stabbed at midnight by the muckfork of a sinuous, tortuous, treacherous Whig. As for the Radicals—poor needy devils !—they would take the last remaining farthing from my breeches pocket, and then leave me to shift for myself. What a patriotic trio ! Poor Britain ! I pity thee from my heart. True patriotism is banished from thy once independent realm. What with Jew, and what with Gentile, thy Parliament House will soon want a Lord Protector with his whitening brush. 'Sir Harry Vane !' The Lord deliver me from Sir Harry Vane.

"I am just returning from Lancashire, where I have spent a most delicious week with the holy Jesuits at Stonyhurst. Their arrangements for the Christmas merriments were so admirably seasoned with ingredients to warn you on your passage to a better world, that it would be almost impossible to say whether the soul or the body received the greater benefit. Would that you had been there. As your unavoidable engagements cut us off from an opportunity of telling you by word of mouth, how sincerely, how fervently, we wished you a merry Christmas, let us hope that nothing will interfere on New Year's Day, to prevent our shaking you by the hand, and saying, at the same time, a 'happy, happy, new year' to one whose friendship is ever dear to us, and whose professional services to us are beyond all estimation.

"In addition, I wish to show you two magnificent toads, which have been sent to me in spirits from Bahia, and which are now ready for a distinguished place in the Museum.

"And lastly, I feel a vehement inclination to gratify you with a view of your old friends, the Reformers of the Church as by law established. I am also anxious that you should invite me to eat a bit of mutton, or even a morsel of bread and cheese with you, under your hospitable roof, any day next week.

"Ever sincerely and faithfully,

"CHARLES WATERTON."

The preceding letter pleasurably reminds me of several very happy hours enjoyed at Stonyhurst College many years ago. Late in the evening, I was urgently summoned to go as quickly as the rail and post-horses could convey me to visit my old friend the Squire, who, whilst spending his week's holiday at the place of his early education, had a sudden and alarming attack of indisposition. Happly, on my arrival a little after four o'clock in the morning, the sufferer had rallied wonderfully, and then appeared to be free from danger, so that instead of my sojourn there, during the day, being one of sorrow, it was truly one of very great satisfaction, there being from the first moment of my entering this seat of learning, an universal anxiety to thoroughly promote my comfort, consequently, during my brief stay among the Jesuits, I was, in every way, really in clover, and I am delighted to have the opportunity, notwithstanding the length of time since this occurrence, to express my heartfelt gratitude for the very cordial reception and hospitality I met with from a body of very agreeable and learned men.

On taking my leave of Mr. Waterton, previously to my departure from Stonyhurst, he facetiously observed, " I am right glad that you have had an opportunity of mixing in the society of those good men. You have, it is true, now and then accidently met with a stray Jesuit or two at Walton Hall, but here you have had a chance of associating with a bevy of them in their natural and familiar lair, and of judging of what sort of stuff they are composed as a body. Surely you are now satisfied and convinced that a Jesuit is an animal neither dangerous nor repulsive of approach, and from what you have seen to-day, are you not confident that our dear Jesuits are always triumphant, that they never stumble, and that one of this body would convey your soul across the Stygian creek more judiciously, and with less fear of an upset than one of those pharisaical Parsons who think it damnation to whistle on a Sunday. I only allude to the pharisaical, recollect."

On the occasion of any official declaration by the sovereign, of a general fast, or any thing of a similar character, I was sure to fall heir to a little good-natured raillery or friendly sarcasm from the Squire, as the following Letter will amply testify :—

Walton Hall, Friday.

"My Dear Sir,—Your Proclamation is excellent, and cannot be mended, saving, that a box of 'Squire Watterton's Pills' ought to be directed to be on the side-board the following day.

"I am just writing to Mr. ——, with a request that he will come and have a drop of broth with us on Sunday. How lucky it will be if you are obliged to be professionally in Wakefield on that day. Kindest remembrances from your patient, who is much better. Thanks for this to the incomparable Doctor Hobson.

　　　　"Believe me, my dear Sir,
　　　　　"Ever truly yours,
　　　　　　　" CHARLES WATERTON."

Anxious, for various reasons, (which it is unnecesary that I should here explain,) not to introduce a greater number of my late friend's Letters than would as much as possible, simply, faithfully, and accurately delineate his true character, I have not, although in possession of upwards of a hundred, and frequently placed in a tantalising and tempting position, yielded to the desire to do so, nor have I indulged in the quotation of a single line, unless, from a stern conviction, that I deemed it absolutely necessary to illustrate some peculiar trait of disposition, natural propensity, or some singularly inherent and pervading spirit of this man, so remarkable in many points of view, and so matchless in his natural history attainments.

It will, I feel confident, be freely and willingly admitted, that no written description, however carefully drawn, short of the Squire's own identical sentences, words, and ideas, could convey to the reader so vivid and correct an imagination, or represent so life-like a form, as the Letters themselves, which are so unique, so pithy, and so original; and it must be remembered, that these communications were one and all, written without the slightest conception of their ever meeting the eye of the public;—therefore, we have here, without a particle of affectation or intentional concealment, Charles Waterton himself, in his spontaneously free, normal, and undressed colours;—for instance,

"My Dear Sir,—If I should have sufficient strength, after this day's Government fast (think of a fast appointed by a Government which ridicules the fast of Advent, and sets that of Lent at utter defiance), I will be with you at the usual time. God bless and protect you.

"Most sincerely,

"CHARLES WATERTON."

Some writer in referring to Mr. Waterton's extraordinary muculiar activity, wonderful nerve, and evident contempt of danger, has expressed surprise at his maintaining his youthful propensities, together with such vast energetic power and unusal daring intrepidity, when verging on forty years of age, substantiating his astonishment by the following quotation from the Squire's own pen.

"During our stay in the Eternal City, I fell in with my old friend and schoolfellow Captain Jones. Many a tree had we climbed together in the last century, and as our nerves were in excellent trim, we mounted to the top of St. Peter's, ascended the Cross, and then climbed thirteen feet higher, where we reached the point of the conductor and left our gloves upon it.

"After this we visited the Castle St. Angelo, and contrived to get on to the head of the Guardian Angel, where we stood on one leg."

I introduce the above quotation now, which had up to this time, singularly enough, entirely escaped my recollection, although Mr. Waterton had often named to me this daring and dangerous climbing frolic. An allusion to it here, is especially made, in order to still further establish and verify the really boyish predilections of the Squire, by reminding and directing the reader's particular attention to a simply sportive freak of his, already recorded by me, namely, his concealing himself under a table, and imitating the growling rage of a savage dog, when his years numbered nearly four-score, which practical joke he not only excessively enjoyed at the moment, but in high glee and with all the animation and gaiety of juvenescence on his part, reported to a friend, who accidentally arrived soon afterward.

On the last occasion of his playing this practical joke, I gently hinted at the fortuitous hazard incurred, stating that many instances were recorded, on un-

doubted authority, when even permanent aberration of
the mind had been the result of such a sudden and unexpected shock to the nervous system.   The Squire, in
perfectly good humour, and with a positively atoning
smile beaming on his countenance as an apparent peace-
offering rejoined, " Doctor Hobson, you have spoken
discreetly, whilst I have acted indiscreetly.   I realise
the danger to which you have alluded, having myself
read of such issues as you state.   If I ever again play
a similar trick, you shall flog me with a cat-o'nine-tails.
It shall not be said of me, as a Yankee observed, when in
conversation with me, ' Things have come to a pretty pass
when a man is not allowed to flog his own nigger,'—you
however, shall have the signal privilege of flogging your
own friend, if such a chastening correction should be
deserved in future."

I have here cheerfully alluded to this perilous ascent
in order to better corroborate Mr. Waterton's statement by
observing that the late Captain Jones himself detailed to me
in the presence of the Squire all the circumstances connected with this sky-larking defiance of danger.

Mr. Waterton's universally acknowledged familiarity
with the habits of the " beasts of the field and the fowls
of the air," was, I suspect, unparalleled, which rendered
him not only a " Triton among the minnows," and
exquisitely amusing to all, but a marvellously instructive
and enlightening companion to any friend partial to the
captivating study of natural history.   If a positive knowledge was wanting of any diffidently stated or un-

authenticated peculiarity, or of a recognition of the habit
of any bird, which had been recorded on equivocal
authority,—or if his memory failed him as to any habit,
which, singular to say, at his age it rarely did, he would
observe, " We must ascertain this point without a doubt
as to its positive accuracy, from actual and careful observation, so as to be sure that we make no blunder, or we
might undeservedly appear in the category of simply
closet-naturalists.   We must carefully and diligently study
nature where she is, and on no occasion by deputy nor
by plagiarism. She is never to be found in the library,
nor in the drawing-room, excepting (if I may be allowed
the metaphorical expression,) through the medium of
the telescope."

> " Thou *Nature* art my goddess ; to thy law
>   My services are bound."

This, the telescopic mode of procuring a sound and
unerring knowledge of the habits of birds and of animals,
is really, in all cases where it is practicable, infinitely
preferable even to that which is generally termed " field "
in contradistinction to " closet-ornithology."   For instance,
all birds assembling on the " little island," in the centre
of the lake at Walton Hall, are in a locality inducing
them to believe that they are free from the haunts of
man, and consequently, under this confident impression
of their undiscoverable privacy and entire seclusion, as
well as being located in a position of entire freedom
from disturbance, appear and act unpremeditatedly and
in a thoroughly spontaneous manner. Having no know-

ledge of a detecting nor of a supervising eye being placed
over them by the telescope, there is nothing to limit nor
to cramp their ordinary acts—their likes or dislikes—
their desires or their objections—which is that precise
condition in nature so desirable to obtain but so difficult
to find within our power.

When there is no human agency, nor unusual external
influence being exercised over them, tending to control
any sudden impulse of feeling, you then see them "*in
puris naturalibus*," that is, in the reality of nature,—and
by careful telescopic observation, you have the rare and
eligible opportunity of acquiring a clear and unerring
insight into the unsuspecting and unbiassed actions and
habits of this branch of organised life, guided by instinct.
You see their habits intuitively directed to adopt beneficial
and reject hurtful operations, not merely for the moment,
not limited to the present only, but by instinct wonderfully and discriminately selected, and hence, extended for
their good to the future.

How nearly do instinct and reason approximate—how
closely they verge and tread on each other's heels—they
are assuredly within immediate call, nay they frequently
appear to absolutely amalgamate.

> " Providence or instinct of nature seems,
>   Or reason though disturbed, and scarce consulted,
>   To have guided me aright."

We see a half-starved and hungry dog pick up a
scrap of offal, thrown from the butcher's stall into the
dirty street, and therefore, offensively and unpalatably

soiled with various impurities. His appetite may be ravenous, yet he refuses, in its filthy condition, to masticate and swallow the prize he has laid hold of, in order to satisfy his craving hunger.

The animal at once recognises the necessity of cleansing the spoil he has obtained, and with his front teeth only, he grasps a small portion of the unsavoury treasure in its then disagreeable condition, and shakes it with a vengeance, until it is freed from its gross impurities. Having effectually carried out the object he had in view, he greedily, and with an evident relish, devours that which was recently offensive, but which is now made sufficiently pure for him by his own device.

Another instance of a close approximation of instinct and reason, may be deduced from the feathered tribe. In the farm-yard among the poultry, we see the male bird, from a feeling of admiration and affection for the softer sex, sedulously scratching the dung-hill in anxious search of worms or of imperfectly digested cereal produce, for his feminine associates; and when his labours are rewarded with success, he stands erect for the moment, with his head raised aloft, loudly calling by a peculiar "chuck, chuck, chuck," for some lady-pet, to whom he may bestow the delicate morsel he has secured and which he holds in his beak for her acceptance.

It must be admitted, that immediately successive and evidently projected intentions are, in many instances, put in force by the male bird in order to accomplish an end, which appears to be foreseen.

The first intention that chanticleer proudly entertains,

is, in his gallantry, to unmistakeably indicate some marked attention to the weaker vessel or, in other and more complimentary terms to the fair sex, in conceiving the idea of procuring a "tit-bit" for some favourite, by adopting Doctor Kitchiner's sentiment, namely, a thorough conviction that "the way to the heart is through the medium of the stomach."

The male bird clearly knows *where* to find the food he requires, and he is equally conversant with a knowledge *how* to procure it; he also knows that he can, by an intelligible signal,—a language of his own,—secure the presence of another, to whom he desires to give the food he finds. Sometimes, whilst actually holding the prize he has discovered, he makes his well-understood signal, by crying " chuck, chuck, chuck ;" on other occasions, immediately on perceiving it, he resorts to his signal, and on the hen's arrival, points to it with his beak, or picks it up and gracefully presents it to her.

Prior says—

> " The philosopher avers,
> That *reason* guides our deed, and *instinct* theirs.
> *Instinct* and *reason*, how shall we divide ?"

Pope responds—

> "Reason serves when press'd ;
> But honest instinct comes a volunteer."

An accurately observing and very intelligent friend, on whom I can thoroughly depend, informs me that he had, some years ago, a goldfinch which was passionately fond of the soft interior of household bread. If however, a crust was offered to the songster, it was always accepted, but the cunning bird, with great sagacity, immediately dropped the gift into his drinking reservoir, and invariably allowed it to remain in the water until rendered sufficiently soft for easy deglutition, when it would artfully, and of its own accord, fish it out, and use it as choice and delectable food. My friend assures me that this was done without any previous instruction whatever.

There is no "glorious uncertainty of the law" existing with birds and animals, "*feræ naturæ*," "in a state of wild nature;" with them might is right, and an admission of this acquired authority or dominion is yielded and permanently established and witnessed on all sides, without the aid of magnifying power. You unerringly ascertain, on both land and water, that there is not merely non-resistance, not simply a capitulation under certain circumstances for the moment, but it is evidenced as a permanency, by a run-away, swim-away, or fly-away retreat. The less powerful or less courageous rival for monarchy on land or on water soon discovers that its position is an untenable one, and, in future, submissively occupies that station in the decree of mastership, in relation to its associates, which a superiority in courage or physical force has awarded it. Nature, in her nude state, has few difficulties to encounter or to contend with, since each species speedily claims and as resolutely maintains its precise and previously acquired and recognised position as regards the various degrees of supremacy, or even despotism in some few species, which appear to inherit an innate spirit of tyranny.

The Squire himself was, for a number of years previously to his death, inestimably indebted to the telescope, for a wholesome correction of many early conceived and erroneous impressions of the habits of various birds, having unwittingly picked up ill-founded impressions, by a sort of universal yet unauthorised consent, that such and such birds were the subjects of such and such habits; whereas, the telescope, when brought to the rescue, soon set him right, as it invariably and infallibly does correct and put an end to all mere assumption and closet ornithological theories, as well as to the speculations of a romantic or fanciful brain.   Unfortunately, sanguine temperaments, when pursuing and professing to closely examine the intricacies of natural history, as in other sciences which require great circumspection and positively absolute facts, take many things for granted which have no existence excepting in a stretch of imagination, or the fumes of fancy, so that no dependence can be, with any confidence, placed on their statements,—hence, habits which actually do exist are passed over without the slightest notice, whilst those existing only in imagination are promulgated as realities.

This is a great and growing grievance, and a lamentable cause of retarding truth and accuracy in natural-history publications, because few authors have the desired opportunity of practically gaining for themselves the accurate information necessarily required for the correction of unfounded impressions, and are consequently, driven (that is, if they are determined to write,) to publish opinions and statements formed by and gathered from their general reading on these subjects, or from direct plagiarism derived from visionary or unauthorised sources,—and thus are errors, or indeed, decided misstatements, perpetuated from one generation to another.

In the ordinary and every-day occurrences in life, we continually find it acknowledged that verbally expressed and even written statements, need frequent, and indeed, severe correction. Now, if common occurrences, which are every body's business, require an expostulating and a redressing influence, how can we reasonably expect to find natural-history statements, which are studied comparatively by few,—and those comprising the sanguine as well as the indolent,—I say, how can we expect so great a medley of descriptions to be in a position entitled to claim exemption from such a chastisement ?

The man who writes a book, on the heterogeneous subjects of natural history, for the sake of pecuniary profit, which is, I suspect, generally an unproductive as well as an infelicitous speculation, or that he may acquire honorary distinction as an author, without being deeply, and I may add, naturally imbued by a devoted and inherent love for the science, and without a thorough knowledge of the elementary details and foundation of this charming study, is not the man to instruct. Ninety-nine out of a hundred of those who peruse such a book, with a view to gain correct knowledge in the varied departments of natural history, may be much pleased and highly *amused*, and very reasonably and justly so, according to the ability, the skill, or the refined taste of the author, but its inevitable inaccuracy and indisputably vague definitions as regards nature, will always debar its being a means by which the earning ornithologist can be safely or invulnerably guided in the attainment of his wants.

Any one, who dares to call himself a naturalist, ought never to be in a position to claim the privilege of sheltering himself under ignorance of a habit of any bird or animal, by using the expression *generally*. The path of nature is undeviating, and may be fancifully assimilated to the skin of the Ethiopian, or to the laws of the Medes and Persians, which change not. Nature always says it is, or it is not. She invariably deals in stern individualities, and never indulges in dubious nor in undefined generalities,—of course, monstrosities excepted.

We should remember that we may, by earnest and assiduous labour, but most assuredly not without it, attain a position to require only a comparatively trifling amount of shelter in consequence of our ignorance in this branch of science. On the other hand, if we calculate upon possessing an accurate knowledge of God's varied works in creation as a congenital gift, we labour under a grievous and a really inexcusable error, and one which can never be compensated by any substitute. Nature no more furnishes us with this knowledge without the utmost exertion of our energies, than she bestows virtue without the shoulder being put to the wheel. " *Natura non dat virtutem; nascimur quidem ad hoc, sed sine hoc.*" "Nature does not bestow virtue; we are born indeed to it, but without it."

Many men in their own estimation call themselves naturalists who have not an atom of legitimate claim to such a distinction.

"Boasting is but an art our fears to blind,
And with false terrors sinks another's mind."

Inasmuch as it is extremely difficult and almost impossible to secure favourable opportunities in order to rigourously investigate some habits, therefore, when we can by means of a telescope, witness any acts absolutely exercised, it is essential, for the sake of accuracy and to prevent the possibility of mistake by trusting to memory, that we should jot down the facts ascertained, at the very moment when such well-authenticated truths are before our eyes, nay are actually discovered and determined, leaving nothing for memory to supply, —a wrinkle is thus added, confirmed, or destroyed in the book of nature for the future.

The Squire, in all his numerous and unusually long-continued natural-history pursuits, had invariably three simple and elementary objects in view, viz., the discovery of a habit hitherto unrecorded—the verification of those already enrolled and generally admitted in natural history—and the irrefutable correction of those resting on hearsay or equivocal evidence, or on the theoretical, the fanciful, and the questionable contributions emanating from the closet, the latter of which provokingly unacceptable consignments to the public were surprisingly numerous.

Mr. Waterton would say, when in a facetious or jocose humour, "If it be necessary to eat a peck of salt at a man's table before you can be said to know him, what length of time and close observation is it reasonable to suppose, would be required to become a proficient in the absolutely practical knowledge of the habits of birds and of animals? On working this out by the

rule of three, you will find the result will be a man's lifetime, and an indefinite period beyond that as a remainder;
and even this remainder, let me tell the off-hand and
take-for-granted naturalist, will be no atom."

Mr. Waterton, I believe, never manifested the slightest
disposition, during any period of his life, to attempt
to tame or domesticate wild animals, and certainly
never sanctioned nor approved of such an essay being
made by any other person in the lengthened span of
our intimacy; indeed, even the simple deprivation of
the liberty of either bird or beast was distasteful in the
extreme to the tender-hearted Naturalist, and was by
him sternly deprecated.

He could not bear to see any creature deprived even
of its liberty without considering it an inhuman torture,
and would bring Burns to his aid by reciting the dying
words of " Poor Maillie " when alluding to her master.

> " Tell him if e'er again he keep
> As muckle gear as buy a sheep,
> O bid him never tie them mair
> Wi' wicked strings o' hemp or hair,
> But ca' them out to park or hill,
> An let them wander at their will ;
> So may his flock increase and grow
> To scores o' lambs an' packs of woo'."

If any one ever suggested or desired the domestication
of a wild animal of any species whatever, the Squire
would instantly and determinedly oppose the proposition, contending against it with a countenance betraying
an inward horror, which was expressive of its being

the *avant-courier*, the harbinger of a future cruelty,
to which he could never be persuaded to consent, much
less approve. He would in a firm but subdued tone
say, that he never could endure to witness desert-nature
repulsively disfigured and painfully tormented during
life by any inhuman brutality.

The Squire also insisted, that if even the mildest
form of domestication, or assuredly of incarceration,
should be once unfortunately conceived and indulged
in—if the thin end of the wedge should be once introduced,
that it would, in a great number of cases, lead to tribulation
or torture, and indeed to his positive knowledge,
had, in some instances, terminated in the greatest
barbarity, but one fortunately seldom seen or permitted
in a civilised country.

The Squire's argument was grounded and uniformly
exemplified by adducing, in his brief but telling phraseology,
"the inhuman cage-confinement of birds," and
especially on that of the bullfinch, which he contended,
if viewed in the most favourable light that any deprivation
of liberty could claim, was nothing less than
imprisonment, nay solitary confinement for life And
callous and unimpressible as all endowed with right
feeling must admit such an infliction on innocent and
unsuspecting nature to be, yet it was but the first act
in the tragedy of the woes of this poor bird.

The second link in the chain of its afflictions, the
teaching it music, he contended, although mild by comparison
had its numerous discomforts and annoyances,
very frequently from the inconsiderate and case-hardened

austerity of its teacher. For instance, when birds are taught to perform or to do certain acts requiring (in order to accomplish such unnatural feats,) severe and long-continued training, it is found necessary to deprive them of all food for a protracted period, so that they may especially enjoy their rations which are given to them immediately after their training lesson as it is supposed that the poor creature, after a little time ascertains that this food is given as a reward or a bribe for its obedience. When it is supposed to be requisite to punish a bird, the trainer takes it in his left hand, and with a flirting or jerking action of his right thumb and long finger, hits the bird on the scalp,—and sometimes these fillips are of a flint-hearted character.

When poor " bully," as the bird-catchers call him, has been made as perfect, under existing circumstances, in the art and execution of vocal music, as human skill can inculcate, his brutal and avaricious teacher, believing that there can be a still further improvement, a more melodious and attractive vocalization secured in his pupil by obliterating his vision, hesitates not to perforate the pupil of each eye with a red hot needle, hoping by this cruel act, to improve his intonation and also secure some other additional refinement, and consequently to obtain a more extravagant remuneration for him.

Mr. Waterton when abroad, had several times seen the bullfinch in this deplorable condition, and there appeared, from what he could learn, to be no doubt but the poor creature, in order to " pass dull time away," when ruthlessly and inhumanly deprived of the faculty of vision, is driven to amuse himself by singing more frequently than he otherwise would do, if his attention were occupied and amused by seeing the various objects around him.   I may add that the Squire stated he was not sufficiently skilled in the science of music, to be able to distinguish with accuracy whether the loss of eyesight certainly tended to improve the acquired vocal powers of the songster.   He also remarked, that he had known many instances in England of the linnet being deprived of vision, but he knew not by what means.   The chief reason for this savage act is grounded on the supposition that by depriving the bird of one sense, namely, that of seeing, the other senses become more acute, perfect, and refined.

I understand that in England, the linnet frequently suffers by bird-fanciers, this merciless and cold-blooded barbarity, by an apparently less torturing, but certainly by a longer-continued, and probably, in reality, by a still more excruciatingly painful operation.   The means these bird-fancying miscreants adopt, is the application of intensely heated iron, or some other metal similarly prepared, for a continued period, in such close approximation to the eyes as to produce a degree of inflammatory action sufficiently intense to entirely destroy their healthy organization, and to induce consequent loss of vision, which is the entire aim of these mean-spirited and mercenary recreants.

Although we can not literally assimilate "poor bully," nor the harmless linnet, however mutilated and disfigured in aspect, to any thing strictly monstrous, even under the most aggravated circumstances, yet we are figuratively reminded of Virgil's line relative to Polyphemus the Cyclops :—

"*Monstrum horrendum, informe, ingens, cui lumen ademptum.*"

" A monster horrible, mis-shapen, huge, and deprived of his eye."

It has been previously stated that Walton Hall did not abound with game ;—and the reason then assigned was, the heavy cost and extreme difficulty of preserving the manor, in addition to the frequently consequent sacrifice of human life. A more matured recollection furnishes me with sundry other representations, creating additional stumbling-blocks in the way of accomplishing all that could be desired in the way of preservation of game, which ought not to be omitted without some explanation.

It is a universally acknowledged fact, that hares, in order to be in a healthy and productive condition, require variety of food and distant feeding ground. Now these essentials, within the park walls at Walton Hall, are necessarily limited, the amount of arable land being trifling, and the feeding ground unfortunately in close proximity with that in which they make their forms in which to squat ; and, whensoever hares are very numerous on a limited space, they soon become infected with what keepers call the " rot," very many dying off, and those that "pull through" are not fit for the table, at all events for six or eight months.

The nesting ground for partridges is good and safe, if

the weasel be "kept under," as the ground is dry, and
there is always a plentiful supply of water, but there is a
lamentable dearth of arable land, and consequently, an
insufficiency of cereal crops to sufficiently attach and
endear them to their birth-place,—and by straying out
of the manor in quest of seeds, turnip and potatoe cover,
as well as basking-ground, they are often picked up on the
outskirts by the straggling poacher.

The male-bird renders no assistance in the act of
incubation, but always remains in close proximity so as
to warn the female of danger, and by a pretended
exhibition of being unable to fly, he half flies and half
runs, in order to lead away any apparently intruding
party from the nest.   Few birds show the same intensity
of parental affection as the partridge.   For instance, in
the wet summer of 1836, Mr. Weir says, "several pairs
were found dead in the fields near Bathgate with their
broods under their wings, having perished under the
influence of cold and hunger rather than expose their
tender charge to the inclemency of the weather."

Pheasants being very fond of roosting and of cover,
if artificially supplied with Indian corn, buck wheat, or
some other equivalent, do remarkably well at Walton
Hall;—indeed, the Squire had, beyond all doubt, ample
proof of this in bygone days.

One day, on paying Mr. Waterton a casual visit,
and immediately observing that his temper was somewhat ruffled,—which irritated condition his countenance
always speedily betrayed,—I enquired if he was poorly,

Y

or if anything had distressed him, when he excitedly replied, "Yes, I am grieved to the back bone; Mr. —— whom you would just now meet in the carriage-road, and who professes to be enchanted and in raptures with the works of God's creation has just left the house ; and, what do you think ? he coolly turned up his nose at my Bahia toad, calling it 'an ugly brute.'

"That a gentleman, avowing himself a lover of natural history, and pretending an anxiety to work in the same vineyard with me, should profanely designate one of God's creation 'an ugly brute,' was enough 'to put me out' for a week,—so I left him in the staircase to his own cogitations."

This was a mode of manifesting indignation or displeasure not entirely free from objection, and was one which, indisputably, few persons would have adopted under similar circumstances, as the Squire doubtless, by his remorseless countenance and unpalatable manner, did not conceal from the gentleman that he shelved him in evident umbrage.

When we however, make charitable and privileged allowances for the peculiar idiosyncracy of the man, in consequence of his positive adoration of the works of creation, and also for the light in which he very probably received the unguarded, and certainly, the unfortunately selected expression of his casual natural-history visitor, there was then much to be said on behalf of Mr. Waterton, and in extenuation of his sore annoyance at this manifestly unintentional offence on the part of the stranger.

This, like some other of our friend's little failings, (and who is free from a sprinkling of imperfections?) had an origin and a foundation grounded on a sacred feeling, which by some might be considered as more than compensating for the intentionally ungracious desertion of a gentleman in his own house, and yet offering no correcting nor reproving observations to the offending party in proof of his disapprobation, which mode of condemnation was not the usual one with the Squire.   In fact, as a general rule, he was instantaneously "down upon" those whom he conceived unreasonably differing in opinion with him, and occasionally, where the dissent savoured of officiousness, and when he had his antagonist fairly "*inter malleum incudem*," "between the hammer and the anvil," in rather a rough-and-ready fashion. He was implicitly impressed with the idea that every thing in nature was beautiful, and consequently, could not see any thing disgusting in the toad, which he would handle, nay fondle, apparently with the greatest delight.   He would expatiate, in evident pleasure, on its eyes, "those brilliant luminaries of vision," upon its utility to man, notwithstanding his ingratitude in return for its destruction of the despoiling insect families.   He would dwell upon its harmlessness, and upon its general appearance, as an object of interest and admiration, although he had no friend to support him, with evident pleasure.

Mr. Waterton always entertained and manifested such a profound respect for the Deity, and indeed, absolute veneration for every thing created by or associated with potentiality or sacred attributes, that he could seldom sanction an expression of even disapprobation of any of God's works, much less endure appellations, in the slightest degree repulsive, to be applied to any object whatever within the range of natural history, without what he termed, giving a "Rowland for an Oliver," yet in this isolated instance, he signally failed in his wonted effective retort, his displeasure being such as to entirely obliterate his ordinary presence of mind, which was usually in the ascendant.

Before my friendship with the Squire, the toad had frequently been the subject of experiment with him, he had buried it in an earthen jar underground with and without food for certain periods of time, weighing it previously and subsequently to its being so immured but my treacherous memory serves me not as to the comparative increase or decrease in weight, showing the variously limited duration of its imprisonment.

CHAPTER XI.

For a very long time I have carefully preserved many of Mr. Waterton's letters written to myself, without any special reference to the character of their contents, not however, until recently, with any idea or pre-determined intention of *my* applying them to their present purpose, but with a hope that they would be useful to some other surviving friend who might, and I doubted not, would feel an anxiety to rescue their hitherto hidden recital, and the good deeds of this extraordinary man from oblivion after death.

> " Death only is the lot which none can miss,
> And all is possible to Heaven but this."

Indeed, at one period, I had entertained a rather confident and certainly a pleasing idea, that some Jesuit or a combined phalanx of that fraternity, to whom the Squire was such a hospitable, considerate, and warm-hearted friend, would have been naturally induced, or in naked truth, would have been irresistibly tempted to have written *the life* of their noble and generous benefactor, and I then determined, that not only should Mr. Waterton's letters to me be at their unlimited service, but that I should have been in addition, delighted to have furnished the author, or the incorporation of authors, with all the information that I was master of, from which they might have selected or rejected at pleasure.

Of course, it would have been little less than an insane
act on my part, to have contemplated, and still more so,
to have attempted to write *the life* of a man, with whose
early antecedents I was totally unacquainted—of the first
half of whose life I literally knew nothing—and of whose
family ancestry I was comparatively ignorant, knowing
little more than what the ordinary newspapers of the day
brought to light, when the good man had ceased to exist.

It will then be evident, that I never meditated any thing
beyond a brief sketch of the retained and deeply impressed
reminiscences of my friend, and I should, in truth, bitterly
lament if a single sentence should have escaped from my
pen which would have been contrary to the wishes of the
deceased.

The Squire's spontaneous, voluntary, and uninvited
acts never failed to be of a noble character. His chief
objects, when fairly relaxed from his various and numerous
taxidermic labours, were by exemplification, directed to the
generous support and relief of his fellow-creatures, and as
the organs of credulity and benevolence were largely
developed in our enterprising friend, we cannot be surprised
to find that he was very often grossly imposed upon, and,
therefore, fully verifying the truth of an assertion of Ovid's,
—" *Quique aliis cavit, non cavet ipse sibi ;*" " And he that
has defended others, fails to defend himself." Let me here
add, that the charities of the Squire's benevolent heart,
carried out in supposed secrecy on his part, were innumerable ; some of which, accidentally coming to light,
thoroughly established that which his intimate friends
never questioned, namely his innate kind and generous
feeling, and always exercised without parade.

If a man, whom he had befriended, behaved rudely or ungratefully, the Squire would hunt up all sorts of excuses and apologies for him, and would not hesitate to plead earnestly on behalf of this sinner.

On a friend once saying to him in my presence, " Really this is casting your pearls too promiscuously," Mr. Waterton observed, "Ah, my dear friend, err on the safe side. You and I have repeatedly had the offer of pearls which we have rejected, why then should not this poor fellow have another chance ? "

Few persons have known Mr. Waterton for so lengthened and uninterrupted a period and so intimately as I had the satisfaction of doing, and the number of individuals would be limited indeed who could advantageously enter into and record any very detailed information with regard to his ordinary and undisguised habits, or with respect to his marvellous manipulating powers; and probably, a still smaller number, *if there be any such* surviving confidants, who were, during the life of my friend, so intimately acquainted as I was with the many interesting *minutiæ* of Walton Hall and its surrounding scenery in its familiar and unaffected attire.

Under his own roof, during our friendship, the Squire's every-day habits were reserved nor concealed from me, whilst his taxidermic skill, as an amateur and practical expert, with all his ingenious arrangements and contrivances, were invariably and even seductively exposed to me; nay I was cordially invited at all times, to share in the interest Mr. Waterton himself experienced in

ornithological operations, in order to endeavour to fathom
all their difficulties, and to attain a knowledge of all their
intricacies, whilst Walton Hall and its many peculiarities,
in consequence of their being so frequently and so unreservedly under my eye, and so precisely harmonising
with my own tastes, were as familiar to me as if I had
resided within the park walls for half a century.

Mr. Waterton, from the commencement of our friendly
and familiar intercourse, was well aware of my ardent
attachment to every thing connected with natural history,
and therefore, when he had obtained any thing novel or
out of the ordinary way; or if he had himself added
any thing by his own handiwork to his collection, well
selected acquisitions to which he was incessantly contributing until the close of life; or if a strange bird had
made its appearance on the lake, or in the grounds, I was
pretty sure to receive a letter requesting me to pay him
a visit, whilst every possibly captivating inducement was
volunteered to encourage and persuade me to drive over
and socially share his prospective pleasures,—the object of
which visit was, without exception, in his letter of
invitation fully entered into and minutely explained, so
as to give me a detailed foresight of his contemplated
intentions; and the more especially, if there was any
knotty or disputed point associated with natural history
to solve, determine, or correct, or any attempt to be
made to unravel by our united effort, any recent discovery
which had been publicly recorded as actually accomplished
and practically displayed, and particularly, if it appeared

to be enveloped in any unusual mystery, or in some degree of incredibility.

The Squire was always in possession of moral courage sufficient in the first instance, to firmly but gently contend for the correction of an error unguardedly or recklessly stated, and if a palpable one was obstinately persevered in, he would then not at all hesitate to support his own side of the argument by very energetic language, and occasionally, by a tartness and an asperity of expression somewhat ungracious, and unfortunately, also by a very decided insuavity of manner.

On my arrival at the Hall on such occasions as I have named, Mr. Waterton was always on the tip-toe of expectation, being as sure as "death and taxes" to be eagerly looking out; and the moment my foot had overstepped the threshold of the entrance-hall door, his anxiety was manifested to introduce the subject of his previously noticed novelty,—probably some unique abnormity in the animal kingdom or in the feathered tribe might be prepared and conspicuously placed so as to create intense surprise or "love at first sight," or it might be some recently and exquisitely mounted rare but normal specimen in some other or collateral branch of natural history. At all events, I was never disappointed by his frequent special invitations, which, on no occasion, failed to be interesting and to afford a gratifying treat to me, independently of a certainty of two or three hours of genuine enjoyment with the Squire himself. Then, to witness his animated manner, his hurried anxiety, and his extreme delight to exhibit any thing new, "fresh from the mint," or recently executed, was such that my heart must have been frigid indeed if I had not cordially shared in his very manifest pleasure and gratification, whilst rapidly recounting or vividly explaining its peculiarities, or nature's necessary and marvellous provisions, with evident heartiness and impetuosity of exposition, and in his own incomparably quaint style.

Mr. Waterton might be fairly, and indeed impartially, deemed in some degree impatient with any one hazarding an opinion at variance with his own, as regarded the attitude or anatomical form of the birds he mounted. In whatever attitude he placed the subject of his labours it was always natural, but seldom deviating from one of repose. It is rare to see a bird of the Squire's "mounting" in an attitude representing a state of surprise, auscultation, or anger. That position in which the bird is evidently listening, is very interesting and adds, in many instances, materially to the appearance of life,—but I recollect very few mounted by the Squire "*arrectis auribus*," "with ears erect."

This excessive degree of sensitiveness and susceptibility, or what I have ventured to designate impatience, or an unfortunate tendency to too readily "champ the bit," which I have frequently alluded to by its proper name to Mr. Waterton himself, was perceptibly indicated, even if merely the most trifling difference of opinion was ventured to be expressed in the mildest and most gentle manner possible, and, in this respect, no one was exempt from the reception of a testy or a somewhat irascible punition, nor did any one possess the slightest immunity from this infliction in consequence of age, friendship, or sex ;—in this, as in other instances, he dealt out equal justice to all.

It has been my most anxious and even ambitious desire, and I may add, my firm determination, in writing this Sketch of the "Home, Habits, and Handiwork" of my late friend, never to tread, nor even, in the least degree, trench upon what writers in the present age would liberally permit me to designate sacred ground, in other words, on a substructure, from which I should have been "warned off" by the Squire himself during his life.

It has also been my inflexible resolution, so far as a cautiously formed judgment could direct and guide me, never to infringe on any subject beyond what even Mr. Waterton himself would have countenanced and sanctioned during life. How far a successful or approved issue has been realised, as regards the object in view, must be left for an impartial and unbiassed public to determine.

Conflicting, prejudiced, and, now and then, ill-digested opinions may be formed, and perhaps, of an obstinate and unyielding character, as to the remarks contained and the sentiments expressed in this volume, probably as to their propriety, and possibly, as to its hazarded publication, and especially I suspect, by parties, in truth, totally ignorant of the circumstances under which I write, and yet of course, speaking as if "*ex cathedrâ*," "coming from high authority."

I quarrel not with any opposing party-spirit, from whatever cause it may emanate, nor even with a jaundiced or malevolent eye, if such should prevail, nor with any diversity of opinion that may be entertained; indeed, it would be unreasonable in me to calculate upon casting my net with such exquisite skill as to secure every variety of fish by a single draught. Such really dexterous management would, in all conscience, require, in reality, "a long pull, a strong pull, and a pull altogether," which combination of good luck and skill rarely falls to the lot of human decision, however cautiously formed and judiciously directed.

If the subject of this Memoir had been a naturally diffident and retiring character—if he had dwelt within his own park walls all his life, and had parsimoniously wrapped himself up in his own sphere of knowledge, niggardly tenacious of its distribution—if he had never travelled— had never encountered the lion's share of danger by land nor by sea,—if he had never mixed in society, nor roughed it in foreign climes,—if he had ingloriously concealed his every-day deeds "under a bushel,"—if he had ever acted, in the eyes of his fellow-men, "as a thief in the night"— in that case, and under such unenviable circumstances, the writing of this volume might have been an irksome and would have been an unwilling and a disagreeable task, as well as a difficult card to play.

The Squire had far too open and generous a disposition to care who might become acquainted with the ordinary acts of his long and well-spent life, and more especially in its later years,—he knew his own singularities, and cared not who shared in that knowledge. The old man never beat a retreat from broad day-light, always abominating "deeds of darkness." He himself, uninvitedly supplied me with *memoranda* as to dates, in order to complete this sketch, and years previously, he hesitated not to publish his own biography, and was then not sparing in recounting his own peculiarities, nor ashamed to describe, in not very complimentary terms, his own personal appearance,—therefore, the basis on which I rest, is a permission more than equal to all my necessary requirements for the publication of this volume.

> *" Si quid amicum erga bene feci, aut consului fideliter,*
> *Non videor meruisse laudem ; culpâ caruisse arbitror."*

"If I have in any way acted well towards my friend, or have faithfully consulted his advantage, I deem myself not deserving of praise ; I consider only that I am free from blame."

As I am anxious to delineate the man in his various characters, I can not refrain copying the following letter which is written in so off-hand a way, and in so cheerful a spirit :—

MY DEAR SIR,—

I am all right again, and should like to show you some of the chief actors of the reformation in the staircase. We fear that you may be mortgaged for Christmas day. Come if possible when it arrives, you shall have a bed and a slice of turkey and plum pudding.

I don't care who holds the helm of our crazy vessel, so long as " Mummery John " does not get hold of it. You did not arrive according to promise. We hope to be more fortunate on Palm-Sunday after you have requested your spiritual adviser to keep a blessed palm for you, when he delivers the sprigs to the assembled multitude from his Altar. Stop, I ought to say table. Many thanks for your communication. I hope that you will pursue the investigation. It is somewhat singular that I have never yet found the large bone in the wings of waterfowl full of marrow. Why is the bone of one waterfowl full and another empty? We shall join heart and soul in wishing you a happy New Year when it comes, and many of them. Keep yourself disengaged.

I returned from the good Jesuit Fathers yesterday. The plant which you sent them flourishes admirably, and blossomed beautifully during summer. In allusion to the Baronet and his daughter, we were delighted with them. We have two fine dusky grebes feeding with the coots close to the boathouse. So Mr. —— wishes to kill the devil. I think it imprudent to make such an attempt as he suggests, as they really cannot do without him in our houses of Parliament. They are very hard up, and it would be cruel to take away their main prop. A multiplicity of out-door work has pressed heavily on me, and to wind all up, Advent has arrived, three days of which are set apart by the Church in order that the body may give its soul an additional shove to the realms above. Dr. H. will have announced this to you.

Should you put in appearance three days hence, your benign countenance will make the fiddle sound more sweetly, and the dance will have redoubled charms. I am still prone to obesity.

Ever yours sincerely,
CHARLES WATERTON.

Mr. Waterton's anxiety to show me "some of the chief actors of the reformation," always convinced me that this, in his own estimation, was his greatest work of art in taxidermy. In allusion to the fiddle and the dance, Mr. Waterton was then shadowing forth an approaching gala to be held in the Park.

The Squire's heart, in allegorical or vernacular language, was infinitely too large "to rest and be thankful" with those amusements or labours which usually terminate by merely affording self-gratification so long as others were in misery. Although always the most happy when putting his shoulder to the wheel in good earnest in favour of his hobby, or when feeding the hungry, clothing the naked, and ministering to the wants of the poor and the desolate, yet his varied, unwearied, and enterprising labours were not all devoted exclusively to the useful, nor all exclusively to the pleasing—not all to the temporary, nor all to the more durable.

His handicraft operations were so judiciously, so suitably, and so reasonably combined, by mingling the agreeable with the useful and the laborious, that they never failed to yield an interest more than commensurate, with certain duties which are necessarily inseparable from some disagreeable, repulsive, and responsible obligations attached to the department of positively practical taxidermy,—but where is the rose without its accompanying thorn ?

The embryonic source of the Walton Hall Museum undoubtedly derives its origin, its initiative inchoation, as regards time, from the summer of the year 1812, when its founder, the "South American Wanderer," literally rambled, unaccompanied by any friend, through the wilds of Demerara and Essequibo, and boldly penetrated the borders of Macousia, in anxious search of the Woorali poison, which at that period he not only fortunately obtained in the Portuguese inland frontier, but actually witnessed its elaborate and mystifying manufacture, and which now, at the expiration of more than fifty-three years, maintains all its pristine purity, and appears not to be deprived of the shadow of a shade of its original virulent intensity, as an effective and a speedy poison, when inserted within the cuticle, even in very minute portions; indeed recently, good and advantageous opportunities, as well as clever, well-informed, and experienced professional men, have tested and thoroughly proved and established the possession of its original efficacy, as regards its immediately and certainly destructive power.

Mr. Waterton has, on several occasions, intimated to me that he was primarily initiated into the fascinating labyrinths of natural history—that the impedient curtain was first raised by witnessing the varied and resplendent plumage of the feathered tribes in Demerara, which gorgeous display of the multifarious and diversified tints of colour, when the numerous birds were flitting from spray to spray, and peacefully and playfully hovering on the wing all around him, appeared, from recollection, at the moment to far excel the brilliant shades of the rainbow,—declaring that he had never entertained the slightest conception of the ornamentation and beauty of colours in nature which he subsequently met with in foreign climes—that he was totally ignorant of calisthenics, never having in his earlier life instructed himself, nor ever having been enlightened by others in the science of the perception of beauty. The Squire on his first and unattended visit to South America when young, powerful, and abounding in physical activity, with a mind equally eagle-eyed, resolute, and energetic, was evidently in blissful ecstacy with the vividly radiating and harmonious colours of the birds he there met with, as he says in his "Wanderings," "The finest precious stones are far surpassed by the vivid tints which adorn the birds," and in after-life, his countenance always vigorously lighted up simply from his own graphic description to his friends of these lustrous, varied, and harmonious colours.

From that date, 1812, to the melancholy and heart-rending period of his death, did the Author of the Walton Hall Museum—that extraordinary and unequalled achievement in natural history — pursue his ceaseless labours with a lively zeal, as agreeable as it was indefatigable, and which, when its originating fabricator was called hence, was I believe, never surpassed, and indeed, was generally acknowledged to have been rarely if ever equalled by any single individual.

I must apologise to my readers for the abrupt introduction of the following information relative to the subject of this memoir. I readily admit that it is, in this part of the

Z

book, somewhat out of place, but it really is a case of " Hobson's choice," not having received it until the page in which it has to be inserted is absolutely in the hands of the printer.

This communication is doubly interesting, inasmuch as it has reference to a period before I knew Mr. Waterton, and has been furnished to me by a gentleman on whom I can thoroughly rely, as well as its having been positively chronicled in black and white at the time, and consequently not depending on a stretch of memory.

The Rev. T. Dixon, now of the Holy Trinity Parsonage, South Shields, was, at the time to which I am about to allude, Curate in the Church at Sandal, and therefore a neighbour of "the Old Squire," who was invariably very attentive and remarkably kind to the clergy, consequently the Rev. Gentleman had undisturbed opportunities of frequently committing his observations to paper at the moment, which he has not only communicated to me, but given me permission to make use of them in this edition.

"SANDAL, 10th January, 1826.

"Having read Mr. Waterton's ' Wanderings in America,' in which he gives a detailed and most interesting account of his four journeys thither, and many months residence in the Forests of Guiana amongst wild beasts and serpents, Caymen and Vampires, in quest of objects of Natural History, my brother and I called upon him this morning to beg the favour of seeing his collection, more especially a creature which he obtained in his last journey, of the monkey tribe, to which he has given the name of ' Wild

Man of the Woods.' He was most polite and attentive ; and showed us this nondescript animal's bust, being the only part he brought over with him. Its face and features are perfectly human : a sweet placidity sits on the whole countenance. Its skin is black : nose, mouth, and chin without hair, but each side of the face, and a good deal on to the cheek is covered with a glossy red hair, inclining to yellow, which forms a thick beard under the chin of an inch-and-a-half, or two inches long. The hair upon the head is yellow, short, and, as upon the human head, with a crown on the top. The animal had hands, and a long tail. Its colour is that of the red monkey. But then this human face ? Some will have it that Mr. Waterton has formed it thus ; others, that it is impossible for any art to compress and placidify the elongated savage countenance of the monkey into that of the dignified and serene Grecian ' *lis est sub judice.*' Nor will Mr. Waterton terminate the contest by stating positively what the case is. To the former he replies, 'If you can, produce any specimen of the art that has under-gone such a change by the hand of the operator, as that the distorted face of the monkey has been converted into a sweet human countenance, then you have grounds for saying that I have thus altered this. Then may you give to one side of the face an age of 70, and to the other side the paleness and youth of a lad of 17.' To the others this is his answer :—' If you think it came thus from nature's hand procure its fellow from his native forests. I should think to establish the fact of its being a newly discovered species would be sufficient inducement for the undertaking.' For

myself I am in doubt whether party has the advantage. Mr.
Waterton's skill in the art is unrivalled; but still in comparing the head of a red monkey, which he put into my hand,
with the other, the latter differed as much from it as my
own, in everything except the colour of its hair and its
situation, in which respect there was much resemblance.
Thus the matter rests, and thus must it remain, till he
decides the point, which he has partly pledged himself to
do at some future period. He pointed out to us the
immense snake 14 feet long, and which he said, when alive
was nearly as thick as his own body. With this he had a
tremendous conflict in the woods; he found it coiled up in
its den; then reinforced by two Indians, at the risk of his
life and theirs he made the assault—he sprang upon it,
pinned it through the neck with a lance eight feet long,
which he immediately committed to one of the Indians to
hold, and threw himself upon its tail to keep it down.
This his own weight was not sufficient, till the other
Indian threw himself upon him, and after a considerable
struggle he got its mouth tied up with his braces, and
then they bore him off in triumph. Shortly after he
found and engaged alone a young one 10 feet long, as
it was crawling along he seized it by the tail; it now
turned about; he took his hat off, put his hand into
it; let the serpent come open-mouthed within two feet of
his face, then he pushed his hat and hand into its
mouth; seized it behind its head that it could not
bite him; and let it fold itself about his arms and
body, as he saw it was not strong enough to break
the former. He says it pressed him very hard, but not

alarmingly so. He had subsequently a tremendous encounter with a cayman or a crocodile, which we also
saw. This monster is 10½ feet long. An Indian hooked
it for him in the river Essequibo. But when hooked,
none of them durst come near it. At last, being
dragged within two yards of the shore, Mr. Waterton
sprang upon its back in the water, and after a perilous
struggle tied its fore-legs over its back, fastening
up its wondrous jaws; and then ordered the Indians to
haul it to land and cut its throat. His preserved tro-,
phical birds, insects, and reptiles, are unrivalled specimens
of the art, being as perfect in form, and as varied in the
brilliancy of their colours, as when nature gave them
the last touch of her plastic art and pencilled skill.
After the politest attention from Mr. Waterton, who
wished me to take a friend at any time, we exchanged
parting good wishes, myself not a little impressed in
his favour. Mr. Waterton is a Roman Catholic of an
ancient family, which has suffered much for its religion. The family seat is Walton Hall on a small
island surrounded by a beautiful piece of water. It
communicates, where the water is narrowest, with the
continent by a beautiful cast-iron bridge. Mr. Waterton
intends to journey again into America after the re-estab-
lishment of his health, which has been very precarious
since his last return." So far my narrative. I find I
have afterwards added the following note : — " The
Inquisition having subsequently threatened to bring
Mr. Waterton to account for killing a man, he was
obliged to confess that the *creature* was made out of

two red monkey's heads, which his skill enabled him to patch together!   Surprising deception !!!

" T. Dixon."

The Rev. T. Dixon says in his letter to me, "It is with peculiar regret, I see with many others, that the splendid and unique museum, which that unequalled ornithologist had collected and prepared with his own hands has been removed from Walton Hall. May I ask why? And whither? as I cannot gather from your narrative an answer to either query. My questions are beyond merely idle curiosity.   I was Curate of the parish of Sandal Magna in 1825, when Mr. Waterton returned from South America, and as such had different opportunities of seeing his most beautiful collection, which I well knew was subsequently much increased. I called upon him a short time after his return and had a most agreeable visit.   He was in his handsome dining-room and had numerous objects of natural history before him on the table ; amongst them the 'Nondescript,' about which we had much conversation, and that was before the secret of its publication came out.   Another was a very beautiful American lark, which he had just finished, and by which he showed me the superiority of his mode of preparation, by just laying his hand over it and pressing it down, when it sprung up again, recovering its former attitude, as soon as his hand was withdrawn, with all the elasticity of life.

"I well remember the great boa constrictor, which used to be coiled up as it were ready to spring at you, just within

the drawing-room door. Shortly after his return from
America he met Thomas Schorey, our parish clerk at
Sandal, whom he well knew, when he drew up his horse
and said, 'Well Thomas we shall now have no more
occasion for priests and clerks, as I have been in South
America and have shot the Devil there, and have brought
him home with me.' Thomas came at once to my lodgings
and told me this, and seemed dreadfully shocked at Mr.
Waterton's 'profane' speech.

"I left the Curacy of Sandal January, 1826."

In the former edition of this volume I did not feel
at liberty to speak in detail as regarded the expropriation
of the subjects of natural history at Walton Hall, nor
did I hazard to inaugurate their induction within the
walls of the Roman Catholic institution at Ushaw, four
miles from Durham, established in 1808, and which owed
its origin to the dissolution of the English college of
Douay, in French Flanders, by the tyranny of the French
Republic in 1794. Now however, there appears to be
no longer any valid reason for concealing the present
location of the unwearied labours of the good old man.
The question is even now being continually put: " Is
the late Mr. Waterton's collection of natural history still
to be seen at Walton Hall?" And on being informed of
its removal, great disappointment is invariably expressed,
and I may add, united with a deep regret, by many
who lament their having lost several irrevocable opportunities from their dilatoriness of being so highly gratified as
they might have been.

The Squire has several times, when speaking of his early pedestrianism and what he called, vagabondising expeditions in South America, insinuated to me, that in admiration of nature in all her varied profusion of modified phases and alluring aspects, with extreme pleasure and with a deep and fervid interest, which none but an ardent admirer of nature could realise — that he had, he observed, in numerous instances, been delighted and influentially animated beyond measure, during a long succession of years, by closely watching simple arborescent vegetation during its gradually advancing growth, from the tiny twig to its umbrageous and approaching ornamental termination of its growth.

With this carefully acquired impression, formed on the absolutely well-grounded information that I have now described, firmly rivetted in his judgment, (and retained in his memory,) and continually in view, Mr. Waterton invariably found himself assimilating, by anxious and frequently repeated comparison, his growing and rapidly accumulating natural-history collection, in a corresponding ratio, to the tender sapling of the forest, whilst gradually increasing, ripening, and expanding into maturity.

During the Squire's whole life, it was his great anxiety to advance and improve the taxidermic art hitherto so imperfect, and it was also one of his inextinguishable objects to endeavour to elevate it in rank, in the widely deviating scale of science.

Mr. Waterton's innate partiality and admitted ability

for this marvellously imitative representation of life was signal and enduring, and always dissociated from every unworthy and selfish feeling.

The professed experts of the day had, up to this period, displayed glaring incapacity in this faculty, generally arising, in all probability, from a combination of difficulties uncontrollably hostile to the accomplishment of any certainty of excellence, and which from their very nature, they could never surmount.

These acknowledged difficulties entirely arrested the progression of artistic skill, as they consisted in a deficiency in pecuniary resources, in an insufficiency of leisure at command, in negligence of that character of literary attainments essentially necessary, and from inattention to the cultivation of refined taste.   Mr. Waterton was, fortunately in a position to check-mate all those trying difficulties, and it must be admitted that they one and all vanished, when tested and aided by his untiring energy, and determination.

The Squire had one very prepossessing endowment, he was largely gifted with the pleasure of pleasing, and this was not limited in its bestowal to the learned, nor to the aristocracy.   It was liberally and heartily distributed to the humble and unlettered, to the poor and needy naturalist on all opportune occasions.

Nor was this noble quality restricted to his own generation.   Mr. Waterton has repeatedly said to me— "I do hope that my labours will afford pleasure in future ages, and if at this moment, I had a well-grounded confidence in such an expectation, I could at once, separate myself from all my handicraft without a single regret."

Now, it can not be denied that this was unvarnished liberality and genuine benevolence. It was a substantial sacrifice of self-gratification for the advantage and pleasure of others, and in reality, charitably extended to those we have neither seen nor known. How unlike the man, who when assailed to contribute something, for the sake of posterity, peevishly replied, "Not a farthing, what did posterity ever do for me?"

After a certain period of life however, it was evident that he who heretofore judiciously selected and determinedly adhered to his own path, was now, not merely less caring to contend against the erroneous opinions of others, but that he was more easily prevailed upon to adopt them. The why? and the wherefore? were not so frequently introduced, not so shrewdly and ingeniously brought into requisition in support of his arguments, nor so pertinaceously persevered in as formerly. Honied words had a more seductive influence as the Squire advanced in years and declined in physical power.

His once favourable impressions were no longer incontrovertible. Alas! the inflexibly independent Naturalist of yesterday was gradually and manifestly declining from the Charles Waterton of an earlier day.

I have hitherto been specially and rigidly careful in limiting my remarks to Mr. Waterton *only*, but in deference to the opinion of many friends, I do now think that I should not deal frankly, nay scarcely in equity, in a second edition, with those who may peruse this volume, if I should refrain from alluding to any of the late Mr. Waterton's acts which might interest my readers, even if it should, although reluctantly on my part, be the means of introducing to publicity parties, concerning whom abstractedly, I do not desire to make any observations.

I have thought it of sufficient interest to the literary world and the public at large, to know the ultimate destination of Mr. Waterton's works of art, and incidentally, of such other property as he had the power to dispose of. I have accordingly, procured an official copy of the will, which is inserted at the end of this volume.   In which it will be seen that the bequest to the two legatees is so framed that on the death of either, the surviving one would take the whole.

That the museum, the absorbing idol of the Squire's whole heart, should, on the demise of the Naturalist, have been subjected to the degradation of being inventoried.— That it should have been arrested *in its natural descent by inheritance* as an heir-loom, to gladden the heart of some existing scion, or even some prospective issue, bearing the name of its founder, was painful to contemplate, but is still more distressing to realise.

It is marvellous, nay almost incredible, that subsequently to the decease of the testator, this noble collection of natural history, should find its way to *Ushaw*, in spite of the vehement attachment of its founder to *Stonyhurst*, in spite also of the Squire's perpetually expressed admiration of this Catholic institution, where he was educated, which place, for a very long period, he preferentially visited, in order to attend to certain religious duties, and which institution, as his numerous writings will testify, he praised beyond all others, and in addition, the existing inmates of which, in their various positions in this establishment, up to the time of his death, he almost adored. How unintelligible,—how mysterious! if not paradoxical.

"This is not thy old language, nor own thoughts."

What greater criterion or proof can we have that the Walton Hall Museum was, in reality, originally and intentionally designed by the Squire himself, as the affiliating link between his continually progressing acquisitions, his untiring labours, and the ultimate completion of this permanent and lasting patrimony in conjunction and in perpetuity with the name of the naturalist?

It is not then, surprising, that this engaging and proselytising series of the rare and beautiful, combined and associated with the unique and abnormal effusions of the animated and organised world, by degrees artificially unfolding, developing, and unmistakeably disclosing innumerably hitherto latent attractions, should have created, affixed, and permanently secured the enthusiastic and permanently devoted attachment of this good old man to the captivating and enchanting objects of his own inimitable handiwork.

This wonderfully harmonious and fascinating accumulation of nature and of art—these numerous and far-famed celebrities, the distinguished offspring of the unwearied labour of the single-minded and perservering "fine old English gentleman," had become, in the eyes

of the people, and indeed, in the unsought but highly
appreciated estimation of naturalists of all grades and
from various nations, as it were an hereditary heir-loom,
a fixed and immovable portion of the freehold of the
Walton Hall territory.

Hence, it requires no great stretch of imagination,
no far-fetched nor extravagant flight of fancy, to forcibly
idealise the pitiable condition of the residents in the
surrounding district, when mourning the loss of the
Museum, its founder and fabricator, that they should
be tempted to exclaim with Ovid, when writing a beautiful and pathetic elegy on the death of his friend,—

> .   .   .   .   *" Jacet ecce Tibulus,*
> *Vix manet e toto parva quod urna capit."*

> .   .   .   *"* See, here Tibullus lies,
> Of one so great there hardly remains enough to fill a little urn."

Painful and grievous as the bereavement of this universally esteemed veteran was, which event passed through
the whole district like a flash of lightning — widely,
deeply, and poignantly as his death was deplored, yet the
completion of an age far exceeding that short span
allotted in Scripture to man, had for some time previously,
forewarned his surviving friends, and indeed, all who
frequently came in contact with him, that they lived
only in disconsolate anticipation of the coming change
at no distant period.

> "The leaves are fal'ing, falling,
>   Solemnly and s'ow ;
> Caw ! Caw ! the Rooks are calling ;
>   It is a sound of woe,
>   A sound of woe."

The manifestly and very distinctly and painfully visible drooping into the grave, so heart-rending to his numerous admirers, had for a considerable time before the fatal accident, gradually and extensively foretold the anticipated fact, its shadow had been previously reflected, and had consequently, by degrees, alleviated the distress of his associates, so as to more calmly and submissively surrender their feelings of anguish to the evidently impending and irrevocable summons—to the fiat of a Higher Power. "*Prævisus ante, mollior ictus venit.*" "Seen beforehand, the blow comes more lightly."

But, that they should be so speedily called upon, and so unexpectedly summoned by a firm and unalterable edict, to sacrifice, relinquish, and surrender the very object they adored—to summarily and so abruptly indisputably realise the perennial deprivation of all the Squire's exquisite handiwork from their immediate neighbourhood, from so appropriate and *naturally* determined a site—to witness the desolating change in the residence and in the grounds of the very birth-place of this remarkable man, once, nay so recently, monopolising a positively magnetic influence and gaining the admiration of all—to yield the Museum, the very idol of the people—the elaborate toil of his own unaided mental and physical powers—the result of the refined taste of this son of nature to another arena, is lamentable in the extreme, and has been productive of the assumption of an aspect of the deepest regret in the surrounding district, and of bitter disappointment to the philosopher and to the man of science.

Is it possible, that the place which I have so recently shadowed forth, and which I have had such inconceivable yet melancholy pleasure in carefully and minutely delineating, should have, in conformity with this description, ceased to be?—that it is at this moment, a myth, in reality a thing of the past—that it was, but is not—that it has been not only deprived of the laudable pride of its existence by the uncompromising hand of death, which no human power can contravene. "*Nulla herba aut vis mortis tela frangit.*" "No herb or power can break the darts of death;" but, that it has at last, been shorn of its pre-eminently attractive position by forfeiture of the handiwork of its great inaugurating master, the subject of the present Memoir, and the unparalleled artificial preserver of nature, in whatever character she presented herself?

Is it possible, that the multiplicity of objects rendering Walton Hall so conspicuously unique and deservedly worthy of its celebrity and world-wide fame—so retrospectively fascinating in natural history to the scientific stranger from every quarter of the globe for so long a period,—Is it possible, that these, the indisputable admiration of all, should have taken to themselves wings, and have literally realised their ever-to-be-lamented flight from their birth-place to another region, —that they should have deserted their native soil and have been transported to a land of strangers, to which there seems to be no indigenous nor connecting link of attachment?

It is now, I grieve to say, no longer a question hanging in anxious suspense, no longer in painful ambiguity, as the days of this splendid and distinguished collection have already been numbered,—it is a grave reality— *un fait accompli*. Each niche, so recently proud of its occupant, the handiwork of "the old Squire," is now left desolate, to exhibit a melancholy blank, a mournful recollection of the past, and an irreparable deprivation of that which was recently so dear to us.

We now know, and most unfortunately to our deep regret, the "ultimate fate" of what cost the Squire an incalculable amount of time, of physical labour, and an age to accomplish. We are cognisant of, and have to reluctantly record a second, nay a twofold grief, which is as unwelcome as it has been unexpected to the surrounding district, and to the many, many, distant friends.

All our grief however, will not restore to us the loss of that for which we vainly mourn. Submission to the "fates decreed" is, or at all events ought to be on all occasions, our sheet anchor, and although "lowering our flag" is seldom an agreeable act, or gracefully capitulated, yet it may be a politic and a just act. Humanly speaking, we find it difficult to train our unwilling minds to kiss the rod that inflicts the source of our heart-ache, and even under wholesome correction, to bravely but patiently meet and endure the worst, yet after all, the only legitimate and I may truly add, praiseworthy remedy we possess, is to "stoop to conquer."

"*Levius fit patientia, quidquid corrigere est nefas.*"
"What we cannot correct, becomes lighter by patience."

It was not my intention to have inserted even another fragment from my abundant store of Mr. Waterton's Letters, but I am reluctantly tempted to introduce the following, because their composition and peculiar character of innate humour so faithfully evince to his old friends an unmistakable recognition of the "old Squire," and afford his deliberately expressed opinions on two or three subjects hitherto not specially alluded to. He thus refers, in an accidental way, to Church-rates, in a letter to me :—

" MY DEAR SIR,

" I return you my very best thanks for your report on my brother's state of health. If it were possible, I could really find in my heart to quarrel with you for refusing your fee. It is well that you are far beyond the want of it, and unlike Mother Church in Wakefield, recently crying out most bitterly for a penny in the pound. Rot her, she has got the day, and this we are informed through the votes of some vagabond Catholics, who have basely lent their shoulders to prop her up, in order that by so doing they might repay the Dissenters, (rot them too,) for their scurrilous abuse in the late affair of the Maynooth grant.

" On the 8th of this month, we left the orthodox and clear blue sky of the eternal city, and reached the gloomy and heretical atmosphere of this tax-ridden country on Wednesday last. We are all well. As for myself, I fancy that I am getting fat and pot-bellied. The frog-soup, goat-flesh, and snail-cream of Italy have been too much for me, and unless I put myself immediately on a

A A

lowering diet, I don't know how long I may be able to "swarm" up the pillar at the portico at the front of the house. The three gentlemen you met the last time you were here dined with us yesterday, and Mr. N—— committed the same rude vulgarity he always does, viz., that of officiously commencing some rubbish when some other gentlemen was, not only in possession, but actually detailing that which was to the point, amusing and really instructive. How this rude intrusion betrays the hairy leg.

"I wrote to you from Rome. The Puseyites are doing well for us. Like Balaam's ass they speak the truth, but do not profit by it.

"Well then, Wednesday next we will punish your larder, praise your cook, and thank you kindly for your hospitality. But I must particularly request you not to allow a beef-steak to be prepared for me on this occasion. I certainly will not partake of it, as I have been living on clover ever since my return to England, and it is high time I should now feed on thistles, unless I should wish to outdo in bulk your Ackworth patient.

"As you liberally leave the hour of dinner to our own disposal, we will say, notwithstanding the heterodox fashion of the present age, two o'clock. Perhaps it might be well to meet Doctor H——k some other day. You know our humour, and we know yours, both perfectly harmless, but should a stranger be present when we exchange shots, he might receive a random arrow which perhaps would cause a wound, and this would not do.

"Ever sincerely,

"CHARLES WATERTON."

Some of Mr. Waterton's friends have been anxious to know his opinion of the Puseyites. The foregoing letter will satisfy them as to the estimation in which the Squire held them.

The following Letter shows the Squire's ardent attachment to the Priests, and his anxious desire that no earthly labour should be spared for their welfare in a religious point of view. It was written in 1847, when so many Roman Catholic Priests were suddenly cut off in Leeds and Liverpool by a virulent fever :

"MY DEAR SIR,

"It was most kind and friendly in you to write to me on this melancholy occasion, and I shall never forget the attention. Could I persuade myself that poor Mr. Walmsley is still alive, I would be in Leeds this morning, and at his bed-side, but the sad contents of your letter convince me that all is over ere this. I got your letter just in time to have him prayed for by the Wakefield congregation.

"What a mistake it is in the friends of sick people to send for the Physician at the fiftieth minute of the eleventh hour. This is too often the case. We are indeed here now and gone in a moment. It is but the other day that I saw Mr. Walmsley in full health, and requested him to let Mr. Wilson come to Walton Hall, for change of air. His reply was that he could not spare him on account of the numbers of the poor sick Irish. I trust that the charity which has most probably caused Mr. Walmsley

ere this to be no longer amongst the living, will have
gained him an abode in the regions of everlasting bliss.
We shall be delighted more than I can express· to see
your horses drive up to the bridge.

          "Believe me,
            "My dear Sir,
              " Ever sincerely yours,
                 " CHARLES WATERTON."

All the *facts* which are stated in this Volume directly
or indirectly, as connected with Mr. Waterton personally,
have been carefully verified by the Squire himself when in
his eightieth year. With regard to the *opinions* that are
here entertained and expressed of the man, I may add that
they are stated by me with scrupulous sincerity, and from
a firm conviction of their real existence, and that they
have been deeply impressed by a frequent, most cordial,
and familiar intercourse of many years' duration. I also
hesitate not to affirm, which assertion gives me extreme
pleasure, that during this protracted "hand and glove"
intimacy, there was between us a reciprocal esteem, an
affectionate familiarity, and a mutually devoted attachment rarely equalled ; and I may now, and I trust to the
last day of my existence, truly say with Cicero, " *Vita*

enim mortuorum in memoriâ vivorum est posita." "The life of the dead is retained in the memory of the living."

There is no necessity in my case, to stimulate nor to officiously jog the memory, although treacherous on many occasions, that it should bear in mind and dwell upon the recollection of the countless happy hours and days that we unitedly enjoyed. Even now, with a mind closely absorbed on a variety of other subjects, the Squire's vividly remembered and deeply impressed figure—his singularly pithy phraseology—his genuine warmth of heart—and his countenance beaming with a smile of inexpressible pleasure on the discovery of any thing new to him in his favourite scientific pursuit,—all uninvitedly, nay attractively, insinuate themselves into my mind's eye and spontaneously flit before me as if scarcely an hour had separated us on this earthly tenure.

Hence, under all the circumstances enumerated, seasonably tinctured with the most agreeable recollections of by-gone days, of felicitous conversations and associations with the ardent admirer of organised nature, it has been a most grateful pleasure, on my part, and I have felt it a duty absolutely incumbent upon me, not to willingly allow the remembrance of my late friend's generous and humane ácts, coupled with his disinterested and meritorious virtues, to pass unnoticed.

It would hereafter grieve me, if I were now to neglect acknowledging the pleasure derived from frequently listening to the myriads of interesting and most amusing anecdotes, and to the variously thrilling incidents recounted by the Squire, relative to the aristocracy of the broad-acred county in which he was born, in which he had lived for so lengthened a period, where he had been distinguished, honoured, and beloved by all grades of society, and where his memory will long be cherished with feelings of a most grateful recognition and pleasure.

It would be ingratitude of the deepest dye, if I could forget how delighted I had repeatedly been by the highly entertaining narratives and adventures related by my late friend with so much genuine zest, and especially on all occasions with such delicacy of feeling for the memory of the dead. It would, indeed, be an unpardonable oblivion of sunny days gone by, the memory of which enjoyment is still fresh and inextinguishably indulged by me, to allow an undeveloped recollection of all these pleasures to silently perish along with the crumbling to dust of their Author.

> " *Quis desiderio sit pudor aut modus*
> *Tam cari capitis ?* "

" What moderation or limit can there be to our regret at the loss of so dear a friend ? "

> " Like the dew on the mountain,
> Like the foam on the river,
> Like the bubble on the fonntain,
> He is gone,—and for ever."

Not being able to do justice to the numerous Paintings at Walton Hall, by any written description of my own, the least that my readers may anticipate, and which expectation they are undoubtedly in a position to reasonably calculate upon, is, that I should furnish them with a copy of a Catalogue presented to me by Mr. Waterton himself.

The interest associated with these Paintings, unfortunately and unavoidably deprived of an artistic description, will be partially compensated by some observations relative to them from the Squire's own pen, and still further enhanced by the introduction of an extract from a Letter addressed to Mr. Waterton, by the celebrated George Ord, Esquire, President of the Institute of Arts and Sciences in Philadelphia, with whom I have the pleasure of being personally acquainted.

CATALOGUE

OF A

COLLECTION OF PAINTINGS,

AS PREPARED BY THE LATE MR. WATERTON, AND EXHIBITED

AT WALTON HALL DURING HIS LIFE, BUT REMOVED

ELSEWHERE AFTER HIS DECEASE.

PREFATORY REMARKS.

ONE hundred and forty-eight of the Pictures in this Museum, came from Bavaria in the year 1830.

I stopped at Wursburg on my return from a visit to Mr. FORSTER, the Prince of Hohenlohe's secretary at Huttenheim; and hearing that there was a very fine private collection of pictures to be seen in the town, I obtained permission to inspect it; not having any idea of purchasing it, as I did not know that it was for sale.

It belonged to Mr. BERWIND, who was eighty-two years of age, and in the bank of Wursburg.

The old gentleman received me with great politeness. He said, his mortal course was nearly run; that he had no children; and that, if he left it to his relatives, they would sell it; and then the government would cheat them out of half of the proceeds;—and they themselves would fight for the remainder.

Wherefore, he had made up his mind to sell it:—and, on saying this, he went and fetched a printed catalogue from a table in a corner of his room;—put it into my hand;—and requested at the same time, that on my return to England, if I had a friend, who wished to become possessed of a most choice and valuable collection of pictures, I would recommend his collection to him.

He added, that he had been unceasing in his exertions to form the collection; and that it had taken him fully thirty-four years of his life to bring together what I saw before me.

He attended all the different sales of pictures far and near, during the revolutionary war, when specimens were choice, and buyers few;—and thus, he had managed to form a collection which was universally acknowledged to be the pride and ornament of his native city.

I spent an hour in his rooms ; and I begged permission to revisit them at four o'clock in the afternoon. This was kindly granted ; and ere the sun had set, I became the purchaser of his collection.

Mr. Berwind sent it down the Rhine to Rotterdam. Thence it went to London ;—and so on to Walton Hall, which, I trust, will be its last resting-place.

Eight other pictures, with an asterisk (*) before them, are an invaluable present from my dear and excellent friend, GEORGE ORD, Esq., of Philadelphia, the elegant biographer of Alexander Wilson, the renowned ornithologist.

CHARLES WATERTON.

[*See his Letter, dated March 22nd, 1841, page 365.*]

How strangely inconsistent has been the removal of this collection with the here expressed "trust," that their then Removal to Walton Hall, " will be its last resting-place."

EXTRACT OF A LETTER FROM GEORGE ORD, ESQ.

" PHILADELPHIA, March 22nd, 1841.

"These paintings are eight in number.

"The largest is a Fruit Piece by Campidoglio, a Roman artist, greatly celebrated in his day for the natural effect of his productions. This picture belonged to Bingham, the father of Lady Baring. It was purchased at the sale of his paintings by the late Thomas M. Willing, and from the last-named gentleman it passed to me. It is a genuine picture; but the name of the artist was not discovered until I got it cleaned when the signature and date became visible. They may yet be seen, although indistinctly.

"The Virgin and Infants Jesus and John was another of Bingham's pictures, also purchased by Mr. Willing, and by me at the sale of the effects of the latter. I know not the author of this picture, but from its style and execution I should suppose it to be the work of an Italian master: it bears the marks of genuineness about it. The English connoisseurs will soon determine its parentage, if it be the production of an eminent artist.

"Tobit and the Angel has been pronounced a Breughel. This is conjecture; but from its peculiar style, it will doubtless attract the attention of those capable of ascertaining its paternity. It was one of Bingham's favourite pictures; it ornamented one of his parlours, and I myself bought it at the sale of his family furniture, in December, 1805. It is a pity that this fine picture was painted, as was customary in the age of the artist, on two boards, so loosely jointed, that they now cease to adhere together. However, it is in good preservation.

"The last picture which I got out of the collection of Bingham, is the figure of an ecclesiastic. This, I have no doubt is a portrait, of some celebrated personage, perhaps one of your distinguished authors. I have somewhere seen an engraved head which resembled it, but can not recall circumstances to mind. Should this prove to be an original portrait of a great man, it will be an acquisition of no mean value. There is something in its manner resembling that of Le Brun's portraits.

"Jupiter and Europa is the work of a French artist. It is a highly-finished picture, and it will be easily recognised by those conversant in these matters.

"The two pieces by Jac. Van Es are in good preservation. This was a celebrated Flemish painter.

"The Fruit and Flowers piece is said to be from the pencil of J. B. Monnoyer, a French artist. I possess no means of ascertaining the fact; but the picture will speak for itself, as to its merits.

"G. ORD."

CATALOGUE.

No.				BY
1	Noah and his Daughters	.	.	*Henri Goltzius.*
2	The Holy Family	.	.	*Sir Anthony Vandyck.*
3	The Fortune-Teller	.	.	*Zaganelli.*
4	Landscape with Figures	.	.	*Vinckenbooms.*
5	Bacchus on a Barrel	.	.	*The Flemish School.*
6	Venetian Architecture	.	.	*Van Hoeck.*
7	Ditto	.	.	*Ditto.*
8	A Landscape	.	.	*Anthony Waterloo.*
9	Ditto	.	.	*Ditto.*
10	A Small Landscape	.	.	*Genoels.*
11	Feast of the Dedication	.	.	*Droogsloot.*
12	The Blessed Virgin, with the Infant Jesus and St. Joseph	.	.	*Moucheron.*
13	St. John the Evangelist	.	.	*Michael Angelo, Buonarotti.*
14	St. James the Apostle	.	.	*Ditto.*
15	St. Francis in Contemplation	.	.	*Francis Franck.*
16	The Holy Family	.	.	*The School of Corregio.*
17	St. Magdalen in Contemplation	.	.	*Dominic Feti, commonly called Domenichino.*
18	A Mountain Landscape, with Figures	.		*Joos Momper.*
19	The Bust of St. Francis	.	.	*Bernardo Strozzi.*
20	St. Sebastian	.	.	*Andrian Vander Werf.*
21	Judith with the Head of Holofernes	.		*Lucas Cranach.*
22	The Resurrection of our Lord	.	.	*The German School.*
23	Falconer on Horseback	.	.	*Augustus Querfurt.*
24	Ditto	.	.	*Ditto.*
25	St. Jerome	.	.	*The School of Rubens.*
26	A Storm at Sea	.	.	*De Vlieger.*
27	Old Woman with a Candle	.	.	*Godefroi Schalcken.*
28	Old Man Warming Himself	.	.	*Ditto.*
29	A Small Landscape	.	.	*Peter Van Bemmel.*
30	Ditto	.	.	*Ditto.*
31	Church in Frankfort	.	.	*Stober.*
32	A Small Sea Piece	.	.	*Jean Bellevois.*
33	Bust of the ever Blessed Virgin	.		*Carlo Dolce.*
34	Charity	.	.	*Francis Floris.*
35	Vessels at Sea	.	.	*William Vandervelde.*
36	St. Francis	.	.	*The Spanish School.*
37	A Portrait	.	.	*Jean Holbein.*

No.				BY
38 Portrait of Louis, Elector Palatine		.		*The German School.*
39 Portrait of his Wife	.	.		*Ditto.*
40 A Landscape	.	.		*Eisemann.*
41 Ditto	.	.		*Ditto.*
42 Abraham and Jacob	.	.		*Jean Zick.*
43 Abraham and Hager	.	.		*Ditto.*
44 A Landscape during a Tempest		.		*Eisemann.*
45 A Landscape	.	.	.	*Bredael.*
46 Ditto	.	.	.	*Ditto.*
47 Entrance into a Town	.	.		*Jean Baptist, Tiepolo.*
48 A Landscape with Turkish Figures		.		*Jean Baptist, Tiepolo.*
49 Lucretia Stabbing Herself	.			*Lucas Cranach.*
50 A View in England	.	.		*Stephonoff.*
51 Ditto	.	.	.	*Ditto.*
52 A Peasant Smoking	.	.		*Brauwere.*
53 A Baker crying Bread	.	.		*Ditto.*
54 Dead Poultry	.	.	.	*Francis Kuyp.*
55 Our Saviour carrying His Cross			.	
56 A Fruit Piece	.	.	.	*Jean Wagenseil.*
57 Ditto	.	.	.	*Ditto.*
58 A Rustic Family	.	.	.	*The School of Teniers.*
59 Country Musicians	.	.		*Ditto.*
60 A Small Landscape	.	.		*William Van Bemmel.*
61 Ditto	.	.	.	*Ditto.*
62 A Knight on Horseback	.			*The Flemish School.*
63 A Sea Piece	.	.		*Backhuysen.*
64 A Table with Bread and Fruit		.		*William Gabron.*
65 A Brood Mare and Foal	.			*Dujardin.*
66 Numidian Crane and other Birds		.		*Roland Savery.*
67 The Holy Family	.	.		*Augustine Caracci.*
68 St. Benedict Curing the Sick	.			*Januaire Zick.*
69 A Beaver	.	.		*Hamilton.*
70 The Birth of Christ	.			*Jean Van Achen.*
71 Adoration of the Three Sages	.			*Ditto.*
72 A Landscape	.	.		*Christian Schutz.*
73 Ditto	.	.	.	*Ditto.*
74 The ever Blessed Virgin and Dead Christ		.		*Jean Van Hemssen.*
75 A Cavalry Attack	.	.		*Christian Lowenstern*
76 St. Sebastian	.			*Raphael Mengs.*
77 An Old Man	.	.		*Adrian Van Ostade.*
78 Ditto	.	.	.	*Ditto.*
79 Dead Game	.	.		*Wengal Brasch.*
80 Ditto	.	.	.	*Ditto.*
81 A Post Boy in the Snow		.		*Watzdorf.*
82 Cattle	.	.	.	*Ditto.*
83 Running the Stag	.		.	*Wouverman.*

No.		BY
84	A Halt in Stag Hunting	*Wouverman.*
85	Landscape in Hungary	*Drillert.*
86	A Countryman	*Artist unknown.*
87	St. Nicholas in Greek Costume	*Ditto.*
88	Triumph of Bacchus	*Francis Franck.*
89	A Landscape	*Peter Molyn, commonly called Tempesta.*
90	Bust of a Persian Prince	*Rembrandt.*
91	The Holy Family and St. Catherine	*Otto Van Veen.*
92	Holy Family and the Three Sages	*Albert Durer.*
93	Countryman with a Pitcher	*Van Helmont.*
94	Ecce Homo	*Sir Anthony Vandyck.*
95	Sketch of St. Mark	*Peter Paul Rubens.*
96	Sketch of St. Matthew	*Ditto.*
97	A Landscape	*Manskirsch.*
98	Ditto	*Ditto.*
99	Shepherd and his Flock	*The School of Berghem.*
100	A Landscape	*The School of Breughel.*
101	Ditto	*Ditto.*
102	A Landscape	*Besschey.*
103	Ditto	*Ditto.*
104	A Nest with Young Birds	*Hamilton.*
105	Goldfinch on her Nest	*Ditto.*
106	Blind Beggar and Boy	*Januaire Zick.*
107	Snails	*Otto Marcellis.*
108	The Last Judgment	*Stolker.*
109	St. Jerome	*Joseph Dorn.*
110	A Landscape	*Hockegger.*
111	Ditto	*Ditto.*
112	An Angel	*Francis Albano.*
113	Fruit Piece	*Catherine Treu.*
114	Ditto	*Ditto.*
115	Bible Piece	*Seekatz.*
116	Interior of a Church	*Hoekgeest.*
117	Ditto	*Ditto.*
118	Dancing Party	*Palamedes.*
119	Crucifixion of our Lord	*Christopher Schwartz.*
120	Flowers	*Deville.*
121	Marriage by a Greek Patriarch	*Paul Veronese.*
122	A Nun at her Devotions	*Dionysius Calvart.*
123	A Military Train	*Christian Lowenstern.*
124	Fruit Piece	*Christian Striep.*
125	Working of the Mines	*Lucas Van Valckenburg.*
126	Martyrdom of St. Erasmus	*School of Poussin.*
127	Bust of an Old Man	*Anthony Arlaud.*
128	Ditto	*Ditto.*

B B

No.				BY
129 Fruit, Vases, and Shells	.			*Catherine Treu.*
130 Ditto	.	.	.	*Ditto.*
131 A Fire	.	.	.	*Christian Schutz.*
132 Ditto	.	.	.	*Ditto.*
133 Sketch of our Saviour, adored by the ever Blessed Virgin, St. Peter, St. Aloysius, and St. Dominick.			.	*Sebastian Conca.*
134 Head of an Old Woman	.		.	*Voelk.*
135 Head of an Old Man	.	.		*Ditto.*
136 Landscape	.	.	.	*Anthony Krimm.*
137 A Battle	.	.	.	*Augustus Querfurt.*
138 Ditto	.	.	.	*Ditto.*
139 Shepherds and Flock	.	.	.	*Francis Londonio.*
140 Ditto	.	.	.	*Ditto.*
141 Ditto	.	.	.	*Wutzer.*
142 Ditto	.	.	.	*Ditto.*
143 Portrait of Guibal	.	.	.	*By himself.*
144 Holy Family	.		.	*Kobell.*
145 Feast of the People, cut in paper	.		.	*Charles Pinterics.*
146 Ditto	.	.	.	*Ditto.*
147 Academy of Sciences	.	.	.	*Stolker.*
148 Entrance of Alexander into Babylon	.		.	*Ditto.*
149 The Itouli, or Nondescript	.		.	*Captain E. Jones.*
150 Head of the Howling Monkey	.		.	*Ditto.*
151 Family Portrait	.	.	.	
152 Ditto	.	.	.	.
153 A Sea Piece	.	.		*Artist unknown.*
154 *Jupiter and Europa	.		.	*Artist unknown.*
155 St. Jerome	.	.	.	*Ditto.*
156 Family Portrait	.	.	.	
157 Edmund Waterton	.	.	.	*W. H. Furze, Rome,* 1841.

158 Sir John Bedingfeld, who, by his personal intrepidity, saved the life of King George III. when attacked in his carriage by the mob in the year 1796.

159 Family Portrait	.	.	.	*Sir Peter Lely.*
160 Ditto	.	.		*Sir Godfrey Kneller.*
161 Ditto	.	.	.	*Sir Peter Lely.*
162 Charles Waterton	.	.	.	*Peele, sen. In Philadelphia,* 1824.
163 Head of an Old Man	.	.	.	
164 Family Portrait	.	.	.	
165 Ditto	.	.	.	.
166 The Ram of Apulia	.	.	.	*Rosa di Tivoli.*
167 An original Portrait of Queen Bess	.			
168 Monkeys Shaving and Doctoring Cats	.			
169 King James II. of England	.	.		
170 Son of King James II.	.	.		
171 The Triumph of Faith	.	.		

No.		BY
172	Pontefract Castle . .	
173	Capture of the Cayman . .	*Captain E. Jones.*
174	Descent from the Cross . .	*School of Rubens.*
175	Sir Thomas More . .	*Hans Holbein.*
176	The Scourging of our Lord .	*Francis Franck.*
177	High Priest of the Jews .	*Supposed to be by Rubens.*
178	St. Jerome . . .	*Artist unknown.*
179	Pope Pius VII. . .	*Carved and bought in Turin.*
180	Canova's Venus .	*Bartolini of Florence.*
181	Head of an Old Man . .	*Artist unknown.*
182	Head of a Man .	*Ditto.*
183	Don Quixote, from Londesbro' House .	
184	St. Catherine of Alexandria .	*Carlo Maratti.*
185	Pork, painted in 1563 .	*J. B.*
186	Dutch Cook . . .	*Jean de Fyt.*
187	Bull-baiting . . .	*Van Limborch.*
188	The Roebuck . . .	*B. P. on the Rock*
189	A Perch . . .	*Adam Van Noordt.*
190	Spanish Piece . .	*Artist unknown.*
191	Ditto	*Ditto.*
192	*Fruit . . .	*Campadiglio.*
193	A Drunken Bacchus and Satyrs	*Luca Giordano.*
194	Wild Boar of Italy . .	*P. Vallatti.*
195	Contents of a Larder . .	*Artist unknown.*
196	*Fruit Piece . .	*Jac. Van Es.*
197	*Lemon and Oysters . .	*Ditto.*
198	Dead Birds .	*Artist unknown.*
199	Portrait of Luca Giordano .	
200	Dead Game from Moscow .	*Beck.*
201	*Fruit . . .	*J. B. Monnoyer.*
202	*Tobit and the Angel . .	*J. Breughel.*
203	*Holy Family . .	*A Copy from Carlo Maratti.*
204	Fancy Piece . . .	*Miss Lucette Barker, of Thirkelby.*
205	Monkey Cramming a Cat .	*Captain E. Jones.*
206	*Portrait of an Ecclesiastic .	*Artist unknown.*

207 Tryptich in Distemper, representing the Blessed Virgin and our Saviour surrounded by Angels. On the right wing is St. Bonaventure; on the left is St. John the Baptist; at the foot is embossed "THADDEVS · DE · SENIS · PINXIT."

208	Madonna and Child . .	*School of Vandyck.*
209	Cock of the Wood, from Moscow .	*I. F. Grooth, 1774.*
210	German Hunting Piece .	
211	Vanity. Painted in 1678 .	*S. B.*
212	Dutchman and his Owl . .	
213	St. John the Evangelist . .	*Antonio Amorosi 1737, in the 81st year of his age.*
214	Fruit and Lobsters . .	

Extracted from the District Registry at Wakefield.

In the name of the Most Holy and Undivided Trinity. Amen. This is the last Will and Testament of me Charles Waterton, of Walton Hall, in the County of York, Esquire, I hereby revoke all former Wills by me made. In pursuance of all powers enabling me, and particularly in pursuance of the power given to me by the Deed of Arrangement between me and my son Edmund Waterton, Dated Twenty-fourth December, One Thousand Eight Hundred and Fify-five. I give the sum of Ten Thousand Pounds, which I am authorized, and empowered to raise unto, and equally between my dear sisters-in-law, Eliza Edmonstone, and Helen Edmonstone, absolutely as tenants in common, and in case of the death of either of them before me, then I give the said sum of Ten Thousand Pounds unto the survivor of them absolutely, and I charge the said Ten Thousand Pounds upon such real estate, as by the said Deed I am authorised to charge the same upon. I give all the rest of my personal estate whatsoever and wheresoever, and all my real estate unto my said dear sisters-in-law, Eliza Edmonstone, and Helen Edmonstone, absolutely as tenants in common, and in case of the

death of either of them before me, then I give the same
personal estate and real estate unto the survivor of them
absolutely. I give and devise unto my said dear sisters-
in-law, Eliza Edmonstone, and Helen Edmonstone, and
to my friend Samuel Fozard Harrison, of Wakefield,
Solicitor, their heirs, executors, administrators, and assigns,
all estates vested in me as Trustee or Mortgagee; to hold
the same upon the trusts, and subject to the equities
affecting the same. And I appoint my said sisters-in-
law, the said Eliza Edmonstone, and Helen Edmonstone,
and the said Samuel Fozard Harrison, Executrixes and
Executor, of this, my Will. And I direct that the said
Samuel Fozard Harrison, notwithstanding his being a
Trustee and Executor of this my Will, shall be entitled
to make, and be allowed his proper professional charges
for all business done by him for my Trustees and
Executors, any rule of Law or Equity to the contrary
notwithstanding. In Witness whereof I have hereto
set my hand and seal, this Fifteenth day of May, One
Thousand Eight Hundred and Sixty-five. Charles
Waterton. (L.S.) Signed, sealed, declared and acknowledged by the said Charles Waterton, as and for
his last Will and Testament, in the presence of
us present at the same time, who in his presence,
at his request, and in the presence of each other,
have hereunto subscribed our names as witnesses, the
words "And I charge the said Ten Thousand Pounds upon
such real estate as by the said Deed I am authorized to
charge the same upon," having been first interlined in the

first page hereof. Richard Browne, Clerk, Leeds. Alfred Smith, Solicitor, Wakefield.

> Proved at Wakefield, the 11th day of August, 1865, by Eliza Edmonstone, spinster, Helen Edmonstone, spinster, and Samuel Fozard Harrison, the Executors.

Effects under £14,000.

Testator died 27th May, 1865.

WOORALI POISON,—SEE PAGE 68.

BEING in possession of some of the Woorali Poison, which was given to me by the late Mr. Waterton, and which he obtained from the Macoushi Indians in 1812, I am induced, for the benefit of Science, to furnish any Hospital, Medical School, or any other Public Medical body, with small portions of this poison for experimental purposes, if desired to do so.

It is obvious that I could not make such an offer to private individuals, as the amount possessed would not guarantee the fulfilment of such an open-handed course, nor could I be at all certain that its use would be exclusively restricted to the purpose proposed.

RICHARD HOBSON.

LEEDS, *May,* 1866.

H. W. WALKER, PRINTER, BRIGGATE, LEEDS.

Milton Keynes UK
Ingram Content Group UK Ltd.
UKHW021325071123
432133UK00007B/81